Sarah Harrison

Sarah Harrison always wanted to write and was the original 'scribbling child'. She read English at London University and then joined IPC Magazines where she worked on *Woman's Own*. During this time she began to write short stories, and after four years she left in order to concentrate on her first love, fiction. The author of nine novels, she has written several children's books, short stories, articles and scripts and is also a regular broadcaster on Radio 4.

Sarah Harrison is married and lives with her family in Hertfordshire. She is currently working on her next novel, *Flowers won't Fax*.

SCEPTRE

Life
After
Lunch

SARAH HARRISON

SCEPTRE

First published in 1996 by Hodder and Stoughton
This special export edition published in 1997 by
Hodder and Stoughton
A division of Hodder Headline PLC
A Sceptre Paperback

A CIP catalogue record for this book is
available from the British Library

ISBN 0 340 69499 8

Typeset by Palimpsest Book Production Limited,
Polmont, Stirlingshire
Printed and bound in Great Britain by
Clays Ltd, St Ives plc

Hodder and Stoughton
A division of Hodder Headline PLC
338 Euston Road
London NW1 3BH

For Jeremy

I prolonged that particular lunch. Like you do.

My friend Susan Upchurch, sitting across from me at our corner table in the Tiffin House in King Street, was blissfully unaware of any procrastination. She never thought to question why she had railroaded me even more easily than usual into sharing the second bottle of house red that I would later regret.

Whatever she might say, there was a lot Susan didn't know, and was not curious about. A sublime self-centredness was chief among her charms. I'd go so far as to say that this, combined with those random flashes of inspired perception, was the reason our odd-couple association had survived with only the regulation number of stops, stand-offs and start-ups, for more than thirty years. From the murky mire of puberty at Queen Edelrath's School for Girls in Watford to the sunny uplands of our middle years, Susan had talked and I'd listened. One of the things she said most often was what a good listener she was, and I always agreed. For when you got right down to the wire, there was no doubt that Susan was a blue-chip friend. I knew that if I were ever in trouble she would leap to my aid with all the furious energy of her naturally spirited nature (latterly enhanced by HRT), and rout my enemies with a thoroughness which would effectively depopulate my life.

The clock on the wall, I noticed, had a long hand which moved forward with a little jerk, flagging the passing of each relentless minute.

Emptying the last of the house red into her glass (the only one in which there was sufficient room), Susan leaned forward, the bottle still grasped in her right hand, and said, 'Did I tell you about Brünnhilde?'

She had told me a great deal about Brünnhilde (not her real name), the business acquaintance who was currently Number One in the Most Hated list, but I was right in assuming there would be masses more.

'The Hun from Hell!' she elaborated with loud and gleeful relish, adding, 'The Teutonic Tart With No Heart!' in case I'd failed to catch her drift.

'What's she been up to?' I spoke very quietly, in an attempt to protect our fellow-diners from my friend's robust revisionism.

'You won't believe this!' she hissed, adjusting the tone but not the volume. 'She invited poor Simon, a widower of barely two months' standing, out to lunch, on her own, without reference to anyone else, purely and simply to suck up! I mean, that is *such* bad form it takes your breath away! She wants to take us over, that's what it is, and she's far too chickenshit to deal with me.'

There was neither rhyme nor reason to Susan's violent, visceral loathings. They were a kind of obsessive hobby with her, like thimble-collecting or bird-watching. The good thing about them was that they went away – usually when some fresh candidate stuck his or her unsuspecting head over the parapet.

'. . . but Simon's not a fool,' concluded Susan. 'He's got her number. The British are so sophisticated like that. Don't you think? I mean, you should know,' she added slyly. I had called a moratorium on discussion of my private life, but she couldn't resist the odd dig.

It was three-thirty. There were now only two other people in the restaurant – a couple of men in suits – and the waiters were beginning to congregate by the till and talk about their social lives. Like all the best condemned women I had eaten a hearty lunch, comprising several trips to the curry buffet, followed by banana fritters, a speciality of the chef. Added to which I was sloshed. I doubted whether I could even make the door. I felt sure that if I did I would leave moist, greasy footsteps on the floor like something out of Stephen King.

'It's been so good talking to you about it,' said Susan, 'because it makes me feel vindicated. The woman's a Nazi. Or she has the mentality that put the Nazis into power. I'm so glad I'm not like that.'

The two men signalled for their bill.

'Now,' said Susan, 'I can see I've depressed you. Let me tell you something really wonderful to cheer you up. I wasn't going to mention this, because it feels like tempting fate, but what the hell?' She grinned tigerishly. It went without saying that whatever the wonderful thing was, it was to do with her, not me. My secret was quite safe. My long dark hangover of the soul would on this occasion remain unillumined by even the smallest glimmer of insight from Susan. This perverse sense of security made me generous.

'Go on then,' I said, 'tell me the good news.'

The grin grew even wider; her eyes glittered. The pleasure and excitement came off her in waves.

'He called!' she said, in a smoky stage whisper. 'The one I was telling you about. At nine o'clock yesterday evening.'

My eyes and throat brimmed with demeaning tears of self-pity. I raised my glass to her and took a swig of wine.

'That's great,' I said, 'I'm so pleased. Fantastic.'

'Thank you,' said Susan graciously. 'And I have to tell you he makes my corny old heart beat faster.'

'Terrific.' Reminding myself of something I'd read about it taking fewer muscles to smile than to frown, I stretched my mouth and bared my teeth dutifully.

'So there you are.' She leaned forward and cocked her head with a teasing expression. 'I'm *not* too old for romance.'

She made it sound as though I'd argued the opposite. 'Of course you're not,' I assured her. 'So what's he like?'

'Let's see. Maddeningly attractive, but definitely different – not my usual type.'

'What does he do?'

'I don't know!' She laughed rustily at the foolhardiness of it all. 'I don't know anything about him! He could be married for all I know. It was a classic case of instant chemistry. I expect,' she went on happily, 'that he'll turn out to be a serial killer and six weeks from now I'll be found murdered in my bed with his

initials carved on my chest and "Every Time We Say Goodbye"
playing on the CD.'

'Probably,' I agreed, and she shrieked with laughter again.

These *coups de foudre* occurred in Susan's life about every
couple of years, and were as necessary to her as the Most
Hated list. I suspected that both had their source in the same
congenital need for emotional excess. In this she was the
opposite of me, and we both knew it. My most fervent wish
(and one which unbeknown to Susan I was about to realize)
was to swap my current emotional Bosnia for the tranquil
Switzerland which ought to have been the prerogative of the
mother and grandmother with twenty-five years of marriage
on the clock.

There was no justice in our respective situations. Susan's
ordered, unencumbered, well-heeled lifestyle enabled her actively
to pursue and enjoy the luxury of an operatic sex life. When
agony followed ecstasy as it invariably did, she would withdraw
into a pale and nun-like purdah simply not available to the
married woman, ameliorated by a full hand of credit cards, a
riverside flat to die for, and a small but infinitely supportive
coterie of friends of both sexes, myself among them.

'Did I tell you how we met?' she asked.

'You mentioned something about it.'

'It was total magic, total madness, total romance!' Susan had
got moved to the back when understatement was being handed
out. 'We know nothing about each other, but I have the definite
feeling we're simply going to fall into each other's arms and bonk
ourselves brainless on the first date.'

She was the only person I knew who still used the expression
'date'.

'I had that extremely unpleasant contretemps with the bus-
driver,' she told me for what was probably the fifth time, 'and
I was aware all the time that *he* was listening in, you know
how one is aware of those things. And at the end – when I'd
won – he gave me this *extraordinarily* sexy smile, with a sort of
implied wink of encouragement. I did nothing. I didn't smile
back. I didn't do anything! Then when I got off he followed
me at the very last minute. And all he said was. "Mind if I
ring you?"'

'You were picked up,' I agreed.

'I was!' She was enchanted by the notion. 'I kid you not, it makes me feel eighteen again.'

'And didn't you tell me he wrote your number on his hand?' I prompted dully.

'He did! That's such a teenagery thing to do, isn't it? But I was completely charmed.'

'Anybody would be,' I conceded. The waiters had all gone now and the Malay girl on the till had put on hornrims and was reading *Madame Bovary*, but I still had one or two tried and tested delaying tactics up my sleeve.

'Aren't you worried,' I began, and was rewarded by an intensifying of Susan's gaze as she prepared to consult her innermost feelings, 'that after such a brief first meeting you'll be disappointed?'

'Not at all! For one thing I trust my judgement – poor old unmarried thing that I am, I do have some experience in these matters.'

'Of course you do,' I said humbly.

'And for another, what does it matter? Fuck it! It was a magic moment. Even if he turns out to have halitosis, nylon socks and a collection of Roger Whittaker albums, that won't detract from the fact that in a few short minutes on the bus and on a crowded pavement he made my heart leap!'

I marvelled anew at Susan's ability to mythologize her experience instantly and at will. Perhaps if I had been able to do that, to make myself the romantic heroine of my own life, I wouldn't feel such a sad case now.

'Do you believe in angels, Laura?' she asked.

'I haven't really thought about it.'

'No, you should,' she said, 'they're all the rage in the States. Everyone believes in them. By angels I don't mean bird-men in white kaftans, but beings who appear suddenly in your life, alter everything for the better, and then quite as suddenly disappear again.'

'I can't say I've ever come across one.'

'I bet you have,' said Susan, another of whose gifts was never to give house-room to a view which did not conform with hers. 'I bet if you sit down tonight and look back over all the really good things that have happened to you in the past few months, especially the unexpected ones, you'll find that at least one of them is associated with a particular individual who touched your life, no matter how fleetingly, at that particular moment.'

This suggestion was free-ranging enough to be almost irrefutable, but for one thing – in my present frame of mind I was pushed to recall any of the really good things to which she referred.

'Maybe,' I said.

'What about Henry?'

'Henry?'

'Yes – I sent you Henry, and romance stepped into your life.'

'I don't know about—'

'I'm sure of it. And the point about my bloke on the bus is, *he*'s an angel!'

'A moment ago,' I reminded her, 'you said he was going to carve his initials on your chest.'

'A dark angel then!' She squawked with mirth. 'Who knows? Who cares?'

Because there was no one left to summon, we paid our bill at the till. Lunch was always Dutch, though we tended to choose the venue to fit in with my more fluctuating finances.

'Thank you, it was excellent,' Susan told the Malay girl, who was marking her place with her finger throughout the transaction. 'I like this restaurant. It was nice of you not to hurry us.'

'You're welcome,' said the girl.

Susan put her card away and nodded at the book. 'Are you enjoying that?'

'I'm reading it for my exam.'

'I don't want to put you off,' explained Susan kindly, 'but it's the most depressing novel ever written.'

'B¹t wonderful with it,' I said.

Susan placed a hand on my arm without looking at me and continued addressing the girl. 'There speaks my friend the married woman! Now quickly, off the top of your head, without thinking, tell me: do you believe in angels?'

With a polite, wary smile the girl glanced from Susan's face to mine and back, and then shrugged one shoulder.

'Sure.'

'There you are!' Susan turned to me in triumph, vindicated once again. 'I told you so.'

The world can seem a chilly, heartless place after lunch, especially when that lunch has been a haven in a sea of troubles. Even on this sunny September afternoon I shivered as I squeezed guiltily behind the wheel of the half-timbered Morris and prepared to sort my life out.

The tall, terraced house in Calcutta Road was untidy and, more surprisingly, empty. Again. In other words, this was my second opportunity simply to go away and let things end by default, but I craved a confrontation. There was a note from Patrick clamped beneath the Fritz the Cat magnet on the fridge door.

'F.A.O. LAURA. WED. P.M. TAKEN PEACHES TO VET.' He always wrote notes in capitals, and I'd always assumed it was because he had the worst handwriting in the world. But this afternoon the habit irked me. It was patronizing, treating me as though I couldn't read. As to Peaches, if she were to be despatched to the great cattery in the skies it was a consummation devoutly to be wished as far as I was concerned. Patrick's attitude towards this indulged Persian with her delicate digestion and her coat that clung to everything it touched was nothing short of unbalanced. For all his Corinthian former sporting prowess, his towering intellect and his earthy charms, I suspected him of turning into an old woman.

Patrick's house was one of a select few that made me feel good about my own. It was untidy in a crazed, large-scale way that left ours for dead. The sitting-room was still in twilight with the curtains half-drawn. The mantelpiece was a dense clutter of old invitations, candlewax, half-eaten apples, loose change, biros, broken watches *objets trouvés*, and cough sweets. The carpet was invisible beneath an unstable drift of paper, slut's wool, and tinfoil takeaway cartons well into their second incarnation as ashtrays. He had some nice things, of course, but they had to take their chances with the general mess. Some paintings were carefully hung in groups, others still stood propped against the wall exactly where he'd left them when he brought them back. Half the bookcases were polished beechwood designed and built by a master joiner in Goose Yard, the other half were MFI white laminate with the obligatory screw missing.

I scrunched to the middle of the floor and surveyed the scene. Awash with red wine, I found myself thinking, what would Susan do? Leaving aside the fact that she wouldn't be here at all, waiting for a man who lived like a pig and took her for granted, she would certainly not fall prey to any knee-jerk compulsion to tidy up.

I flopped down on the sofa with my feet up. The cushions were still disposed and dented to accommodate Patrick's large body last night. I knew if I simply allowed my hand to drop to the floor I'd find the television zapper, and there, sure enough, it was, between the empty Boddington's can and the *London Review of Books*. With tears trickling backwards into my hair I pressed a couple of buttons and found an indoor tennis match, some celebrity event from a conference centre on the south coast. It was a men's singles between a seeded American in funny shorts and hair extensions and a workmanlike young Swede. Grunt-pop-biff-ping-grunt-oh-I-say!

The Swede held serve and the players changed ends. The American threw a large towel over his head but the camera stayed doggedly at its post, filming his shrouded, expressionless form while the pundits speculated as to his frame of mind, his intentions, his old knee injury and his relationship with the famous chanteuse who watched inscrutably from the celebrity box. I thought how good it would be if in everyday life you could simply throw a towel over your head and leave everyone to guess what was going on inside.

The umpire said time was up and the Swede bounced to his feet and moved briskly into position to receive. The American, as befitted a much-loved idol of the crowd, rose more slowly, adjusted his headband and walked pensively with his distinctive rolling gait to the base-line, amidst tumultous applause, rejecting the first two balls sent to him by the ballboy for reasons that only he would ever know.

The American delivered an ace. The crowd exploded with

delight. The Brits' traditional support for the underdog flew out of the window before their passion for this cuddly clown and his withering ground-strokes. Amidst the jubilation the camera picked up the chanteuse, but she remained impassive and after lingering hopefully for a few seconds it slunk away again, deprived of its prey.

I admired her steely sangfroid, with which my own behaviour compared unfavourably. After all, I had come back here to confront Patrick, to say my piece, and to walk out of the door with my pride and integrity intact. Instead of which I was behaving like the ultimate saddo. It wasn't my fault, I told myself. If he'd been here when I arrived it would all have been over by now. There again, if I hadn't been putting off the evil hour in the company of Susan I might have caught him before he left for the vet . . .

The American held his serve to love, and by way of a flourish sent one of the balls up to his opponent with a courtesy ace. He followed this with a pretended prayer of thanks and a self-deprecating gesture. The crowd berserked. The camera, sneaking another quick look at the chanteuse, was rewarded with the flicker of a smile.

I didn't hear Patrick come in. The first I knew of his return was when he appeared in the doorway, cat basket in hand. He was even more rumpled than usual and looked glum.

'Hallo,' I said, 'how did it go?'

He mumbled something and retreated into the hall. The next I heard of him was a clanking in the kitchen.

I glanced into the hall. The cat basket stood on the carved teak chest he'd picked up in Thailand. It was empty.

I sat down on the sofa and waited for him to reappear. There was silence. It was ridiculous, but I went out to the kitchen. He was sitting at the table with a glass of some disgusting Dutch eau-de-vie, and a lighted cigarette resting on the rim of a striped saucer. This was quintessential Patrick – an exhibitionist neediness that bordered on arrogance; raffishness hinting at ruin; his grizzled hair in need of cutting, his blue chin in need of shaving, his large body and old clothes crying out for a woman's touch . . . which they would not, I reminded myself, be getting from me.

'Did you have to leave her there?' I asked.

'Yup.' He took a swig of the firewater and picked up his cigarette with a hand that trembled slightly.

'Poor old Peaches.'

'Yup.' He coughed. 'I was offered the option, but I couldn't face burying her down the garden.'

For some reason, and in spite of my earlier unkind thoughts, it had not crossed my mind that Peaches would be put down. She was indestructible, surely? I was seriously wrongfooted. The bloody animal had stolen a march on me from beyond the grave. It didn't make my task any easier.

'Oh God,' I said. 'I'm sorry.'

'Can't be helped,' he said tersely.

'What was the matter with her?'

'Kidney failure.'

'So it was the best thing,' I said firmly.

'Yup.' He coughed again, his eyes watering. He had a constitution like an ox and a build like a grizzly, yet he had the brass neck to affect this consumptive air.

'You wouldn't want to see her suffer, surely?'

'I wouldn't, no.'

Casting around for a displacement activity under cover of which to change gear, I approached the sink. As one does. I washed up what was there – two mugs and a cereal bowl – and ran hot water into a porridge saucepan, amidst a silence you could have spread on bread. I'd moved on to picking the sludgy bits out of the plughole when he coughed again, and that proved a cough too far – it triggered me into action.

'Patrick,' I said, turning to face him. He looked up at me and raised his eyebrows. Exhausted but doing his best. Please. 'Patrick, I'm going.'

'You are?'

'Yes.'

He sighed, and stubbed his cigarette out. 'I'm sorry to be poor company.'

'It's not that—'

'And you're doing the fucking washing up!'

'That's okay—'

'Come here, tresh.'

As he said this he pushed his chair back and stood up. I suppose he must have taken a step forward but it seemed as though he simply stretched out an arm and pulled me over.

Habit and ambivalence made me ineffectual. Lack of the least suspicion or insecurity made him unstoppable. My feeble 'No' was smothered by his familiar, self-confident embrace. He snuggled his face into the side of my neck. I mumbled something about this not being the time or the place, and he grabbed my bottom and kneaded it appreciatively. As I bowed to the inevitable I entertained a mental picture of Peaches, in her prime, wearing that plump-cheeked, slit-eyed, smug expression that said, unequivocally: sucker.

One thing I will say for Patrick, he was not one of the turn-over-and-snore-noisily types that one reads about. Post-coitally speaking, he was the gnat's pyjamas. But then why wouldn't he be, when that constituted the only purely social part of our meetings? We never went anywhere and I never needed feeding – I was wonderfully cheap to run. On this occasion I could actually have made good use of a snooze-period during which to summon my resources for the ordeal which had been postponed yet again. But he was like a child after food – cheered, revived, raring to go.

'Don't go away,' he admonished, sliding his faithless arm from beneath my neck and padding downstairs to the kitchen. 'Get you anything?' he called.

'Water.'

He sang 'When I'm Sixty-four' as he waited for the tap to run cold. He never hummed, but sang properly, with all the twiddly bits and most of the right words. There was a practised twang to his singing voice which I imagined came from exposure to too many Irish show bands as a child. He was still singing when he came back in, carrying the Dutch gut-rot beneath his arm, my water and his glass in one hand and the striped saucer containing cigarettes and matches in the other. He stood by the bed, still holding everything, and went into the big finale.

'If I stayed out till quarter to two, would you close the door?' He leaned towards me, eyes rolling beseechingly. 'Will you still need me? Will you still feed me? When – I'm – sixty – four!'

He handed me the water and got back under the duvet with a series of self-satisfied bounces and grunts. Then he sloshed some liquor into the glass, lit a fag, balanced the saucer on his chest and said, 'I've got it all back in perspective now, you'll be glad to hear. You were absolutely right.' I held my breath, but he went on with scarcely a pause. 'It's just that she seemed like a perfectly healthy cat when I took her in and within seconds she was under sentence of death. On the other hand, she was in a very real sense *already* under sentence of death, and this dispensed painlessly with what would have been a distressing lingering decline.'

It was that 'in a very real sense' which nudged me back on course. Like the cough earlier, only this time I was on safer ground because he'd shot his bolt and there could be no smothering of the issue. I hoisted myself into a more commanding position, put my water glass on the floor by the bed, and held the duvet firmly in place over my torso.

'I'm glad you were here though,' he said. 'I'm glad you waited.'

'That's all right. Patrick—'

'They've got *Doctor Feelgood* on at the Multiplex. They say it's a hoot. Have you seen it?'

'No. You know I said earlier I was going—'

'Sorry about that, was it urgent?'

'No – yes,' I said, incisively.

'I love you when you're overbearing. If I'm a very naughty boy, will you beat my botty with a slipper?'

'Shut up!' I shouted. 'Be quiet, why don't you, for five seconds? When I said I was going, I meant as in leaving.'

He paused, as if considering this, and then nodded. 'Ah. Right then.'

'I'm not coming back.'

'I see,' he replied a little over-promptly. And then, quizzically: 'After all this time?'

'After five months, yes.'

He stubbed out his cigarette and put the saucer on the floor by the bed, nudging aside a slithering pile of paperbacks. With his back to me he asked, 'Now will you beat me with that slipper?'

I got out of bed and began dressing. He watched me, with a thoughtful frown. That morning I'd put on a black M&S suit with an edge-to-edge jacket and a short skirt – a snappy, sassy, businesslike look designed to carry me through lunch with Susan and on, coolly confident, through the anticipated vicissitudes of the afternoon.

'That's a good get-up,' he commented, as though the frown had been occasioned by my clothes. 'Have I seen that before?'

'No.'

'It's new, then?'

'No, but you haven't seen it.' It was truly astonishing how he gave no credence to my life beyond these four walls – this bedroom, for goodness' sake.

I put on my shoes and from habit gave my reflection the once-over. Patrick didn't own a full-length mirror, so I had to tilt the old-fashioned stand-and-frame model on the chest of drawers. I ducked to fluff my hair, and then straightened to smooth my skirt, run my thumbs beneath my shirt collar and shoot my cuffs. Beyond my reflection I could see his, arms folded over his chest, cigarette held before his face.

'Do you have any idea,' he said musingly, 'how sexy that little pantomime is?' When I didn't answer he went on: 'I do love a dash of testosterone in a woman.'

I turned to face him. 'But do you understand what I'm saying?'

'I think so.'

'It's over.'

'If you say so.' With a sudden and rather unnerving briskness he stubbed out his cigarette and lurched out of bed. 'Would you hang on just till I get some strides on? I feel at a disadvantage.'

I should have been out of there before he even asked, but now that he was hopping and tugging into his rumpled bags I felt I had to wait. He sucked his stomach in to hoist the fly, released it comfortably (he was disarmingly un-figure-conscious) and said, 'There we go.'

Annoyingly he left the bedroom first and jogged, flop-flop-flop, down the stairs in front of me. I felt prissy mincing down in my high heels, carrying the glasses and the saucer that I'd picked up from force of habit. Turning at the bottom he barred my way, one hand on the newel post and the other braced against the wall. He was never particularly clean, and he exuded his usual fragrance, essence of pub. The hand on the wall was inches from my face. Blessed understanding swept through me like a chemical high.

Nothing could stop me now. 'Excuse me.'

'Come on, tresh, this is silly.'

'Get out of my way.'

He stood aside, and immediately went to the front door and stood in front of that. I took the glasses and saucer out to the kitchen. When I came back he was still in front of the door. I picked up my handbag from behind the empty cat basket – there was a certain gloomy poetry in that – and rather than ask him to move again, remained where I was and said, 'Sorry, but I won't be part of your glee club any longer.'

'Glee club? That's rather good.' His face lit up with a surprised, admiring smile. The admiration was mostly, I knew, for himself.

I was absolutely sure he'd use the phrase again, quite soon, and pass it off as his own. That gave me the strength to walk briskly towards the door – so briskly that he'd have had to use force to stop me – and open it.

'Goodbye, Patrick,' I said. 'And all the very best.'

From the corner of my eye as I passed I saw him tilt his head.

'No kiss?'

What sort of question was that? I was no longer under any misapprehension. He was a monster of self-regard. He may have claimed to be turned on by my dash of testosterone, but it was pure oestrogen that saw me out of his front door, and his life, with his corkscrew and bottle-opener in my handbag.

I've no idea whether he watched me till I turned the corner, the way people are supposed to do. I rather doubt it. My guess is he closed the door, padded into the kitchen to fold a piece of bread round something tasty, and phoned the glee club's newest recruit to see if she fancied *Doctor Feelgood* at the Multiplex.

Even then, through the beginnings of a crunching wine-and-stress headache, I thought: 'And the best of British.'

When, six months before that, Glyn and I had reached our twenty-fifth wedding anniversary, it was with a start of surprise. We had been jogging along with our eyes on the ground for so long that we hadn't realized we'd reached the top of this particular hill. In fact it was only when we were invited to Old Edelrat Bunny Ionides' silver wedding party that we realized we too were up for a long-service award.

Bunny was loosely tethered to George Ionides, who owned an international children's wear chain and didn't care what she did as long as it didn't get in the way of making a profit. Their bash in north Herts was an eye-smacking explosion of conspicuous expenditure with orchids, caviar, Bollinger, a flotilla of ice swans holding the strawberries, two bands with an American magician in between, fireworks, a separate sixties disco, full English breakfast, and a thousand giant pearlized balloons released, with extravagant vanity, into the thick dark of early dawn.

'Did you meet your old school chums?' asked George in his amiably pompous way as we did a sedate rock 'n' roll to 'All Shook Up'.

'I've seen Lucilla. She looks wonderful.' Lucilla had turned into a honed Home Counties châtelaine with a manicure to die for and a jawline you could cut cheese with.

'Annette's here too, somewhere,' said George, subjecting me to an inexpert twirl, which gave my dorsal muscles a painful tweak. Annette – cussing, puffing, mutinous Annette – had become the biggest thing in social work (in every sense).

'She's done awfully well,' said George, who hadn't an ounce of poetry in his soul. 'She's one of the top people in her field.'

'So I understand,' I said. It was typical of him to apply the buzz-talk of commerce to the badlands of social work.

'Do you see any of the other girls from the old days?' he asked, mopping his face with a large hankie as the music stopped.

'Only Susan Upchurch,' I said. 'I see a lot of her.'

'Doesn't ring a bell.' George took a glass from a passing tray. 'Bunny can't like her.' This didn't surprise me, but Bunny didn't know what she was missing.

Back at our table Glyn was having a lovely time. 'Should *we* have a party?' he asked me, beaming, as I returned.

'Of course!' cried Bunny, who was doing her hostessly rounds, bursting out of a puce Alaia body-tube. 'You must! There aren't many of us diehards about.'

Empowered by 'Hi-Ho, Silver Lining', she towed Glyn on to the dance-floor, and I thought, as I watched them sway and chant with boisterous abandon, that still being married after a quarter of a century meant different things to different people.

We found one of Bunny and George's gleaming balloons in the car park of the South Mimms service station, thirty miles from its launching place. It was losing air and looked like a used novelty condom.

I told Susan we were having a party, and that she was invited. She expressed herself thrilled, charmed, and definitely committed. I knew she wouldn't come.

'You know what I think you should do to celebrate all those years of blameless union?' she said, grinning satanically at me over the *saltimbocca*.

'No, what?'

'*I* think you should have an affair.'

Our party was nothing like the Ionides'. Glyn's music agency, Guys 'n' Dolls, was successful, but not to the full-band-and-Bolli extent. We first contacted all the usual suspects, and then everyone we'd known for more than ten years (taking a charitable line on whether we liked them or not, since even quite obnoxious people tend to be agreeable when invited to a do). Not wanting to appear grasping, we didn't tell them what it was in aid of, but secretly hoped that a good number of them would realize. The take-up was good. Of the A-list, only Simon and his companion Richard were unavailable, destined to be taking a short break in Marrakesh at the time.

We opted for Sunday lunchtime, on the basis that expectations of a daytime party tended to be lower, and therefore less likely to be dashed. The month being April, we thought it unlikely that we could expect everyone to be outside. But we didn't want seventy-odd people confined to the house, and couldn't afford a marquee. In the end, and fittingly, we compromised. The Dog and Duck in Stoke Newington, where our elder daughter Becca's current boyfriend Nathan worked as a barman, had a lean-to tent which they hired out for peanuts provided the hirers could transport, erect and return it themselves. Nathan, having obtained the evening off, duly drove out on the Saturday with several hundred square metres of stained and tattered red canvas stuffed into the back of his Hyundai van.

'Is that it?' I asked, peering in.

'Yup.' Nathan, who had the physique of a gladiator and the face of a debauched angel, opened the back doors of the van. 'This is it. Where do you want it?'

It took the two of us, and our other daughter, Verity, twenty minutes to manhandle the tent with its accompanying sheets of resistant tarpaulin and plastic, and several sheaves of rusty pegs, hooks and nails, round to the back of the house where it lay on the patio with a sullen and intractable air, daring us to make sense of it. When our son Josh finally fell out of bed he and Nathan began erecting this unpromising structure against the rear wall of the house, assisted in due course by Glyn when he returned from London, and supervised by Becca who sat in the kitchen with a Southern Comfort and a fag while Verity bathed the children. Sinead, just three, and Amos, rising five, were staying the night so their mother could go clubbing.

'It's really dark,' Becca said as I opened the cans of beer which had been selected in preference to tea.

'It'll be fine when it's up properly. And remember it'll be the middle of the day.'

She peered out. 'It's the colour.'

'I quite like it.'

'Do you?' She sounded astonished.

'Yes, it's snug. Like a pub.'

'Oh, it's like a pub all right.'

Josh came in for the beers. 'That thing stinks,' he declared unambiguously.

'Let's have a sniff.' Becca went out and wrinkled her nose questingly. 'Jesus, Nat – what have they been doing in this down at the Dog?'

'Not hosing it down with Dettol, that's for sure.'

'Je-sus!'

The dim interior of the tent did in fact have a dank, graveyard odour. I looked up at Glyn, who was perched on a stepladder where he'd been fastening the roof lacing.

'What do you think?' I asked anxiously.

'It's fine.'

'It is a bit niffy.'

'Nonsense. It's cosy. Get everyone tanked and they won't notice a thing.'

Verity came down with the grandchildren, all sweetly powdered after their bath.

'Say goodnight to Mummy,' she instructed, 'she's going out with Uncle Nat.'

''Night, sweeties!' cried Becca at her most winsomely maternal, holding wide her arms.

'Ugh!' said Amos. 'It smells *gross* in here!'

I thought of the Ionides' lavish pavilion with its swags and bows, its orchids and chandeliers, and told myself that if it was sunny on Sunday we'd pull down the lean-to and brave the April weather no matter what.

Glyn and I made love that night, for the first time in six weeks. We both just knew that we would, slipping into each other's arms with a pleasant accustomedness and lack of urgency, and melding together. Sex with us was the expression and confirmation of our mutual fondness. We were not bonded by it, and its decreasing occurrence and importance in our lives was not a source of tension. It was as if we were returning, by gentle stages, whence we came. As we moved and murmured it was, like our first handshake more than twenty-five years earlier, impossible to tell where my body ended and his began. As we slipped apart, the clock of St Stephen's College struck twelve, and Glyn kissed me.

'Happy anniversary, Laura.'

Afterwards we lay as we always did, facing in opposite directions but with our backs pressed together, a metaphor for the nature and solidity of our marriage.

I was tired after a day of intensive party preparations, but I was also high, and couldn't sleep. We lay in the dark in silence for a while and then Glyn said, 'Twenty-five years is quite something, you know.'

'It is,' I agreed.

'Cy was saying it's a bit like running a marathon – if you can do five miles you can do ten, and if you can do ten you can do twenty. If you can do twenty you're barmy or bloody-minded enough to manage the last five.'

'So what point's he making?'

Glyn nudged my backside with his. 'That if we've lasted this long we're probably destined to stay the course. Till death us do part.'

Funny how even then, in the calm and companionable small hours of our silver wedding, as we heard the pounding backbeat of Nathan's van returning in the street outside, this remark seemed like tempting fate.

The morning dawned bright and mild but a bit queasy, with showers forecast, so we rolled up the sides of the tent and retained the roof, from which we suspended some balloons – not elegant ones, but a job-lot of children's party balloons in primary colours, including several of the sausage-shaped ones which are hell to blow up and result in a dark, nipple-shaped protuberance at one end.

The rain never happened, and no one mentioned the smell. Our party was a big success. The encounter which, with hindsight, was to bathe it in a lurid glow, didn't happen till the later stages, and did not at the time seem all that untoward. When a person is sloshed and celebrating, everything is heightened, and it's not until the hangover has bitten and receded, and the last bowls of leftovers have left the fridge, that the really meaningful incidents float to the surface and bob there, radiating ripples of uncertainty.

My brother David and his wife Anthea arrived early, at about eleven, because Anthea wanted to know if there was anything she could do. She had brought two bowls of *tiramisù* and some garlic bread. David dropped her and the contributions at the door before public-spiritedly parking the Jag fifty metres up the road. He was a partner with international accountants Dorling Toomey, and absolutely rolling. Channings, their spread near Godalming (referred to *chez* Lewis as the Ponderosa) was surrounded by white-painted paddocks full of expensive horseflesh which my sister-in-law licked into shape for other, even richer people. One of her equine pupils, Morgan Misty III, was reputed to be a probable for the next Olympics, which didn't surprise anyone, since it was hard to conceive of a living creature who would flout Anthea Beech, let alone when she had a whip in her hand. In late middle age she was still enviably taut and wiry, but she had the outdoor-woman's leathery complexion and flyaway hair, and her chin was becoming fluffy. In riding gear she was a sculpted centaur: in her Windsmoor shirtwaister and velvet hairband, with a scattering of David's dull but priceless diamonds, she was plain.

'Thought these might come in handy,' she said, putting the dishes and the bread on the kitchen table. 'Now tell me what I can do.'

'Well, I really don't expect . . .' I murmured.

'I know, but here I am, so point me at something.'

I pointed her at washing lettuce and polishing glasses.

'Where is everyone?' she asked, rotating a cloth inside a tumbler till it squeaked.

'Oh, round about. Upstairs.'

'I hope they're putting their shoulders to the wheel.'

'They've done a lot already,' I replied. (Well, some of them had. Verity, who had made two spinach lasagnes and her special apple and raisin cobbler, was at church, Glyn was listening to Radio One in the bath, the grandchildren were in Josh's room watching him get dressed – a welfare officer's nightmare – and Becca and Nathan were still in bed.) 'Do you fancy a drink?'

She glanced at her watch. 'Sun's not over the yard-arm, and anyway I'm chauffeur, but I'll have a coffee if there's one on offer.'

'Did someone mention a drink?' asked David, coming in from parking the car. He kissed me and placed a large, flat, badly wrapped parcel on one of the kitchen chairs. 'Many happies, well done. Hope you like it.'

'They're hardly going to tell you if they don't,' said Anthea abrasively. 'Open it, why don't you, you don't have to wait for Glyn.'

I gave David a glass of red wine and began tugging at the parcel tape. I was actually quite pleased to be opening it without Glyn, since I had misgivings about what it might contain, and it's always so much easier to deal with one's own embarrassment without the added burden of someone else's.

It was an oil painting of a white – sorry, grey – horse. I really couldn't have said whether it was good or bad, but the horse was discernibly a horse and the frame was gilt.

'What a superb present!' I cried, kissing them both warmly.

'Steady on,' said David, sitting down at the table. 'No need to go overboard. We know you don't give a monkey's about horseflesh, but it's actually worth a bit.'

'The horse or the painting?'

'Both, as it happens.' He tweaked his trouser leg and placed his right ankle on his left knee, revealing a smooth stretch of wine-coloured silk sock.

'You're very naughty,' I said, propping the picture up on the dresser. 'You must have spent a fortune.'

'We wanted to give you something you could flog if you wanted to,' explained Anthea in her no-nonsense way.

'Good heavens, we'd never dream of it!'

'Never say never,' advised David. 'Mind if I have a cigar?'

'Of course she minds!'

'Not at all.' I liked to see my brother looking the part of a fat cat.

'It's your funeral,' said Anthea. 'By the way, do you recognize the nag?'

I might have known there was a catch. 'No, should I? It's not . . .'

'It's old Misty, God bless her, looking as though butter wouldn't melt in her mouth.'

I was genuinely touched. 'We'll definitely never flog it,' I promised.

By twelve, I had admitted the caterer – a good-value lady from up the road – and set up the bar, and Anthea had redistributed such flowers as I'd bought and arranged so that they looked more.

Glyn came down, wearing a yellow blazer and a yellow and red bow-tie – he believed in dressing up for parties. He was not in the least embarrassed by the portrait of Morgan Misty III.

'Oh, I say!' he exclaimed, holding it first at arm's length and then close to, as if checking for forgery. 'That is just so smart. I really love that.'

'Good,' said David, smiling benignly upon Glyn whom he regarded as a kind of jolly mascot, not to be taken too seriously. 'By the way, you know Emma's in Cape Town at the moment, so she won't be here.' He referred to their plain and bumptious daughter, who had been on the way at our wedding, and who now fronted for a company who ran balloon safaris in the Kruger National Park.

'That's a shame,' said Glyn, adding with backhanded gallantry, 'we only asked you so we could see Emma.'

Anthea allowed this to pass and said to me, 'Jass is coming under separate cover, and picking up your parents on the way, so that Peter can have a drink.'

'That's kind of him,' I said. Jasper at twenty-eight had turned into an exceptionally nice young man, though a slight disappointment to his parents. His lack of academic achievement wasn't a problem – Anthea in particular would have been both startled and disconcerted if he had excelled in the classroom – but lack of drive was quite another thing. Jasper had no ambition, and following a series of aborted further education courses, in photography, media studies and performing arts (all about as comprehensible as Sanskrit to David and Anthea) and a brace of paternally instigated apprenticeships in the city, he was happily selling theatre tickets at the Barbican and living in a sagging mixed let in a bedraggled terrace in Hounslow. However, even I had to admit that none of this had succeeded in altogether removing the Etonian gloss from his manner, which was poised and personable. Unlike his sister he had plenty to be vain about, with long eyelashes and a winning smile, but his charm was the greater for being self-deprecating – a legacy, perhaps, from years of failing to meet parental expectation.

Both Emma and Jasper were unattached, and I sensed a very slight irritation in David and Anthea that Glyn and I had, in our unorthodox and thoroughly undeserving way, beaten them to grandparenthood. They also (according to Glyn, in whom David had confided at a Pimm's party at the Ponderosa) feared that Jasper might be gay. Personally I thought these fears were groundless. Jass was not gay, but cautious. He was in no hurry to embark on another potential failure, and who could blame him?

'I told him to get them here by twelve-thirty,' said David, looking at his watch, 'so that they can be comfortably disposed before the rabble arrives.'

'What rabble is that?' asked Glyn.

'We know your friends,' replied David, and the two of them laughed, each awfully happy that he wasn't the other.

Verity had returned from All Saints, meeting as she did so Nathan, departing stealthily to man his post amidst the lunchtime frenzy at the Dog and Duck. She came into the kitchen, her flowing green Oxfam dress enlivened by an AIDS-awareness ribbon. Her silvery-brown hair, too pretty to be called mouse, was very long and very straight, and she held it back with her hands as she kissed her uncle and aunt. 'Hallo, Uncle David . . . Auntie Anthea . . . Jesus saves.'

They mumbled sheepishly. In their village near Godalming David was chair of the Friends of St Botolph's, Anthea organized the flower rota, and the Ponderosa was the venue for the annual church fête – but Verity's brand of unabashed spirituality made them horribly embarrassed.

Verity was unaware of this. She bestowed the same greeting on me and on her father, and then exclaimed, 'What a sweet horse, is that a present?'

'Isn't it lovely?' I said.

She looked at me. 'Mum, you haven't changed.'

I thought she was complimenting me on my youthful appearance, till I looked down at myself and saw the XXL grey rugger

shirt and baggy ski-pants that I'd been wearing with only a brief
break since 7 a.m. the day before.

'Oh God!'

'Our fault for talking to her,' said Anthea, adding, 'not that
you don't look perfectly okay anyway.'

'That's what I thought,' agreed Glyn. 'Come as you are.'

I met Josh coming down from his eyrie on the top floor. He
had obviously spent hours deciding, with the help of Sinead and
Amos, what was the right note for a seventeen-year-old genius
to strike at a zimmerfest. Unsurprisingly he and his advisers had
come down in favour of black, the only colour Josh ever wore.
The sole relief was some discreet white lettering on the left breast
of his T-shirt. A closer inspection revealed the legend: DON'T GET
SHAFTED, GET LAID.

'David and Anthea are down there,' I warned.

'All right!' he intoned, 'Let's party!' And cantered down the
stairs.

Sinead and Amos were still in Josh's room, watching the
Jurassic Park video which to my certain knowledge was already
overdue to the tune of five pounds.

'Come on, you two,' I called from halfway up the second flight,
'switch that off, the party's about to start.'

Sinead came out and looked down at me. 'Are you going to
get dressed up?'

'Yes.'

'Can I come and watch?'

'That'd be nice.'

Sinead came with me and sat on the bed, trying on necklaces
and pulling out the hairs on her forearm with eyebrow tweezers,
while I changed. Becca had ensured that her daughter looked
sweet in a faded, old-fashioned smocked dress with kicker boots.
Like her mother, she was a hard act to compete with. In the end
I followed Josh's what-the-heck example and put on a red Jeff
Banks dress, expensive in its day, now amenable with use and
mellowed by many convivial occasions. To show that the old
dress was a choice and not a necessity, I added one of my rare
follies, a pair of Dolce e Gabbana black suede 'fuck me' stilettos,
with ankle straps and a single diamanté stud on the back of the
left heel. I finished things off with Glyn's anniversary earrings,

a couple of big twists of solid silver like Walnut Whips. I fancied that this combination, particularly of a Sunday lunchtime, would be enough to confuse the most sceptical guest.

Putting on my make-up in the full-length mirror, with Sinead standing in front of me putting on hers, I thought of Susan and fancied I could hear her voice saying, 'Very nice, Mrs Lewis, almost like a single woman.' I wondered if this time she'd defy all precedent and turn up, and whether it would be a good thing if she did. On the one hand, there was no one more fun, or whose company in the right circumstances I relished more: on the other, there was no one whose particular perspective on twenty-five years of blameless, uninterrupted marriage might more surely curdle my pleasure in the occasion.

I finished the make-up and stood back, sucking in my stomach and tightening my calf muscles. 'How do I look?'

Sinead, copying, held out her arms, lipstick still in one hand. 'How do I look?'

'You look gorgeous,' I said, knowing how this game worked. 'The belle of the ball.'

'You look gorgeous,' responded Sinead obligingly. 'Belluva ball.'

I relieved her of Desert Dawn and put the top back on. 'Shall we go down?'

'Yes!'

Without prompting, she put up her hand to take mine. Glowing with a sense of privilege, I led her out on to the landing, where we met Becca and Amos, his mother having succeeded where I had not in prising him away from t.rex, velocoraptor and co.

Becca, night on the tiles notwithstanding, presented her usual *bella figura*, in skin-tight black jeans and an emerald-green silk shirt tied at the waist. Her hair was piled up in a wickedly artless Bardotesque topknot, from which a few blonde tendrils escaped, and her Nubian-queen face, with its haughtily upthrust jaw, full, sculpted mouth and slanting cheekbones, was made up with model-girl brilliance. Earrings like cascades of golden coins jingled almost to her shoulders. My two daughters were alike in a way which displayed their differences. If Verity was the moon – pale, modest and serene – then Becca was the sun.

Amos, with his father Roberto's coppery colouring, seemed to have been burnished by his mother's glow, and Sinead, unlike her father Liam, was like a plump little peach ripened in her heat. Perhaps because today I knew I was also looking good, I was bowled over by the beauty of my family.

Becca picked up Sinead. 'What a babe!'

'Sorry about the lipstick,' I said.

'Why? She looks a real star.'

My eyes stung. Becca was no one's idea of the perfect mother, but there were some things she did divinely right. Putting Sinead down, she threw me a look. 'Not so dusty,' she said.

By one-thirty the party had achieved its own momentum. The decibel-count had reached that level which denotes lift-off, the body language was devil-may-care and the atmosphere heady with smoke, alcohol fumes and people getting loose as the proverbial goose. The proceedings had reached the point where I wondered why I had worried even for a split second about the smelly tent. The food – Verity's and Anthea's contributions aside – was Indian in orientation, and going down a treat with not too many shards of bhaji and samosa being trodden into the carpet. The music – well, I had overlooked music, but we had been infiltrated by a couple of Josh's friends who had assumed responsibility for saving us from ourselves with the latest sounds. Even the realization that in this crush no one would notice my diamond-studded shoes could not spoil my mood.

I didn't exactly work the rooms, but I did cruise them, blissfully surfing the crest of the party wave. By the buffet I found my father deep in conversation with Bunny. She had rifled my table-centre and now there was a daffodil in my father's buttonhole and one in Bunny's cleavage – of which there was more on view than is customary at lunchtime.

'May I kidnap Peter?' she asked me.

'By all means.'

'Not so much a kidnap, perhaps,' said my father, 'as an octogenarian-heist.'

Bunny held his tie and waggled it back and forth. 'I don't care if you've got a telegram from Brenda, you're still the most attractive man in the room.'

'I aim to please,' said my father.

My mother was having a similar effect on Cy Boseley-Thwaite and Hugh Heaton, who had married Old Edelrat Lucilla. Dressed in a vibrant turquoise shirtwaister and impeccable pearls, with Sinead perched decorously on her knee, she invested even our nice-but-naff sixties peacock chair with her ineffable brand of glamour. Cy – Glyn's best man and business partner – was still a bit tottery in the backwash of a messy divorce. He and Hugh, unaccustomed to such high-octane charm, were obviously in thrall.

'Darling,' said my mother, taking my hand and holding it as if I were eight years old, 'darling, help. I've started telling Simon and Hugh about the frightful dives Peter and I used to dance in before the war, always a bad sign. They're much too polite to shut me up, so I think you should rescue them before they keel over absolutely rigid with boredom.'

Both men protested. 'That's not all she told us,' said Hugh. 'I had no idea Diana was a Bluebell Girl.'

'Well, you wouldn't, you've never met her before,' I pointed out.

'*I* knew,' said Cy, pulling Best Man's rank. 'And even if I didn't it wouldn't take a genius to guess – check out those legs.'

My mother released my hand and tweaked her hem, glancing down at what were still, without doubt, among the best legs in the room. 'Oh yes, the pins have held up pretty well, but being this height can be a curse too. What size shoe do you take?' She looked up, eyebrows raised, at Cy.

'Nine,' said Cy.

She directed the look at Hugh. 'And you?'

'Ten.'

'Snap. And you cannot imagine the nightmare of being an elderly body trying to find pretty shoes with plates that size. Herring boxes without topses would be no exaggeration, though on this occasion Charles Jourdan rode to the rescue. Didn't he?' she added rhetorically, kissing Sinead's cheek.

'And now,' she added with her most warm, regretful, melting smile, 'you must take these two chaps as far as possible from my skinny hand and glittering eye. With a whole roomful of good-looking women to talk to, they don't want to be doing old-lady duty for a second longer.'

The protests began to swell once more, but I took the hint. 'Come on,' I said, interposing myself and linking my arms through theirs. 'Circulate. Put yourselves about. You didn't come here to enjoy yourselves.'

I bore them reluctantly away, and they were at once replaced by George Ionides, armed with a bottle of Sauvignon and a soppy smirk. As usual my mother had, with an enchanting display of self-deprecating humour, achieved exactly the outcome she desired – or at least a change of company, because I rather doubted that George's charms would be enough to keep her amused for long. All Diana's life, men had been drawn to her as wasps to an ice-cream, and she had learned to cope with this *embarras de richesses* with a silken tact that never failed her.

'I think I may be in love with your mother,' said Cy, a bit red-eyed, gulping wine. 'Is she spoken for at all?'

'They don't make 'em like that any more,' agreed Hugh. I suppose it was bound to be said, but only he would have said it. Cy gave him a look which was only one drink away from blistering rudeness. In another age it would, I suppose, have been pistols at dawn. Now, unless I brought my hostessly skills into play, it would be verbals over the *tiramisù*.

I took Cy to be soothed by Verity and Jasper on the sofa, and Hugh out to the tent where Lucilla and the other Edelrats had convened to chew the fat.

'Sorry,' said Lucilla, on seeing the two of us. 'This is a girls-only tent.'

'Don't be mean,' I said. 'And anyway, he's with me, and it's my party.'

'"It's my party and I'll cry if I want to!"' we chanted. Hugh looked distinctly nervous in the presence of this witchy sorority.

'Ah – can I get anyone another drink?'

'What a good idea,' said Lucilla. 'No, don't prat about with glasses, Huggers, just get a couple of bottles.'

Hugh withdrew. Bunny, who had torn herself away from my father (or more probably he from her), put her arm round my shoulders.

'Now, tell me, Laura,' she said. 'We were just saying, you and I have got to the big two-five, don't you think we've earned a rest? Don't you think we should pack it in and turn sapphic, like Daffs?'

Daffs's haircut hadn't changed one iota since our schooldays, but the word was she was reborn since trading in her RAF dentist for another woman. She blushed scarlet and shook with laughter. 'Oh, for goodness' sake, Bun!'

'No, sell it to us, Daffs,' said Mijou, whose exotic Persian lustre was remarkably untarnished by serial marriage (she was between husbands), a partying habit that would have finished off most people, and personal tragedy (her son, stepson and third husband had been killed in a skiing accident). 'Tell us why we should all become gay. You've got a captive audience.'

Daffs turned an even deeper shade of red. 'I *don't* think you should all become gay . . .'

We jeered noisily. Hugh, rejoining us with two bottles, smiled bemusedly. 'May a mere man know what the joke is?'

'You may, my love, but you won't like it,' said Lucilla, 'Daffs is going to tell us all how to become happy, carefree lezzies.'

'Go on then,' said Hugh, filling our glasses. 'I'm all ears.'

'Except you. Bog off, Huggers.'

I spotted Becca, hypnotizing David near the tumble-dryer, and pointed them out to Hugh. 'Would you go and help out my brother? My daughter's painfully shy and it can be rather hard work . . .'

'My pleasure,' said Hugh, and went off like a lamb to get the vamping of a lifetime.

'. . . I don't think anyone *ought* to be gay,' Daffs was saying. 'It was the last thing I wanted with Jamie still at Cirencester, and Gordon due for retirement, we'd even bought a house near Devizes—'

'So what happened?' asked Bunny.

'I met Ruth—'

'How?' asked Mijou.

'Where?' asked Lucilla.

I supplied the 'When?'

'She's a district councillor—' began Daffs, answering the one question we hadn't asked.

'Sleaze!' we cried. 'Scandal!'

'She's a district councillor, and we met at a public meeting about eighteen months ago . . . about the motorway loop—!' Daffs had always been wonderful tease-fodder. She was now in a St Vitus dance of giggles, with tears streaming down her cheeks, and we were almost as bad.

Lucilla got a grip first. 'Okay, so your eyes met across a crowded council chamber—'

'Village hall,' corrected Daffs, dabbing her eyes with a Devon Violets hankie.

'Whatever. And then what?'

'Well, nothing to speak of, not at that stage, I mean, we got talking about the loop and so on, she was collecting signatures, we got on really well . . .'

Bunny put her arm round Daffs. 'Cut to the chase, Daffs. You know what we all want to know – when did she first put a match to your fire?'

It was at this crucial stage in the conversation that I caught sight of Anthea, grimacing and semaphoring over the heads of the people in the kitchen. Her madly jabbing arm seemed to indicate that something or someone needed my attention at the front of the house.

Most unwillingly, as Daffs was urged on to describe the details of her courtship, I dragged myself away and elbowed through the party to the hall, where Anthea was waiting. The front door was open and a tall young man, in a glum mac buttoned to the neck, stood there with a black case on the step next to him. He conveyed the impression that he was being messed about but was suffering in silence.

Anthea moved in close with her back to him and spoke urgently and low. 'Sorry, I can't quite catch the burden of his song, so it's over to you.'

She withdrew. I advanced. 'Can I help?'

'Probably. Are you Mrs Lewis?'

'Yes.'

'It's your silver wedding, correct?'

'That's right.'

'I've come to play.'

The way he said it was so exactly like the way the children's friends used to talk that I half-expected him to stride in and begin making a mess with Lego.

'Play?'

'For you – and your guests.' He glanced over my shoulder at the heaving party, assuming a wincing expression as he picked up Josh's sounds. 'Music,' he explained.

'Oh, I see . . . But what – who – I mean, did my husband book you? Because I don't believe I—'

'I'm so sorry. Hang on.' He took a card from his pocket. 'This should explain everything.'

The card showed The Wedding of Arnol Fini on the front, and on being opened it read: 'To Laura and Glyn – so sorry I can't make your celebrations after all, but Henry is guaranteed to give your party lift-off, which is more than I ever could. He comes all bought and paid for, and with lots of love – Susan.'

Glyn had appeared at my shoulder and was taking in this message at the same time.

'How do you do, Henry,' he said. 'Come on in. What do you play?'

'The fiddle,' replied Henry, picking up the black case.

'Terrific,' said Glyn. 'What a smashing idea. Let me get you a drink – what sort of fiddle would that be, classical, Appalachian, Country, Cajun . . . ?'

In seconds he'd relieved Henry of the sad mac and taken him and his instrument to the bar in the kitchen. Glyn was always good with performers, and the more unsure of themselves they were, the better he handled them. I was only too happy to let him get on with it, because frankly I was browned off. Yet again Susan was a no-show. Yet again she had bottled out – or turned her nose up – at the thought of having to compete with my family and friends and the other Edelrats, and yet she hadn't been able to resist getting her oar in. Susan, I thought uncharitably, should either have made the effort to be here or settled for a bunch of flowers and butted out.

My mother's younger sister, Caro, swam into view (a liquid metaphor was the all-too-obvious choice) and I directed her to the first-floor loo. I went back into the sitting-room where Josh's jocks, relieved of their duties, were grouped mutinously round the CD player debating whether it was worth staying a moment longer in the face of such blatant culture-terrorism.

'Who is that bloke anyway?' asked Josh.

'Henry,' I said.

Only 'John Smith' would have raised a more scornful smirk. 'Henry who?'

'I'm afraid I don't know. He's a friend of a friend. A professional musician. He's going to play for us.'

Something in my tone gave me away.

'Come on. I thought this was supposed to be a *party*, not a wake.'

'I'm sure he'll be very good,' I said with a calculated hint of implied reservation.

'Oh yeah . . .' Josh and the jocks went back to discussion of their contingency plans. I took a weaselly satisfaction in their discontent.

Caro came back into the room. Her family resemblance to my mother did her no favours. She wore one of those droopy skirt-and-tunic outfits in brushed cotton which although voluminous, only look good on the slim, short-haired and vibrantly well-groomed. In hers, which was maroon, Caro contrived to look like an article of furniture with slightly sagging springs. Her pale, fine hair, not subjected to the same expert trimming and tinting as Diana's, gave her round face with its expression of amiable anxiety a distracted appearance. She was also tiddly.

'Have you seen Steph?' she asked, putting a hand on my arm.

'No. I didn't know she was coming.'

'Well, initially she said no,' explained Caro, 'but then she thought it was time she appeared in public with Monty.'

'Oh well then,' I said, 'I'll look out for them.'

I reflected that this was pretty typical of my cousin. Her twin sister Ros had emigrated to Canada and led an outdoor life with her husband Brian, a geology professor at Vancouver University and their two square-jawed, clear-eyed kids. But Steph had hung around, not giving anyone in the family the time of day but at the same time insisting that they be riveted by her life. It was unfair really. Once every couple of years Caro was whisked over to Vancouver, all expenses paid, and given six weeks to remember – trips to the Rockies, whale-watching, rodeos, Red Indians, lakeside cabins, cookouts, you name it. But it was Steph she always talked about. In her capacity as a professional fundraiser Steph was smart and opportunistic, with a nose for the sexiest good causes. Now that we were middle-aged the gap between us cousins had narrowed and I realized that whereas both girls had been fairly obnoxious in their teens, in Ros's case it had been the normal effect of biology in uproar but in Steph's it was something more. The Monty to whom Caro referred – and I disliked myself for even knowing this – was the television newsreader whom Steph had recently stolen from his live-in lover of many years' standing.

I joined the general drift towards the garden. Glyn was drumming up an audience for Henry. I was shamed by his willingness to enjoy Susan's contribution. It was therefore comforting to see two other people who obviously had no intention of moving. I approached the sofa where they were sitting and realized too late who they were.

'Laura – congratulations!'

'Hallo, Steph, I was looking out for you actually. I didn't realize you were here till I spoke to Aunt Caro.'

'Well, no,' said Steph, 'you wouldn't, because I wasn't originally intending to come, but Monty hadn't met any of the family, so here we are.' She lifted Monty's hand to her lips and kissed it. It was hard to know where to look. Monty was taller and thinner than he appeared on TV, with an unexpectedly chinless profile and hair that curled on his collar. He got to his feet a touch bashfully and offered me the hand Steph had just kissed.

'What can I say? I'm a gatecrasher.' His voice had an actorly timbre.

'Every halfway decent party has one.'

'That's true.'

We shook, and I resisted the urge to wipe my palm on my skirt. There was a burst of laughter from the garden.

'What's going on?' asked Steph. 'Have you got jugglers or something?'

'Not a juggler. A fiddler.'

'What a nice idea,' said Monty politely.

'Not mine, I'm afraid – a present from a friend.'

'In that case,' said Steph, 'you won't take it personally if we stay here.' She gave Monty's cuff a tweak so that he sat down next to her again.

'Not at all.' I began to move away. 'Can I get you anything?'

Monty dropped an arm over the side of the sofa and lifted a half-full bottle. 'Well supplied, thank you.'

It was no good – I couldn't escape the impression that my party had been hijacked. And to underline the situation I heard the front door slam on the departure of the disaffected DJS.

I had literally to elbow my way through my own guests to reach the garden. Their attention was focused elsewhere. My ill-humour made me slow to react, or I should have noticed the music sooner.

None of Glyn's suggested styles was right. Henry played jazz. As I reached the front of the crowd, and emerged from beneath the awning into the garden which was now bathed in spring sunshine, I was doused in a torrent of glittering notes which stopped me in my tracks. The number was 'Ain't Misbehavin',' but Henry seemed to have more than the regulation number of hands, for the tune skipped and swooped on its way adorned in a virtuoso swirl of improvised melody. He was standing on the grass like something that had grown there, tall and skinny in grey trousers and an RAF surplus sweater. Amos and Sinead sat on the ground at his feet. His music filled the air with exuberance, and delight, and sheer frolicsome happiness. It was the music of lasses and lads, and young men and maids, of sap rising and fancy lightly turning – but with a wistful, worldly edge that snagged the heartstrings. I stood and listened, captivated. I felt my shoulders relax and my expression soften. Glancing round at the faces of my friends and family, I saw they too were transformed. Gone were the rag-bag crew of individuals whose only connection was knowing us. They had become a happy and unified throng, their eyes alight with pleasure and a sort of – I searched my mind and this was the only word I could come up with – innocence. It was more than the power of cheap music, because this music wasn't cheap. It was sophisticated, bittersweet, full of dazzling wit and heartfelt sentiment, although Henry's eyes remained downcast and his face inscrutable. Only a slight working of the muscles round his mouth showed that there was any conscious effort at all in his playing. He seemed to have no notion of the effect he was having on us.

When he finished the number there was a burst of applause, followed by something unusual – a kind of murmur of delight and longing. People's glasses were empty but no one moved away. Arms crept about waists, some people joined the children on the ground. Everyone wanted more.

Henry didn't so much as look up in acknowledgement. He simply paused, before lifting his bow again and holding it poised it for a split second. When an enthralled silence fell, and he began once more to play – 'Can't Help Lovin' That Man of Mine' – I felt an arm around my shoulders and Glyn's hand turned my face to his as he kissed me.

'Well done, Mrs Lewis,' he whispered. 'I love you.'

'Me too,' I said. The music lapped us as we stood there together, my face against his cheek, his arm encircling me. It was a moment of sweet content.

As the last attenuated notes spiralled up into the blue like larksong, Glyn gave me a squeeze. 'Clever old Susan, eh?' he said. 'The girl done super.'

Henry launched into 'Maple Leaf Rag' and Glyn and I drew apart. Glyn grabbed my mother and began to dance, moving his arm up and down like a pump-handle. As I walked towards the end of the garden everyone joined in, a wild antic hay like a bunch of peasants in a Brueghel painting. Someone shouted 'Laura, come and dance!' but I waved a hand over my shoulder to show I'd be back in a moment.

I just wanted to sit and listen a bit more, and to observe the party from a distance. I also wanted to see off my earlier uncharitable thoughts about Susan who had indeed, as Glyn said, 'done super'.

Ours was not a large or distinguished garden. The lawn was mainly composed of plantains, moss and daisies, and most of that was taken up with Josh's old green metal swing (dug out and reassembled for the grandchildren) and a sturdy but unaesthetic red plastic climbing frame which I'd bought with good-customer points accumulated on a mail order catalogue. Glyn had made a pond, which was as green and greasy as the Limpopo but which seethed with wildlife, and we had two apple trees which supported a hammock in summer. Our herbaceous border was jolly with daffodils at this time of year and then despite our best efforts turned completely blue in the summer, as it filled up with self-seeded larkspur and canterbury bells which crowded out everything else.

The far end of the garden was divided from the rest by a screen of forsythia, not yet in full flower but green and bushy enough to hide the dilapidated shed, the overflowing compost bin, and the spreading pile of leaves, weeds, twigs and old newspapers which would be Glyn's next bonfire. The garden was bordered by a high fence with a green wooden gate in it beyond which was the twitten that ran between the two rows of houses. When younger the girls had been absolutely forbidden – fruitlessly in Becca's case – to use the twitten after dark because it struck me as exactly the sort of place where unpleasantness would be most likely to lurk.

Today it seemed that my worst fears might turn out to be justified, for as I came through the gap in the forsythia a stranger was standing just inside the gate. At least I was practically certain he was a stranger, but because the house and garden were full of people some of whom I hadn't seen in years, I hesitated momentarily before accusing him of trespass. This allowed him to speak first, which he did with a disconcerting lack of embarrassment.

'I do apologize – I was lured in by the music.'

'Really?' I said weakly. 'He is rather special, isn't he?'

'A faery fiddler,' said the stranger, advancing and gazing down the garden to where the dancers jigged and jumped, their arms waving madly in the air. 'Wonderful stuff.'

On the basis that both of us could now actually be seen, I decided that this irregular situation posed no threat.

'He was a present from a friend,' I said. 'It's our silver wedding.'

'Congratulations.' He held out his hand and we shook on it. 'Patrick Lynch.'

'Laura Lewis.'

'How do you do, Mrs Lewis. Please forgive the intrusion.' He didn't sound in the least like someone begging forgiveness. He stood next to me – presumptuously close to me, in fact – gazing down my garden at my guests as though he had as much right to be there as me. He was tall and broad with a burgeoning gut, a rower, perhaps, or rugger-player, just past his prime, dark, unshaven and smelling faintly of beer – I guessed he was on his way back from the pub.

Without asking, he fished out a packet of cigarettes and lit one. 'I take it you don't?' he asked, raising an eyebrow. 'Nobody these days does.'

I wasn't sure I cared for his assumption that I was like everyone else. If I hadn't been completely certain that it would send me into a paroxysm of coughing I'd have accepted one. His air of indulged self-confidence stopped only a whisker short of arrogance. An ostentatious scruffiness underlined his manner – his matted guernsey was frayed at the neck, and balding cords sagged over desert boots shiny with age. The impression was of a man who could well afford not to make an effort. A man who could take it or leave it, because it was always on offer.

Henry was playing 'Smoke Gets In Your Eyes'. Patrick Lynch began to warble along with the words.

'Why don't you come and join us and have a drink?' I suggested.

'Hellfire, no,' was his response. 'I'm on my way.'

He went to the gate and opened it. Then he paused and looked me up and down. 'You're a beautiful woman on your silver wedding day, Mrs Lewis,' he remarked with a blarneyish lilt. 'Mr Lewis is a lucky man.'

Oh, the cliché! Oh, the bullshit!

But how they made my heart beat faster.

Glyn was a Barnardo's boy. By an odd coincidence the home he had been brought up in turned out to have been only a few miles from my old school, Queen Edelrath's. He claimed to have had a happy and secure childhood, but it didn't take a psychologist to deduce that his subsequent career in the emotionally charged world of showbusiness, and his happy immersion in my own family, stemmed from his lack of personal roots.

I met him at a Rolling Stones concert in Exeter in 1965. I was nineteen and reading English at the university, and he was two years older and gophers for the road manager of the bottom-of-the-bill support group, an outfit called the Fallen Idols. The *folie de grandeur* implicit in their title was carried through in the Idols' stage gear, which was by Georgette Heyer out of Carnaby Street, with long dandy jackets, stand-up collars, ruffled shirtfronts, Cuban heels and hairdos like dralon tea-cosies. This was their big moment without a doubt, but their strenuous glamour compared ill with the Stones' ineffably rebellious crew-necked jumpers and unpressed cords. The Idols's set, comprising a brisk canter through not so much their greatest but their only hits, was played against a burble of inattention and impatience.

Ike and Tina Turner were the chief support act, trailing clouds of transatlantic glory, all tigerish eroticism and snarling vibrato. My memory of their set was tinged with revulsion at what Tina must have been going through at the time. Did Ike actually beat the bijasus out of his wife in some chintzy hotel room in the West Country the night before the show? It didn't bear thinking about.

I and my then-boyfriend Stuart, a chemist taking his Dip. Ed., had seats about halfway back in the stalls of the Gaumont, a cinema bravely masquerading as a concert hall for the occasion. There were very few men in the audience and we were a conservative pair, a little ill at ease with the frenzy of adulatory lust inspired by Jagger and co. The screaming began in earnest while Ike and Tina were still taking their curtain calls, and rose to an ear-splitting sonic chatter like the amplified roosting of a million giant starlings. It intensified as the curtains closed on the Turners, and again as a dozen locally recruited heavies ranged themselves in a row before the stage with a studiously cultivated air of menace.

Because of being with Stuart I didn't like to join in, and he adopted a look of nervous academic interest as our eyes watered under the onslaught of noise, and several girls in our immediate vicinity collapsed in full-blown hysterics. We had to stand up, because everyone else had and we would not have been able to see the stage otherwise. But since we had been impelled by simple necessity rather than feverish excitement, we stood amongst the screeching mob rather sheepishly, our arms folded, necks craning, hoping it would all be worth it and each of us conscious, I'm sure, that this embarrassing experience would mark the end of our relationship.

The curtains were held apart by an anonymous arm to allow the MC to step through. These were not high-tech days. There were no lasers, gantries, metal towers and walkways; no dry ice, holograms and giant screens; no squads of half-clad sexually ambivalent dancers; nothing, in fact, to winch up the existing levels of excitement except the wavering house lights, a rather tinny drum-roll from the orchestra pit, the row of local lads in vests – and now this cheeky chap in a dj, carrying a mike that trailed yards of flex. He was a dapper, peanut-faced man with more than a passing resemblance to Norman Vaughan. He was going to make the most of it.

'Okay, ladies and gentlemen, I thought I'd give you a song.'

There was a brief lull of disbelief followed by a growl of disapproval. The band – such teases! – struck up with a slithering cascade of violin notes, and the growl turned into a mutinous roar. The MC laughed and waved his hands in the air. He was like a drunk who'd wandered out of a window on to a tightrope and still hadn't realized the danger. It was terrible to watch.

'Sorry, what's that?' He cupped his hand to his ear. The clamour was deafening – they didn't think it was funny. 'Sorry, you want who?'

'The Stones!' we bayed. I felt it was legitimate to join in with this particular game, but Stuart was still po-faced.

'Pardon? Who?'

'The Stones!' we screamed. The heavies unfolded their arms and took a step forward, their scowls a fraction less convincing than they had been on entering, as who could blame them? They probably wished fervently that they were at home eating a fish tea in front of the telly with their mums instead of stuck here in front of a thousand teenage banshees.

The MC held up his hand again. 'Hang on a tick, I'll take a look.' He parted the curtain, stuck his head through, and withdrew it again. 'No one there, I'm afraid.' We screamed and stamped and waved our arms in the air. The heavies held their arms away from their sides as though about to draw six-guns and waste the lot of us. It was impossible at this stage not to be infected by the general fervour. Only Stuart still evinced a lofty immunity to it all, confining himself to adjusting his glasses and – I could not hear, but could tell by the movement of his Adam's apple – swallowing nervously.

The MC went through his routine once more, this time toying with us to an almost unbearable degree. With his head and shoulders hidden by the curtain, he communicated through the hand, first flapping it up and down in a pretended attempt to silence us, then waving it from side to side to indicate that nothing was happening, then lowering it wearily . . . only to raise it slowly once more, the thumb lifted in triumph.

We were beside ourselves. Even at the time I realized how horribly easy it was to get caught up in a mood of mass hysteria. When Stuart and I had entered the Gaumont an hour and a half earlier it had been in a spirit of curiosity. I had some Stones records but I was a John Lennon girl myself and had never fantasized about tying Mick, let alone Brian, Keith or Charlie, to the bedpost. But now I began to feel that when the curtain parted to reveal these undernourished subversives I might be unable to prevent myself from leaping knickerless on stage and forcing myself upon them. And Stuart's cringeing superiority only made matters worse. Who did he think he was?

'We want the Stones! The Stones! The Stones!' we roared. Talk about putting on our very own Nuremburg Rally right there . . . it made my blood run cold to think of it.

The MC withdrew from the curtains and scythed his hands back and forth, palms down, to quieten us. We subsided into a rumbling silence.

'You want to see the Stones?'

'Yeah!' we screeched.

'Well, I've got news for you . . .' He glanced behind the curtain teasingly. 'They're here!'

We went ape. The heavies took another step forward looking still more wary, since common sense must have told them that any real advance on our part, fuelled as we were by a ferocious hormonal rush, would have resulted in them being trampled underfoot by a myriad Saxone slip-ons and left for dead.

The curtains indulged in a certain amount of jerky foreplay and finally parted, to reveal the stars in their pullies. Richard, Jones and Watts were thumping out the opening chords of something but it was virtually inaudible. Jagger twitched and cramped like a man attempting not to wet his trousers.

Their performance was something of an anti-climax since we'd left ourselves with almost nowhere to go in terms of noise, and amplification was in its infancy so we had no idea what they were playing. For Stuart, though, it was better. He could now legitimately sway and nod with the preoccupied air of the serious student of rhythm and blues. I decided then, if I had not done so before, that he was a complete prat.

To complete this revelatory moment I felt a pressure on my shins and looked down to see, crawling on all-fours along the row, among the sweet papers, stamping feet, hairslides and urine on the floor, at considerable danger to life and limb, the man I was destined to marry.

At first I thought he was some pathetic representative of the weaker sex enjoying a free peep-show – hemlines had climbed rapidly over the past year – until he suddenly got to his feet, forcing himself upward between me and the back of the seat in front. Our bodies were crushed uncompromisingly together and I couldn't see the stage. I had to brace one arm against the back of my own seat to prevent myself from falling over into the row behind. It didn't escape my attention that Stuart continued to bob about, indifferent to my plight.

'What are you doing?' I yelled in his face.

'Mercy dash!' he yelled back, jabbing a finger in a direction along the row to my left. 'Sorry!'

'Go on then, get on with it!'

He began squeezing crabwise along the row, attracting the opprobrium of everyone along the way, and I saw that yet another girl had collapsed. There was no centre aisle at the Gaumont, and he was obviously going to attempt to drag her out the way he'd come to the St John's Ambulance team who hovered near the exit. The girl was built on an epic scale and I found that in spite of myself I kept glancing away from Jagger's gyrations to see how the intrepid Samaritan would tackle the problem.

There was no attempt at heroics. He grabbed her round the upper chest, beneath the armpits, and began hauling her back along the row, her vast legs in lacy tights bumping along like a couple of bolts of cloth, one shoe missing in the mêlée. I remember thinking her rescuer did well to hold her like that without, intentionally or otherwise, taking a purchase on her enormous sagging bust. She slid further and further down, until by the time he reached me her arms stuck straight up and he was more or less pulling her by the chin. He was sweating profusely. The Stones were doing another quick reprise of 'Not Fade Away' but he looked as if he might do exactly that unless he got some help. On an impulse I picked up the girl's legs, one on either side of my waist like a competitor in a wheelbarrow race, and together we lugged her to the side aisle and thence through the exit into the narrow corridor.

As the St John's people got to work with kind words and capable hands, the Samaritan said, 'Thanks. Excuse me,' and headed up the narrow passage to the Gaumont's rear door. I followed.

It was a summer evening, damp and cloudy but still light. He leaned against the wall, breathing heavily, offered me a cigarette which I refused, and lit himself one.

'Well done,' I said. 'She weighed a ton.'

'If it wasn't for you I'd still be in there,' he replied. He had a pleasant voice with a fashionably urban twang. This was the heyday of working-class glamour, when all the smartest people came from the wrong side of the tracks. The only childhood photograph of Glyn, taken when he was about twelve, shows a boy who would have been perfectly cast as the Artful Dodger. When I met him he bore a slight likeness to Terence Stamp, with shaggy dark hair and blue eyes, but less patrician features than the cockney star. He wore a white collarless shirt and a black leather waistcoat, with jeans, all of which bore testimony to the current state of the Gaumont's five-and-nines.

'Glyn Lewis,' he said, holding out his hand.

'Laura Beech.' We shook. I couldn't tell where my hand ended and his began.

The back door on the other side of the Gaumont opened and the Fallen Idols emerged with suits on hangers, guitar cases and a couple of hardbitten functionaries. The Idols in mufti looked less ridiculous but more vulnerable: dwarfed by their luxuriantly styled hair, they were just four peaky, undernourished youths whose lucky break had not amounted to as much as they'd hoped, and who were in consequence occupying the slippery edge of only modest success. It was taking all their effort, concentration and hard graft to walk that edge and not fall into the black hole of obscurity below. I felt embarrassed for them. I was easily embarrassed then.

'Hey, lads!' called Glyn. 'I'll be right there.' He dropped his cigarette end and trod on it. 'Got your phone number? I'll be back this way in a couple of weeks.'

'Um, yes . . .' I realized I'd left my bag under my seat in the auditorium, but he was already holding a chewed biro and a dog-eared concert pass. I gave him the number and he scribbled it down.

'I'll give you a bell. Thanks for your help.'

I stood and watched as he helped the Idols load up. And then I waved to him as the vans pulled away, like some western farmer's wife watching the stagecoach clatter out of town.

I left the handbag – and Stuart – where they were, and wandered home in the afterglow to my flat in Heavitree where my flatmate, expecting at least another hour to herself, had her boyfriend in our shared bedroom and was busy setting in train those events which would lead to her second abortion.

The next time I saw the Stones it was on their *Voodoo Lounge* tour, and Mick, Glyn and I were all grandparents. I considered that given Mick's fiscal advantages, we bore the comparison pretty well.

We were married eighteen months later, in church, from my parents' house in the Surrey Hills. It was Glyn, a susceptible agnostic, who was sold on the church idea. He had an open mind where the Almighty was concerned, but thanks to Barnardo's he had a surprisingly sound knowledge of the Anglican calendar and liturgy.

My father was a bank manager with the Westminster, who read the lesson once a month with a dry, crystalline credibility; my mother brought her stage experience to bear on music and movement with the Sunday school, the slightly irregular results of which were presented to the local congregation at family services and feast days. But neither was particularly pious, and my father in particular took the view that mortification of flesh and spirit in the form of church attendance was essential to the full enjoyment of Sunday lunch and whatever stand-up-and-shout preceded it.

I had intended Glyn, with his irregular work on the fringes of the pop world, to be my pretext for a little mild snook-cocking in the form of the register-office-and-King's-Road-bistro option in town. But he confounded my assumptions.

'Oh no, don't let's, everyone's doing that,' he said, adding disarmingly, 'I've told everyone you're a Home Counties toff, they'll be terribly disappointed if we don't have the whole works.'

It was typical of Glyn to present his own preference as an indulgence of the preferences of others. But then the two usually coincided because he was an enthusiast who took on the colour of whatever group he was currently enthusiastic about. This puppyish desire to be taken in and approved of was one of his most endearing characteristics.

My parents liked him, in my father's case rather in spite of himself. He was both sceptical and admiring of Glyn's chameleon quality. When Glyn told him he'd applied for what both men referred to as a 'proper job' (it was on a listings magazine), I remember my father saying, 'What as? Primate of all England?' As for my mother, she liked men, and the more they conformed to her picture of them as sweet boys, the more she liked them. But both parents had the sophistication of their generation, where much was acknowledged though little said, and I was prepared to bet that at the time of our marriage they understood him rather better than I did.

So the full works it was. The dash of testosterone was not, I must tell you, in evidence on that occasion. I harbour no illusions about my looks. With my big bones, broad shoulders and large, emphatic features I'm no one's idea of a beauty. With a bit of effort and a following wind I can be striking, but on my wedding day my mother's genes must have been in the ascendancy, and I believe I came close to being pretty. I wore full-length white brocaded satin, empire line and trumpet sleeves, with my hair up and an elaborately coiffed hairpiece with white ribbons intertwined in its coils. Round my neck was a pale green velvet choker with my mother's peridot brooch pinned to it, and I carried white roses. I was Elvira Madigan, and Patti Boyd, and Julie Christie in *Far From the Madding Crowd* . . .

My mother wafted in as I was putting on the final coat of lip-gloss, and laid her hand on my shoulder as she looked at our combined reflections in the dressing-table mirror. She was nothing short of a fantasy Mother of the Bride in a broad-brimmed hat of pleated black silk with a single turquoise flower, and a dress and coat of floating silk organza in black and turquoise.

'Darling, you look absolutely lovely,' she said.

'So do you.'

'Thank you! You're quite sure I don't look like the cook on a day out . . . ?' I didn't bother to reply to this, one of her rare, and quite involuntary, glints of snobbery. 'I'm just going, so I'll see you in church.' She made a *moue*, careful of her lipstick, and I inclined a cheek, careful of mine.

She straightened up and gave my shoulder a little pat with her silk glove. 'He's a nice man, Glyn. I want you both to be extremely happy.' She ducked briefly to catch my eye in the mirror once more. 'You be sure to be a good girl.'

It's awful to admit, but I was flattered by this piece of advice. Though I might not have been had I known how prescient it was.

It was April, with the weather hovering between smiles and tears. Glyn wore a pale green suit with a white shirt, a green-and-white patterned bow-tie and a gardenia – we were winsomely colour-coordinated. Cy, who was then editor of the girls' monthly magazine *Hipster*, wore a cream chalk-striped three-piece with zip-up canvas boots.

My older brother David (grey morning dress, silk stock, gardenia), then no more than a gleam in the corporate eye of Dorling Toomey, was chief usher, and the three-year-old Jasper was page. Spawn of Satan though he seemed to me at the time, Jasper was small enough fry to be under his mother's thumb. Anthea was always an absolute brick of a woman, scion of a dauntingly county family, who was still riding in three-day events at five months pregnant. She thought nothing of putting the maternal frighteners on her son, who in consequence looked uncharacteristically seraphic in green breeches, white hose, and a white ruffled shirt.

My twin teenage cousins, Ros and Steph, were bridesmaids. They were about to take O-levels and were even stroppier than usual, what with not having done a stroke for the past five years, and having to fall in with what they perceived as my unreasonably draconian demands about dress. Aunt Caro was a less reliable ally than Anthea, being fairly daffy to begin with, long divorced, and worn down by many years of bootless struggle. It was left largely to me to police the twins. From the neck down I got them looking almost virginal (if I could do it, so could they), in pale green-and-white sprigged cotton with scoop necks and full sleeves. From the neck up they remained dolly-birds – pasty-lipped, sooty-eyed, and brain-dead. (It always struck me as odd that in the sixties, that period of emancipation and the Pill and opportunity for all, the prevailing female fashion simpered: Look at me, I'm an underage sex toy.) Their sculpted Cilla Black bobs, rising smoothly over a nest of backcombing at the back and falling into two lacquered points at the front, utterly failed to accommodate my wired alice bands of white flowers, which had to be jettisoned. The unobtrusive Bally pumps obediently purchased by Caro were also rejected at the last moment in favour of cloggy white patents which I only spotted as we foregathered outside the church porch for our entrance, when it was too late.

'What a bevy of beauty,' said my father, dapper in his morning dress, as I glared at Steph and Ros to show I'd noticed.

My father wasn't a handsome man, but he was an attractive one. He brought irony to bear on what in another man might have been grave disadvantages. Aware that others probably saw him as a dry stick, a number-cruncher who after a dull war had sat tight and risen effortlessly through the ranks of the Westminster, he simultaneously accepted and undermined this view with a frosty courtliness which, allied with a sharp, glancing wit, made him rather devastating. I had seen gorgeous women glued to my father's side by the minutely raised eyebrow, the quizzically inclined groomed head, the finely judged murmured remark, the scholarly adjustment of gold spectacles with finger and thumb.

My mother, a renowned beauty standing six foot-plus in her stilettos, had been with him since 1937 without a word of complaint or a moment's discontent that anyone knew of. My father's reference to the bevy of beauty was the comment not just of a quietly satisfied man, but of a connoisseur.

We stood in the capricious spring breeze – my father and I and my mutinous train – waiting for the off. Inside the church the organ played the *largo* from Handel's *Water Music*. Ros and Steph were like waxen images in their briskly billowing muslin. David hovered in the porch to receive signals. Anthea, in an elastically expanded blue suit (Emma) and a petalled toque, hovered over Jasper, occasionally removing the questing hand he thrust down the front of his breeches.

'I've got a Mason Pearson in my bag, Jass,' she told him,

'and if you do that again you're going to feel it on your bottom.'

'I'm frozen,' complained Steph.

'Stamp up and down,' suggested Anthea abrasively. She had done bridesmaid duty almost annually in all weathers since the age of four and saw no reason why these two whingeing horrors should be pandered to.

'What are we waiting for?' Ros was querulous. 'I thought they were all waiting for us.'

'Ah, but we all in our turn await the vicar,' explained my father, 'who only arrived a moment ago.' This remark was edged with a certain caustic relish, since he regarded the clergy in general as not worthy of their calling and only imperfectly trained. It pleased him to say that he had yet to meet a vicar whom he would willingly have employed in his branch.

A second later David advanced to the entrance of the porch with the long, creeping strides of a man being painfully discreet.

'Flag's gone up,' he said. 'It's all yours.'

'Hold your horses,' cried Anthea, 'while we dash behind a tombstone!'

A scattering of rain fell as we waited, and the accompanying small drop in temperature made Jasper's urine steam exuberantly as it hit the granite.

'Cheers,' said Anthea. 'We're ready for the off.'

'Thank God for that,' muttered Steph, 'I've got goose-pimples like the Andes.'

'All right?' enquired my father. I nodded, and we strode purposefully forward. I didn't have even the smallest twinge of nerves or anxiety. But as we entered the porch, and I could smell the flowers, and the scent, hear the creak of the organ pedals and see the rows of faces turned sideways to greet us, something compelled me to look over my shoulder.

And there, beyond my sulky handmaidens, I saw Susan sauntering up from the direction of the lychgate. She wore a black-and-white checked trouser-suit, a yellow polo-neck jumper, black patent shoes with a gold buckle, and a black butcher-boy cap pulled down jauntily over one ear. When she caught my eye she pointed, covered her eyes with her hand, and then waved both arms in the air and capered up and down like a mad baboon, her Mary Quant shoulder-bag flapping wildly in the wind.

Unsettled, I almost dragged my father up the aisle to meet my groom.

After the wedding it was two years before we met Susan again. We were living in Willesden Green with Becca aged twenty months and Verity on the way. Glyn was working as a stringer on the diary column of the London listings magazine. Every week there was a distribution of whatever freebies had been sent to, and rejected by, the heads of department. On this particular occasion Glyn, at that time the lowest form of editorial life, had come home with two tickets for a film premiere. On the day I deprived Becca of a nap, laid in a supply of chocolate digestives and prevailed on the churchy lady from the flat upstairs to babysit.

The film was the first foray into directing of a South African actor who had made it big in Hollywood by growing a natty moustache, taking elocution lessons and assuming quintessential Englishness. It was a dire comedy of the high seas called *The Plimsoll Line* ('One woman on board is bad luck. Twelve's a bonanza!') and concerned the pranks, romps and escapades occasioned by the transportation of a troupe of chorus girls aboard a Royal Navy frigate. It was stupefyingly energetic and coy – the last gasp of those toothsomely smutty but naive British pictures that films like *The Knack* and *Blow-Up* saw off for ever. In the following weeks it died a lingering death at the box office, but on the night in question it was enjoying its hour in the sun. The ersatz Englishman had got his well-preserved chums and their popsies out in droves, and backing them up was the usual squad of dolly-birds, chancers, hairdressers, photographers and sportsmen. Never were so many heavy fringes, headbands, elephant loons, beaded waistcoats and false eyelashes worn by so many to so little purpose.

I was no slouch myself. I wore a purple panne-velvet Biba shift with lilac suede platform-soled ankle boots. Though not new, it had been sufficiently ahead of its time when it was, to pass muster now. My five-month pregnancy was obvious enough to disguise my slight ongoing weight problem, and the dress had a halter neck with a plunging 'keyhole' décolletage which displayed my hormonally enhanced cleavage to advantage. Glyn, now aware of the Terence Stamp comparison, wore a lilac suit and a tie-dyed silk handkerchief round his neck. God, but we were as cool as all-get-out.

Or that's what I thought until the after-show party. Glyn and I were standing near the buffet (we were not among the shining ones allotted places at tables in the ballroom) talking about how disappointing the stars looked in real life, when I heard a familiar rasping cry like the call of an exotic parrot in the jungle canopy. Or at least the tone was like that – the content mimicked the title of another undistinguished film about the Japanese bombing of Pearl Harbor.

'Laura, Laura, Laura!'

'Susan!'

'How are you? Who's this?'

'This is my husband, Glyn. You came to our wedding.'

'I did, yes, but we scarcely exchanged two words, and anyway I don't expect these things to last.' She hung on to Glyn's hand for a moment, grinning excitedly. 'Tell me, Glyn, do people tell you you look like Jess Conrad?'

'Not usually,' said Glyn bravely. Only I could tell quite how crestfallen he was, but fortunately there were other matters to draw our attention. One was Susan's outfit, a backless-to-the-rear-cleavage palazzo-pants number in gold lamé. The other was her companion, whom she now seized by the elbow and introduced.

'And this is Jimmy Mullaney who is *not*, I'm happy to say, my husband.'

'Hallo there,' he said, giving us both a short, sharp tug of the hand.

We were no longer cool. We were shamefully impressed. Jimmy Mullaney was the undisputed king of Formula One, three times world champion, twice back from the dead, with enough metal in his body to build a family saloon. Even in this company he was by far the most glamorous person in the room, trailing clouds of Grand Prix glory and standing about shoulder-high to Susan in her gold wedge heeled sandals.

'Wasn't that film the most unspeakable load of shite you've ever seen?' said Susan loudly.

'We thought so,' agreed Glyn. 'Thank God there's plenty to drink.'

Jimmy Mullaney swirled the contents of his glass as though it were medicine. 'If you call this stuff drink.'

'Take no notice,' said Susan. 'He thinks champagne is for spraying over people when you've notched up another few points in the championship.'

We laughed, but he only smiled coolly and asked, 'So how do you two know each other?'

'We were at school together!' cried Susan.

'Laura doesn't look old enough,' he remarked with mischievous gallantry.

'Oh, she's centuries younger than me,' explained Susan generously. 'We once completely ballsed-up an egg-and-spoon race together.'

'Did you?' asked Glyn.

Susan reached across and laid her hand on his forearm. 'You must let me buy you a drink some time and I'll tell you all about it.'

'It was the house relay actually,' I said.

Jimmy raised his eyebrows. 'Such recall . . . it must have been a formative experience.'

'It was all too boring for words,' declared Susan, 'and best consigned to the dustbin of history like this dog film.'

She spoke as always *con brio* and it was impossible not to notice this remark being registered on several faces in the surrounding crush.

'Why don't you come and join us at our table,' she went on, 'so we can talk properly?'

'We're not allocated table places,' said Glyn thinly. 'I'm working.'

'No! You're an actor – no, you're in films – no, no, no, don't tell me, you're a photographer—'

'I'm a journalist,' explained Glyn.

Jimmy raised an eyebrow. 'I hope everything I say isn't going to be used in evidence against me.'

'Christ, no. A five-line précis in the listings is all that will be required of me in return for this sumptuous evening's entertainment.' I was proud of my husband's selflessness, for this chance encounter must have seemed like the portals of preferment.

Jimmy looked relieved. Susan beckoned vigorously. 'Come on, there's a no-show at our table!'

We followed. Glyn had long since forgiven the Jess Conrad blunder and looked happy and thrilled. He was more than a bit star-struck and loved to feel he was at the centre of things. I wondered if there would be an embarrassing scene with the muscular flunkey at the doorway of the ballroom, but I was to witness the power of true fame. Jimmy simply walked through without a word and the flunkey was too polite even to glance at the rest of us.

There were eight gilt chairs round each table, and the other couple were dancing when we got there. Dinner was over, but champagne on ice was on a stand by Jimmy's chair and he poured us all a glass and motioned for more. Emboldened by the high life, Glyn said, 'Isn't he a short arse, that star?'

I turned hot and cold, but Susan screeched with laughter and put her arm across Jimmy's shoulders. 'Hear that? You've got competition.'

Jimmy submitted to Susan's squeeze with the relaxed good grace of a man who, although only five foot two in his shoes, knew he was the absolute embodiment of fearless machismo.

Glyn blundered on. 'No, but it's different with film stars. You expect them to be larger than life, and when they're not it's a disappointment somehow.'

'I couldn't agree more,' said Jimmy. 'I like someone to look up to.'

'So you see he's *extremely* content!' said Susan. We laughed.

* * *

A little later, in the glass, marble and quilted-leather wastes of the ladies' powder room, I said to her, 'He's really lovely, where did you meet him?'

'At a drinks party given by a friend of mine who has the knack of bringing interesting people together,' said Susan, with no trace of false modesty. 'And yes, he is a little darling, isn't he? I must say I thought any racing driver, let alone a dwarf one, was bound to be an arrogant pig, but he really isn't.' She cast me a sidelong glance as she finished retouching her lipstick. 'He knows what he likes though.'

'Does he?' I remained in neutral, awaiting a flow of salacious confidences to discuss later in bed.

'Oh, yes.' Susan smacked her lips. 'He spotted your Glyn across a crowded room.'

It took only a split second for the implication of this to hit me, with all the messy impact of a kitchen cupboard collapsing. As the door of the powder room swung shut behind me, Susan's rusty squeaks of laughter rang in my ears.

After the churchy lady had returned to her flat we lay in bed with Becca slumbering between us (she had an uncanny understanding of when conjugal rights might be imminent, and interposed herself accordingly). I drank tea and Glyn smoked a joint. I knew he was flattered.

'He behaved like a perfect gentleman,' he mused, 'more's the pity. If he'd put his hand on my knee then I'd really have had something to write about. It could have been the making of me, in every sense.'

I sipped my tea. 'What did you think of Susan?'

'A gas,' said Glyn. 'But I wouldn't want her as an enemy.'

A year later as we sat in a heap on the sofa with both girls one wet Saturday afternoon, trying to persuade Verity to take a nap, we saw Jimmy's Renault spin off the track during the Hungarian Grand Prix and watched, horrified, as his dead body was prised from the wreckage. Reports of the memorial service, held in London, contained no reference to a 'constant companion' or 'lifelong friend' and we reflected in the slightly smug way of married couples that he must have been lonely. In one newspaper photograph of people outside the church we saw Susan in the background in dark glasses.

That was when she and I began having lunch regularly.

.

4 ∫

Two days after our party I met Susan at Pizza Parade and we
ordered the Four Seasons for two with garlic and herb bread,
and a bottle of Valpolicella, to be brought at once.

'We can't thank you enough,' I said. 'This one's definitely
on me.'

'No, no, you can't do that. Rules are rules.'

'Rules are made to be broken.'

'Not these ones. Once we start to make exceptions there'll
be no end to it.'

'Well . . .' It had only been a token suggestion anyway.

Susan lit a cigarette. She liked being thanked. 'So you enjoyed
my little Henry, did you?'

'He was wonderful. Where did you find him?'

She tapped her nose. 'I have my contacts. No, I heard him
play at an otherwise boring party before Christmas, and as
soon as you mentioned your celebration I knew he'd be the
very thing.'

Hearing her say this in person, it seemed incredible that I
could have been so miffed about it at the time. 'He was.'

She poured the wine with what seemed to be an especially
gleeful giggle.

'What did you think when you opened the door and saw
this saturnine stranger standing there?'

'Well, actually—'

'Because he is, don't you think? A little bit mad and bad?'

'I don't know about—'

'You can't believe when you see him that he can play like
an angel. But it's all part of his charm, I think. That out of

the whatever comes forth sweetness – out of the what?' She hesitated momentarily, allowing me to take a short, sharp breath and plunge in.

'Strong,' I said. 'Out of the strong.'

'Really? Well, that isn't what I meant. So much for free-ranging quotation.'

'And it wasn't me that opened the door, as a matter of fact, it was my horsey sister-in-law—'

'Is that horsey in appearance or persuasion?'

'Both. She and David regard us as some sort of sub-culture anyway, so nothing would surprise them. But when she fetched me I admit I was pretty gobsmacked. He doesn't exactly launch a charm offensive.' Susan chuckled. 'Anyway, he was a smash hit. Glyn asked me to say a special thank-you.'

'And how is Glyn?' asked Susan searchingly. 'And the rest of the tribe?'

'Oh, they're fine.' It was always hard to know how much to say on this subject, or how genuine the enquiry was in the first place. For once, Susan allowed a short pause to elapse as if trying to tempt me into indiscretion, before asking, 'What did Glyn give you on your anniversary?'

'These earrings.' I turned my head so she could see.

She fingered them appreciatively. 'They're nice. You may continue to wear them in my presence. What about the children?'

'They made us an album of special occasions.'

'Good for them!' This accorded well with Susan's hopelessly idealized picture of how offspring should behave. I didn't bother to add that I suspected the album had been almost entirely the work of Verity, while Josh's and Becca's contributions had been confined to a pro rata financial donation and the presentation itself, when Verity had stood blushing in the background with Sinead in her arms while Becca took centre stage.

'Did they make a speech?' asked Susan.

'Becca did, sort of—'

'What did she say?'

'She said we must be completely bonkers—'

'Bet she didn't use bonkers—'

'She said we must be mad but she admired us for it anyway.'

'Right on, Becca. Any sign of her marrying anyone?'

'Not at the moment.'

'Either of her children's fathers, for instance?' Susan laughed piercingly, but she knew she'd touched a nerve and adjusted her expression to accord with my pained smile.

'What did Glyn do, did he make a speech?'

'No.'

'Goodness, I thought he'd serenade you in front of the guests or something.'

'Hardly.'

'Gosh,' sighed Susan, 'what a foolish old romantic I must be . . .'

The herb bread arrived and we dug in, tearing off delicious greasy chunks and losing all our lipstick in the process. We neither of us made any secret of our liking for Pizza Parade. No pretensions, pure pig-out.

Susan scrubbed at her mouth and hands with a paper napkin. 'You're looking terribly good by the way.'

'Heavens.' I looked down at myself, surprised but pleased. 'I thought I might have put on weight.'

'You have a bit,' said Susan, with the gracious candour of the true friend. 'And about to put on a bit more,' she added as our giant, deep-pan Four Seasons with extra peperoni and black olives hove in view. 'But that doesn't matter. You're lucky you carry your weight in the right places. And there is an indefinable sparkle . . . What have you been doing?'

'Nothing.'

'Or perhaps I should ask,' she leaned forward and looked up at me from beneath her brows, 'what has Glyn been doing?'

'Nothing.' Her brows shot up. 'No, I don't mean nothing, but honestly – we're just another year older and deeper in debt.'

Susan screeched. 'You're the only person I know who'd admit to a quoting acquaintance with the songs of Tennessee Ernie Ford—'

'Who?

She screeched again. She was in cracking form. 'Well . . .' She sat up and glugged out more wine. 'One of you must be doing something right. Tell Glyn I said so. If he looks half as good as you I'm going to be straight round to your place in my crotchless knickers. It's not fair that you married people should keep all the talent to yourselves.'

It was at that moment, tempted as I was to unbosom myself, and old and valued friend though she was, that I decided to keep *schtum*. I did not mention the short handwritten note which had appeared on the doormat the previous evening, addressed to 'Mrs Lewis' and signed 'Your admiring gatecrasher, Patrick Lynch.' Secrets, however slight and incomplete, are erotic.

'I meant it when I said that about Glyn,' she continued. 'I need a little romance in my life. I need *sex*, for crying out loud, and if it comes without the carnations and the box of Black Magic I can very easily put up with it. You're a woman of the world,' she announced contentiously, 'what do you recommend?'

I was happier now the conversation had moved into familiar territory.

'For heaven's sake, you have to ask me?' I said. 'Get out your little black book.'

'I could,' she conceded, 'I do know several who would be only too happy to do the honours, but Laura, I need someone *new*.'

'What about Simon? Hasn't he got any ideas?'

'He's nothing but ideas, both of them are, but it's not exactly their field. When they do come across someone they think would suit me they generally wind up staking a prior claim. It's like buying people presents you want for yourself.'

'Yes.' I pondered. 'I can see that.'

'I suppose,' said Susan, wagging a slice of peperoni at me, 'I suppose I could join a dating agency.'

'Not quite your style, I'd have thought.'

'Not in the least my style, but desperate times need desperate measures. Maybe I could go on one of those late-night cattlemarket TV shows.'

'Maybe.'

'I mean, be honest, I could knock most of the no-hopers you see on those things into a cocked hat.'

'That's true.'

'*Blind Date*!' She was warming to her theme – the peperoni

slipped from her fingers without her even noticing. 'They do middle-aged Blind Dates from time to time, don't they? That would be far more fun – I shall audition for Cilla, have a free weekend in Tenerife and be thoroughly outrageous on the sofa afterwards!'

'That could be fun.'

'Limiting, though. And there might be rather a high fake-tan and chest-wig count.'

'You never know.'

At last she put in a large mouthful, and I took advantage of this natural break to ask, 'What about at work? I'm always reading about the workplace being a hotbed of sexual liaisons – I mean, the CAB's not like that, but I'd have thought in your line—'

'Some of my best lays have been clients,' she agreed. 'But it does leave one open to the charge of massaging the sale.'

'He'll walk into your life any day now,' I declared. 'And your eyes will meet, and you'll know. It happens all the time.'

'Does it?' she asked, darting me one of those warm, shrewd looks which showed she paid me more attention than I thought. 'Does it now, Mrs Lewis?'

Although she was a little older, Susan had arrived at Queen Edelrath's after me, and left a couple of years later, having made twice the impression in half the time. My own early days at the school had been a slough of homesickness and incompetence. It was several terms before I began to fit in and when I did it was with a slavish need to be as inconspicuous as possible.

QE's was a jolly, middle-rank, uncomplicated sort of place on the northern outskirts of London, with a relatively enlightened headmistress and a good reputation for sports (lacrosse, tennis) and music (the choir and orchestra took their budding libidos on tour each spring). The uniform, available from Gorringes, was in a colour then unflinchingly known as nigger-brown. Long cloaks for winter – seniors only – were brown with a yellow lining. Summer dresses were beige and white striped cotton with a detachable white collar. Hats were panamas – brown felt with a yellow band for winter, beige straw with a brown ribbon for summer. There was no really serious bullying, the staff were mostly sane, the food edible if not palatable, and the plumbing adequate. There was a dance at Christmas for which the older boys of nearby Harefield Hall were bussed in, accompanied by a squad of rumpled masters who were the unwitting cause of a hundred humid gussets. Up to three teddies were allowed on the bed and pin-ups 'within reason' on the cubicle walls. These had to be vetted, but only by Matron, who was a broadminded divorcee with tinted hair. Even she had been scandalized by one girl's picture of a pouting, acne'd teenage rocker named Cliff Richard, and asked what on earth we saw in him when there were gorgeous hunks of men like Rock Hudson about. If dear Matron were still extant today, I wondered what she would have made of the recent ennobling of our idol and the death, from Aids, of hers.

Parents' consciences were salved by the much-repeated mantra, 'It's such a *happy* school,' and it was – up to a point. What QE didn't allow for was girls who were not happy: wet, moping, disconsolate girls were beyond its collective comprehension. In consequence I was a pariah for most of my first year, not so much vilified as utterly ignored, like one of the more disgusting beggars on the streets of Calcutta. When I did begin to cheer up there was an almost audible sigh of relief, as girls and staff alike realized they were no longer going to have to get stiff necks looking the other way.

So I settled down, but remained big, and shy, and unexceptional. You couldn't say I built up a circle of friends. What I did was hover on the edge of an existing circle until, by a process of osmosis, I became part of it. There were Annette, Mijou, Lucilla, Daffs and Bunny. Mijou was Persian (as then was), and had an angora cardigan with pearl embroidery and a sister who'd caught the eye of the Shah; Annette was fat and insubordinate and smoked; Lucilla took up with a ski instructor, left before O-levels and was later seen modelling nursing bras in the Mothercare catalogue; Daffs was incorrigibly giggly and got married young to an RAF dentist; Bunny was vivacious and busty and could pull even in school uniform.

Hierarchies were strictly observed at QE, and the six of us were all in the same class. Friendships across form barriers were rare, and generally denoted a 'pash'. A true pash had to be at a distance of at least three forms. So it was hardly surprising that Susan, with her cavalier disregard for these conventions, caused quite a stir.

She came for the sixth form only, because she'd been at a school in Hagley Wood which had closed down, and QE had an understanding with the trustees. The other girls from the Hagley Wood school were perfectly unexceptional, so Susan's differences were clearly genetic. She was virtually tone-deaf and hopeless at games, but neither of these shortcomings prevented her singing loudly in chapel and taking on the suicidal role of goalie in lax. She was a gifted actress, who could laugh and cry on stage at will, which QE found somewhat *de trop*. When she landed the role of the Dauphin in Anouilh's *The Lark*, she gave herself a historically accurate pudding-basin haircut which caused the Maid of Orleans to corpse in all three performances. She conducted an entire current events assembly on the rise of the Beatles, and got away with it. Until, years later, my daughter Becca became a teenager, Susan was my sole exemplar of a person who could bend and stretch the system to her advantage without ever actually falling foul of it.

It was astonishing for the rest of us to see this proof that you could be yourself and survive. For when the Head, Mrs Puddifut (we suspected the 'Mrs' of being a purely honorary title), spoke of girls being 'natural', she did not mean naturally themselves, but natural in some generic, wholesome way of which she approved. Susan was not exactly a rebel – that would have been too much like work – but she didn't conform, and for the six terms she was at QE the staff seemed hypnotized by her.

It would be overstating the case to say that she and I were friendly, but we were more friendly than was usual between girls in different years. I took part in an end-of-term revue of Susan's devising, rashly entitled *Stir Crazy*, and on Sports Day we were both obliged to be in the same team for our house, Edith Cavell. I think it was this that provided the seedcorn for our later friendship. We were both atrocious at PT, but the liberal regime at QE stopped well short of allowing girls to duck these healthy and character-forming activities. On sports day, rabbits like us were entered for low-status, high-manpower events such as the house relay, where our ineptitude would, in theory, attract the least attention. In practice it meant that one invariably took the baton from the sinewy hand of the meanest, fastest thing on two legs, and was then exposed to the onlookers' screams of despair as one proceeded to throw away a hard-won lead.

Lining up for the relay, I found I was behind Susan.

'Shall we run away to sea?' she asked.

'Jolly good idea.'

'Except for the running bit!' She screeched with laughter, and then was suddenly serious. 'I hate this. I really *hate* this.'

'Me too.'

'If I ever have children,' she confided, 'not that I intend to, I shall make bloody sure no fat teacher with hairy legs and BO has the nerve to tell them what's good for them.'

'Quite!'

It's hard for anyone who didn't attend a girls' boarding school at that time – it was the early sixties, but at QE the fifties lasted well into the next decade – to appreciate the sheer dazzle of a sixth-former who spoke freely to a girl two years below, let alone one who 'bloody-ed' in that casual and comradely fashion. I was ensnared.

We both ran. Susan, I remembered, laughed for the whole hundred yards, flung the baton at her waiting team-mate and threw herself, howling with mirth, into the arms of the rest of them. The baton came back to me at alarming speed. I snatched it, dropped it, and finally lumbered down the field, fiery with humiliation, to ensure that Edith Cavell got the wooden spoon.

As I trudged back up to school-house for tea with Annette and Mijou, Susan hove alongside once more.

'Traitor!' she said. 'You went like a bloody train!'

'I was still last,' I pointed out.

'That's true.' She poked a long finger at me and waggled it up and down. 'So honour is satisfied.'

This was the trick I came to associate with her of making everything suit her ends. I, poor hidebound creature that I was, would rather like to have won. In the face of all evidence and experience I nurtured a Mallory Towers-ish fantasy of myself, head back, chest out, arms pumping, flying down the field to breast the tape an inch ahead of my nearest rival. The thrill, even in this fantasy, consisted not in personal glory, but in saving the honour of the house. When Susan spoke of honour being satisfied, she meant something diametrically different. Honour consisted in making a virtue of necessity, a triumph of your failures, and a positive *blitzkrieg* of your strengths.

I was essentially a team player. Susan, like Groucho Marx, wanted no part of any team that would have her.

From the time of Jimmy's death she became a feature of my life, and mine only. 'How's Susan?' Glyn would ask, but he only needed the briefest token run-down. And when she asked about him it was either to commiserate presumptuously with my plight, or to build up sufficient credit to hold forth for the next hour. She very flatteringly believed I was too bright to be anything but bored and frustrated hanging around at home with the girls. When I fell pregnant with Josh she evinced sufficient pity and horror to sustain several Greek tragedies. You'd have thought Glyn – in reality the most sensitive of lovers – was some drunken Victorian wife-abuser, reeling home of a Saturday night, belt at the ready and flies gaping, to ensure his threadbare little wife remained safely up the duff.

'Do you come from a big family yourself?' she once enquired, fixing me with a look of tortured puzzlement.

'Only two. And this will only make three.'

'I'm an only,' she said.

'I thought you had a sister.'

'Oh, my sister the cow, I don't count her.'

'That's cheating,' I protested.

'No it's not.' She inveighed happily against her sister for a while and having returned, via this scenic route, to the point, leaned forward and tapped me sharply on the forearm.

'The thing is, when are you going to get some time to yourself?'

'I have time to myself,' I protested.

'No you don't!'

'Yes I do.'

'When, for instance?'

'Now, for instance.'

'Oh, *well*.' Susan took out a Rothman's King Size and held

it questingly aloft until a lighter was magicked to her side. She took a drag. 'Oh, *well*, if you're going to pretend the odd hour's browsing and sluicing with a girlfriend constitutes real freedom . . .'

'It does,' I insisted, adding spiritedly, 'And so does the option to have six children if that's what I want.'

'God in heaven, don't do it!' she cried, with every appearance of genuine dismay. 'You mustn't! That's not just reproducing, it's reproducing in order to opt out of the rest of life!'

'Rubbish.' I laughed. 'And anyway I'm not going to.'

She looked sceptical. 'Nothing would surprise me.'

If all this makes her sound unfeeling, it shouldn't. When Josh arrived, Susan came to visit me, bringing a cold-box with the ingredients for Black Velvet ('I've read stout is good for nursing mothers but I won't touch it without champagne') and a gigantic gonk with a Zapata moustache which Josh kept in his room well beyond the age when I would have dreamed of commenting on it.

After Josh I lost a baby, stillborn. Another little girl. Susan wrote me a letter full of such fiery feeling that it actually made a tiny difference where all else had failed. I have kept it. In the letter she managed what no one else had dared attempt – to speak of Isobel as a real, whole person.

'*I want us to have a wonderful, long lunch, and I want to know all about your youngest daughter* [she wrote]. *I want to know who she looked like, what she weighed, what colour her eyes were, and her hair (if any). I want to know what name you've given her, and all about the godawful funeral service. I wonder if I might be her godmother? I'd make a lousy godmother in real life and I don't have any of the right credentials, but I know I'd be good at thinking about your lost little girl, and talking about her so that she stays in the family . . .*'

Susan's words breached the dam and allowed me to cry. Even Glyn hadn't been able to do that because he was as paralysed with grief and despair as I was. Six weeks later we did have lunch, and I did tell her about Isobel, and she listened, without a murmur, through two hours and three bottles of wine, and that time we both cried. Afterwards we went to Kensington Market – this was when Susan was still based in London – and she bought me a Victorian locket and arranged for it to be engraved with the names of all our children, including Isobel. A couple of weeks later I received, by special delivery, a white rose bush named 'Isobel' after our youngest daughter.

If I ever needed proof that Susan was a true friend, that alone would have provided it. Maddening, egotistical and dictatorial though she often was, she had heart. And, more importantly, soul.

Susan took the view that marriage – any marriage, but of course mine was the one she knew best – was by definition dull and stifling. But I believe that deep down she was ambivalent about it. The mere idea of being, as she put it, 'banged up with the same man for thirty or forty years' filled her with real horror, as did the interdependence, the responsibility, the compromise, the mild, necessary hypocrisy, and (Isobel notwithstanding) the kids. At the same time her scorn was tinged, I felt, with a slight anxiety that in the twilight of her years she might miss someone to drink cocoa with. I believe it was this anxiety that made her increasingly judgmental, and me endlessly forgiving. For despite living a life high on the post-Pill hog, Susan displayed the classic double standard of the child-free. No hint of irony coloured her 'don't-do-as-I-do-do-as-I-say' philosophy. She stood in her glass-house, Rothman's King Size between her lips, large gin and Schweppes at her elbow, and lobbed boulders. When Becca shacked up with Roberto, a Brazilian dancer and the first of her boyfriends brave enough – or not sufficiently fluent in English – to invite her, Susan professed herself shocked to the core.

'You're actually going to just *let* her?' she squeaked as we stool-perched in a tapas bar in Long Acre.

'What else can we do? She's nineteen.'

'Yes, but at nineteen I was still a *virgin*!'

I was sufficiently surprised myself not to be put off my stroke by the ripple of turning heads. 'You weren't, were you?'

'Believe it or not I was!' Since she had already effectively caught the barman's eye Susan gave him a speaking look and nudged our glasses forward. 'I may have been a late developer but I'd never have *dreamed* of moving in with some foreigner, let alone telling my parents that was what I was doing!'

I spoke in a determinedly lowered tone in an attempt to lower hers. 'Isn't that hypocrisy?'

'It may well have been hypocrisy,' she declared, not taking the hint, 'but it kept me out of harm's way!'

'It's all very different now,' I said in what even I could tell was a battle-weary tone. 'The whole culture is towards openness.'

'Okay.' Susan took delivery of our next round and settled into the argument with relish. 'Okay. But if everyone's being so open, what I want to know is, why doesn't Glyn go round there and bop this dago on the nose?'

I flinched. Heads turned away to conceal smug smirks. Once again she was painting a picture of Glyn which lacked only tattoos and a pitbull to qualify as Hardest Man in Town.

'It's not his style,' I said wetly.

'Maybe that's the problem.' She drove me crackers in her psychoanalytical mode. 'Maybe you should both of you be heavier parents.'

It was characteristic of our relationship that I never paused to consider what qualified Susan to lecture me on how to raise children. 'But Becca wants to be with Roberto,' I said. 'He makes her happy. He's done nothing wrong—'

'Except steal your daughter's innocence.'

'Oh,' I laughed, 'that was given away with stamps years ago—'

'QED,' crowed Susan.

Sometimes her subversion of the marital status quo took the form of these swingeing but grossly unfair indictments of our competence. Sometimes they were more subtle.

'Of course,' she would sigh, having described some particularly trying weekend when the demands of her social life had proved too exacting and she'd been reduced to lying alone on her bed with *Kiri Sings Cole* and a glass of iced coffee, 'of course, you blissfully married ladies don't have to worry about times like that, because there's always someone there for you.'

'I suppose so,' I'd mumble cautiously.

'No, but come on, there is. When I feel bleak I have to dig

deep and find the answer inside. When you feel bleak you have a shoulder to cry on.'

'It depends what it's about.'

'Surely not,' she'd scoff. 'A partner for life is a partner for life. What's marriage about if not being there for each other?'

'That's meant to be my line.'

'But I don't hear you saying it, Laura.'

I forebore to tell her that I wouldn't stoop to using such a hackneyed old cliché, because of course she knew it was a cliché and that's why she'd used it herself.

'What does Glyn do?' she'd ask.

'When?'

'When he's down. When he needs a friend. I bet he comes straight to you.'

'Sometimes,' I conceded. It was impossible to convey the intricate weave of long-term marriage, its tacit conventions and assumptions, to someone who could not conceive of it.

'Sometimes?' She looked aghast.

'It would depend what the problem was.'

'There are times,' she would say solemnly, 'when I feel I know nothing about you, or about marriage.'

She didn't, of course, so all I could do was look humble and reflective.

'I think,' she went on with the utmost satisfaction, 'that I must be an incurable old romantic. I could never tolerate being cooped up with one other person for years on end, but I always assumed that people who did derived endless emotional comfort from it.'

I did occasionally try to explain to her about Glyn and me but her inattention never allowed me to get into my stride. Her method of stopping me was simple – she conceded defeat with the blasé good humour of a woman to whom the battle itself is already of no consequence.

'I know, I know, I know,' she would say, tapping my wrist to indicate 'time' as she refilled my glass. 'Laura, you don't have to tell me all this, honestly. I know you Lewises have an absolutely solid marriage. I talk about it to my friends. I do! You are a legend in your own lunchtime. Please, not another word. It's very naughty of me to tease you the way I do, when what I *really* want to do is tell you all about my exquisite Nicole Farhi shift . . .'

Susan looked enviably good in Nicole Farhi. She was the same height as me – around five feet ten – but was always a good stone lighter. I put this down partly to luck and heredity, and partly to the fact that as a single woman she didn't have to have a kitchen permanently stocked with calorific foods. I knew I could keep the family on a completely healthy diet at relatively low cost, but that presupposed that I wanted to cook every day. There were days – to be honest they may even have constituted a majority – when I would rather have bungee-jumped than turn on the stove. That meant that the family were in the habit of conducting fridge and cupboard raids and foraging for themselves. For this to be possible you have to maintain a solid base of fats, sugar and carbohydrates. When the kids were at junior school I took the view that if there was bread, cereal and baked beans in the house no one would starve, no matter what my state of mind. No. 23 Alderswick Avenue was comfort-food heaven.

Susan's fridge contained bags of vegetables and salad, cartons of live yoghurt, occasional packets of smoked salmon and skinless chicken breasts, dry white wine and tonic water. Her cupboards held herbs, spices, Gordon's gin, pasta, wild rice, coffee beans, extra-virgin olive oil and balsamic vinegar. Ask for a strong cuppa and a fig roll *chez* Susan and you'd be disappointed.

So she was bound to be thinner than me. Also, she was a completely different build. People imagine that tall people are automatically leggy. I am not. I'm broad-shouldered and long-bodied, with a tendency to be pear-shaped. My legs are not awful, but they stop at my bottom, not my armpits. I have squarish hands and feet which are small for my height. In other words, I'm a tall endomorph. Susan was a classic ectomorph, slim and rangey, with long limbs, elegant tapering hands and feet, and a swan-like neck. She had wilfully curly dark hair, short-sighted, slighty protuberant brown eyes, and a beaky, vivacious face. Her pronounced nose and chin, and extremely well-cared-for teeth gave her smile its devilish quality. Like me she was not a beauty, but her basic equipment was of the sort that takes much less effort and expense to bring up to scratch, and since she was in a position to spare neither she was generally well ahead on points. On what might be termed the minus side she was rather flat-chested, and wore glasses. But the former actually added to her Hepburnesque air, and she employed the latter with such style that it made you feel like dashing out and buying a pair or two so as not to be left out. I made the mistake of asking her once why she didn't use contact lenses.

'Why should I?' she retorted.

'I wasn't implying that you *should* . . . It's just that most people these days do.'

She removed her specs and leaned forward, poking one of the arms at me. 'Exactly.'

Every time a coconut.

It must be said that Susan was generous about the way I looked, and free with compliments. She frankly admired my bust, my thick, straight hair and my easy-tanning skin, but allowed that she had better legs. She almost always began our meetings with 'You do look nice' or something like it, and she was honest about what suited me and what didn't. She was always right, as well. There was never any attempt to flannel me into wearing something grotesque, or inappropriate, or both, in order to benefit from the comparison. And as any woman knows, that is no common thing in a friendship, and of no small value, either.

She delighted in what she considered to be our complementary good looks. 'Take a look round, Laura,' she would stage-whisper gleefully, grabbing my hand, 'and tell me honestly if we're not the smartest broads in this whole goddamn restaurant . . .'

When Susan talked like that, she was irresistible.

She was less approving about my involvement with the Citizens Advice Bureau, which she considered ghastly beyond belief.

'How on earth can you stand it, all those deadbeats, day after day?'

'They're not deadbeats.'

'Come on, they must be or they wouldn't be there in the first place.'

'They're just people who need answers to questions. They're all sorts.'

'There you are then,' she said. '"All sorts" means deadbeats. And for nothing! I tell you, Laura, you're the last outpost of *noblesse oblige*.'

Susan most emphatically did not deal with deadbeats, and her income reflected the superior nature of her clientele. Her initial line of business was interior design, which developed into estate agency, which in turn developed into 'Ideal Homes' – something rather more exclusive. 'We are the personal services of the real estate world,' she was fond of saying, without a hint of irony. She and Simon thought of themselves as matchmakers, bringing particular customers and particular properties together, even occasionally persuading people to part with the house they were living in because someone else wanted it more, and anyway they could (through her good offices) find something better. Many of their clients were foreign – overseas businessmen looking for something for a couple of years, or American rock stars in search of a moated grange with attitude – and all were loaded. The business was not only profitable but served as a highly selective dating agency for Susan, who was not squeamish about forming liaisons with the customers. Simon lived an elegant pink-economy lifestyle with his older partner Richard, a one-time heartthrob of the British cinema, first in Fulham and subsequently in the village of Mutchfield, ten miles from our town.

Susan and Simon were an unholy alliance, always abuzz with scurrilous gossip, and alight with a deliciously elitist self-satisfaction which was based on a simple premise: they had life sussed and the rest of the world did not. Simon was a handsome, *soigné* man, and he and Susan took great delight in 'letting people think they were a couple'. They seemed unaware that this conceit was predicated on the assumption that people a) watched their every move and b) cared whether they were or not. But it did no one any harm and they derived a lot of innocent pleasure from it.

It was well into their personal services phase that Simon

and Richard decided to move out of London, and acquired Gracewell, the small but perfect sixteenth-century manor house in Mutchfield. Having rubbished this development up hill and down dale at the time, it didn't take Susan long to reach the conclusion that she, too, needed a more tranquil setting from which to operate, and that anyway much of what was quintessentially English and stylish was these days to be found outside (but within easy reach of) London. Her change of heart did not extend to the sort of rural grandeeism aspired to by Simon and Richard, but she exchanged her flat in Lancaster Gate for a larger one overlooking the river in Litherbridge. Had it been not for the fact that Simon had taken this step first, I might almost have suspected her of wanting to be nearer me.

But of course that was ridiculous.

5

A week after the party I got back from the Bureau at lunchtime to a calm, empty house. Glyn was having a London day. Verity was filling boxes for war-torn Central Europe in Tesco's car park, Josh was at college and Becca and the kids had not dropped in. There were no messages on the answerphone and nothing protruding from the fax in Glyn's office. Our cards and flowers still decorated the mantelpiece and bookshelves. Verity had washed up, cleaned the kitchen floor and hoovered. Morgan Misty hung in the hall, lending it a spurious grandness. I rather wished that someone – Susan, perhaps, or my mother – would call in unexpectedly at Alderswick Avenue and be pleasantly surprised. I had a little wander in order to pleasantly surprise myself. I should have known the household gods don't like a person to get complacent . . .

The house was big – one of those tall, shambling semi-detached places which seems to be holding itself up by leaning against its neighbour. It had a basement and an attic, and three floors in between, and the kitchen was a rather unlovely back extension. We'd selected it for its capacity, and originally had great plans for the proper deployment of the space. Glyn's office, for instance, would occupy the attic, where he would be insulated from the noise of the household. This did not allow for the fact that Glyn did not wish to be insulated from anything. He lasted only a week at the top of the house, during which time he made such frequent forays into 'the real world' as he called it that it became obvious he'd have to move. He opted for what must at some time have been the dining-room, off the hall to the right of the front door. Here he could answer the doorbell, earwig on the comings and goings and keep the street under observation. When it came to work Glyn wanted the very opposite of an ivory tower. Deprived of the buzz of new bands he had to have the next best thing, which was us.

His office looked like precisely what it was – a grown-up playroom. An inflatable palm tree rocked gently on its rounded axis whenever the door opened. On his desk was one of those flowers that moved when you spoke, and a trio of plump ceramic pigs flew across the wall between the magic-eye posters and the floor-to-ceiling photo-collage of family, friends, clients, and permutations of the three. His chairs were red corduroy, his cushions had Mickey Mouse on them, and the expensive technology was completely swamped by an enormous volume of paper – cuttings, magazines, box-files, dog-eared lists and jottings and a blizzard of yellow and pink stick-its. Glyn didn't employ a full-time secretary at home. The theory was that he could E-mail any necessary responses to Guys 'n' Dolls in London for the company's hard-pressed amanuensis to deal with. In practice Verity and I, and very occasionally Becca, with degrees of computer literacy ranging from nil to barely adequate, did a good deal of ad hoc clerical mopping-up. I kept the books in a big old ledger of my father's, and only transferred them to a computer spreadsheet at the end of the financial year, for the benefit of the accountant.

The children all featured in his celebrity photo-collage. But I was captured in a frame all to myself, forever twenty-one, in a pastel portrait done by a street-artist in Brighton. That was my husband for you.

Glyn, though different in all sorts of ways from the usual run of long-stay husbands, and from a background as different as possible from my own, could always fit in anywhere. It was a miracle our marriage survived in the face of such complete compatibility. The pretty compliments of the itinerant Patrick Lynch, I fancied, would add no more than a retrospective lustre to our silver celebrations.

After our gorgeous, toffish, Home Counties wedding we returned abruptly to normality and a one-bedroom rented flat in Queen's Park. Shortly before Verity was born we graduated to two bedrooms in Willesden Green. Glyn's adaptability, aptitude and charm saw him up to Diary Editor at the magazine, whence, through the good offices of Cy, he moved to be Show Business Editor of *Hipster*, then enjoying its heyday as *the* teenage monthly. By the time Josh started primary school we were in a three-bedroom house on the Archway fringes of Highgate and invited to more showbusiness parties than we knew what to do with.

When *Hipster* folded Glyn was in the happy position of being able to turn down another similar job in order to do what he'd always wanted, and set up a small management agency, Guys 'n' Dolls. He was really going back to his Fallen Idols days, mixing with what he called 'the real music people', doing deals, seeing people right, pursuing dreams – his own and other people's – and generally playing in the showbiz sand. He bought premises near the Post Office Tower and made a go of it – just. He was too nice, too concerned with making things work for clients he liked (which was by definition all of them) instead of taking on clients who would make things work for him. It was something of a relief when the entrepreneurial Cy, who had been in another part of the forest unsuccessfully punting ideas for a pre-teen weekly (he was ahead of his time) came back on the scene and into partnership in Guys 'n' Dolls. Cy's business acumen, allied with an altogether less sentimental view of what would now be called wannabees, freed Glyn to do what he did best, which was keeping clients and managements happy, talking up – and to – new acts and disseminating favourable publicity.

The agency became solidly established, and in the mid-eighties we moved from the house off Archway Road to the university town of Litherbridge, and 23 Alderswick Avenue. Cy and the troops ran the office by the Post Office Tower and Glyn continued to play happily and productively, based at home but zooming back and forth up the A1 in his beloved racing-green four-wheel drive two or three times a week. Launches and previews, bashes and binges, hyping and hustling, moving and shaking, remained meat and drink to Glyn: even under the influence of the more sceptical Cy he remained touchingly wide-eyed about artistes. When Isobel 'was born' or 'died' – I never know which to say since they were both the same thing – I received expressions of sympathy from several pop stars and a major impresario.

I practically never went to the bashes any more. Our daughter Becca was the girl for that job. Her big hair, small clothes and drop-dead body were ideally suited to the company, and she could work the room to deadly effect, scattering smiles which, like the dragon's teeth of legend, sprouted into erections in her wake. In fact it was at one of these dos – to promote the crucial follow-up album for the ragga band Anko Limited – that she met Roberto, who was to become our first sin-in-law, and father of our grandson Amos.

All this time I was not simply presiding over hearth and home – what am I saying, could anything be less simple? Once Josh was at school I cast about for a good and remunerative reason not to keep the paintwork pristine. I had a 2:1 in English, a self-taught knowledge of the QWERTY keyboard, a clean driving licence and the average parent's appreciation of the human condition and just how much of it could be fixed. The Citizens Advice Bureau took me on. I survived the course – one day a week for three months, plus homework – and found what I was good at.

By the time we moved to Alderswick Avenue there was nothing I didn't know about advice to citizens – no leaflet, benefit, grant, nor legal wrinkle with which I was unacquainted, no contingency which I could not, after a fashion, handle. This was the work for which my nature – unambitious, liberal and non-specializing – ideally qualified me. After the trauma of Isobel's death it helped to ease me back into life. I loved it, but the satisfaction (great) was in inverse proportion to the material rewards (nil). We weren't pushed for money, but I was sensitive to the widely held notion that an unpaid job was no job at all. I took a business and finance course at the local Poly and did a bit of book-keeping for local freelances, of which there were plenty in Litherbridge, Glyn included. My fitful bursts of number-crunching effectively financed my twelve hours a week at the Bureau.

Glyn, unlike Susan, thought my involvement with the CAB fitted me for canonization. 'If it was me going into one of those places,' he said, 'feeling insecure, not knowing my rights, looking for reassurance, you're exactly the kind of woman I'd be hoping to find.'

'What kind is that?'

'Intelligent, experienced, mature, liberated—'

'That'll do. But a bit less emphasis on the mature.'

Our three children grew up in their variously unpredictable ways. Becca, who at school had been strong, stunning and bright, became a single mother, twice. Verity, who had been dim and uncommunicative, took Jesus into her heart and became a shining example to us all with a job at the night-shelter, where she converted psychotic drunks on a regular basis. The jury was still out on sarcastic, clever, idle Josh. And I learned the truth of the runic saying 'It's not over till it's over'. With families, it was never over. Like a town when the picturesque old centre has been ripped out by some brain-damaged planners in the sixties, it was no good mopping and mowing over what was gone. The past was not necessarily the repository for all that was good, beautiful and upstanding. The present, after all, was where one lived. Childhood may no longer have been all ankle-socks, *The Wind in the Willows* and china horses, and pubescence carried six times the dangers and scarcely any of the fear. But your children grew up, and even matured, in spite of you.

The attic was now Josh's lair. Verity's room, Becca's old room and the family bathroom were on the second floor, and our room, the smarter bathroom and the main spare bedroom were on the first.

Our bedroom, like the rest of the house, had never quite achieved the dizzy designer heights I'd envisaged for it. I'd wanted coolness, and quiet, and ordered calm. We still had the Portobello Road brass bedstead we bought when we were married. And certainly my well-chosen leafy greens and cottony whites were a start. But our combined untidiness and Glyn's late-night phoning, viewing and listening habits meant that the room was usually hijacked by the hurly-burly I had so much wanted to avoid.

Verity's room was chaste and sparse, with a picture of Our Lord and a statue of Our Lady (as I'd learned to refer to

them) and several well-tended plants. Verity did not believe in
having any more clothes than one actually needed, and would
donate any surplus to the night-shelter or the charity shops
the moment it occurred. Which was just as well because Becca,
even with a place of her own, was well on the way to filling
two wardrobes and several square metres of floor on her old
room at Alderswick Avenue. Constrained by income support
and fitful handouts from us, she bought extremely cheap
clothes on a wear-and-chuck basis, and would occasionally
offer castoffs to her sister. 'Want these?' she'd say, appearing
in Verity's doorway with an armful of stained and scented
garments, none of them more than a few months old. Verity
always accepted, and washed and ironed everything meticu-
lously. What the dossers and bag ladies made of these random
harvests of basques, micro-skirts and shiny leggings it was hard
to imagine.

My children's rooms perfectly illustrated their relationship
to the parental household. Verity, who spent the most time
at home, was almost painfully clean and contained. Becca,
with a perfectly good house of her own, had still succeeded
in colonizing vast areas and contaminating them with dirty
underwear and make-up with the tops off. Josh in his eyrie
was with us but not of us. About twice a year I ventured into
his territory, armed with the domestic equivalents of a whip,
a chair and a flame-thrower, and emerged in a state of shock.

Our living-room should, like our bedroom, have been a tranquil zone in which music might be listened to, books and papers
read, selective television watched and intelligent conversation
engaged in at our leisure. In the décor I had striven for the
atmosphere in which these activities could flourish: clusters of
large plants, a big mirror opposite the window and another over
the fireplace, a polished wooden floor, fan-shaped uplighters and
large copper lamps, two deep sofas, like gondolas, to lounge in in
privacy among berry-coloured cushions . . . But this delightful
environment was not enough to counter the habits of a lifetime.
Glyn's amiable restlessness and my own inability to set any kind
of firm precedent were far more influential than my aspirations.
The living-room had a transitory, excitable feel like a railway
station. It was never tidy, nor tranquil, and probably the only

time it served the kind of purpose I'd dreamed of was when we had friends for dinner. I had to admit Glyn and I did nothing to help ourselves. We were never the sort of parents who insisted on our routines, our space, and quality time together. And as ye sow, so shall ye find half a dozen spaced-out teenagers occupying the comfortable chairs, or one's grandchildren eating kettle chips in front of *Dumb and Dumber* when the classic serial is on . . . We were our own worst enemies.

I made myself a coffee and went out into the garden. I sat down on the peeling green park bench outside the kitchen window. The daffodils and narcissi were out and in a week or so the grass would need cutting. From the house next door where our neighbour taught Suzuki violin came the endlessly-repeated strains of 'Twinkle, twinkle, little star'.

I had originally planted 'Isobel' against the south-facing fence to the left of the kitchen. But like her namesake she had failed to thrive and I had since transplanted her three times, with an increasing sense of desperation, and at the moment she occupied a corner of the raised bed at the edge of the patio. She was hanging in there – just. Each summer one or two frail white roses appeared and trembled for a week or so until their waxy petals fell. There were never more than two, and no second flowering. This saddened me. When Susan asked how her present was doing, I lied.

The squeaky little violin next door kept plugging away. Glyn had alternative words: 'Starkle, starkle, little twink, who the hell you am I think?' I got up and was stooped over the bare rose twigs, examining them for signs of life, when the phone went.

'I have a call for you from a Miss Lewis, will you pay for the call?'

Becca was in a towering rage. 'Mum? Is Verity there?'

'No, as a matter of fact she's—'

'Then can you please come and take the kids off my hands? I've got this bloody stupid man harassing me—'

'Doing what?'

'I've had an accident in the car. It absolutely wasn't my fault—'

'Is everyone all right? Are the children all right? What about you?'

'*Mum*! We're all fine except that the car's a write-off.'

'What happened?'

'Does it matter? Can't you just get over here? Like *now*?' Becca's tone implied that I was focusing, typically, on trivia like life and death instead of the far more pressing matter of bailing her out.

'Well – where are you?'

'I'm – Christ, *I* don't know —' I heard her open the door of the call-box and ask impatiently, 'Where is this? No – what's the name of the road?' During this interval I heard Sinead wailing in the background.

'Is Sinead okay?'

'She's perfectly okay, but this idiot keeps picking her up—'

'Which idiot?'

'Look – can you just *get here*?'

'You still haven't told me where—'

'For fuck's sake!' She was exasperated with my nit-picking need to know the facts. 'It's the corner of Selwyn Street, near Planet Burger!'

With Sinead's wails ringing in my ears I drove like a doctor on call, and arrived with my legs shaking and my heart pounding at the corner of Selwyn Street. There was no mistaking the place – a small crowd had gathered. I pulled up in the cycle lane and left the car with its hazard lights on. Becca's battle-scarred purple Mini and a black Granada Scorpio had come to rest in the side-street. The Granada was in front, and unmarked as far as I could see. The Mini had a bloody nose. So not only had it been Becca's fault, but she'd come off worse, a state of affairs perfectly calculated to send her ballistic. On the other hand this was also the sort of situation she could manipulate to good effect with her eyes shut and one hand tied behind her. She was holding the tearful Sinead (presumably rescued from the idiot) in one arm, and an enraptured Amos by the hand. In her black shirt, skin-tight Levis and fringed Red Indian boots, she quivered with righteous indignation, a tigress in defence of her young.

'We could all have been killed!' she asserted vehemently as

I came round the corner. The focus of her attention was a plump middle-aged man in a grey suit, his pleasant face pale and concerned.

'It's all very well for you, driving around in that great tank,' continued the incandescent Becca. 'But not all of us are so well protected!'

'I am sorry,' said the man. I bet he was, too.

'Becca?' I ventured. 'Darling?'

'This is my mother,' said Becca. The emphasis on the first word indicated that she'd been giving me some sort of build-up. 'She works in the Citizens Advice Bureau.'

'Do you?' asked the man, smiling with anxious politeness in my direction.

'Yes, actually—'

'She knows the law,' added Becca threateningly.

'Granny!' whined Sinead. 'Granny!'

Becca let her slither to the ground and Sinead rushed into my arms. I picked her up and stood at Becca's shoulder, completing without really meaning to, an affecting family tableau.

'Look,' the man took a wallet from his breast-pocket and fished out a business card, 'this is me. If I can just take down your name and address this whole thing can be sorted out and over and done with.' It occurred to me that under Becca's onslaught he was beginning to revert to the language of the nursery. She snorted like a palfrey. 'It was an accident,' he went on. 'These things happen. You were driving a tad too close—'

'No, no, I'm sorry – you weren't paying attention to the lights!' Becca retaliated. 'Big fast car, too much attitude—' how did she have the nerve? – 'you thought you'd slip across on amber and then changed your mind, with the result you had to slam on your brakes – I never stood a chance of stopping!'

'Perhaps you were thinking of slipping over on amber too,' suggested the man with a commendable but foolhardy glimmer of spirit.

One of the bystanders made a 'Who-ah!' noise in anticipation of further fireworks. Never one to disappoint her public, Becca narrowed her eyes and stepped forward.

'Don't you dare try and tell me what I was thinking!'

'Becca,' I said, catching her sleeve. 'The police are here.'

'And about bloody time.'

'Now then, love,' said the first officer, who was young and hunky. 'Take it easy. Why don't you just tell us what happened?'

I told Becca – or rather, I told the second police officer to tell her – where I was going, and then piled Sinead and the extremely reluctant Amos into my car, parked it on a meter, and went to Planet Burger. It was packed, with several queues snaking back from the counter and not a free seat in the place. We loitered next to a group who seemed about to finish their Family Fun Meal, but they were quite impervious to hints. The glares and fidgets of the children, my weighty sighs and repeated declarations that 'We wouldn't be long' did nothing to prevent them toying with their last few fries as if they were alone on a Cornish beach. At last they got up, pointedly ignoring us to show that their decision to leave had nothing to do with us, and I thrust Amos into the banquette.

'You stay right here, don't move, and say these seats are taken, all right, love?'

'Okay!' He was completely sunny – his day so far had been almost perfect.

'Sinead, you come with me and we'll choose.'

Normally Sinead would have taken the Granny option like a shot, but on this occasion her eye was caught by a Family Fun Hat which the previous occupants had left behind. It was a kind of cardboard forage cap densely decorated with Ray Robot, the Planet Burger logo, in the corporate colours of red and green. At the very moment she reached for it Amos snatched it up and plonked it on his head. If Sinead had wanted the hat before, she would now willingly have died for it.

'I want it!' Her yell split the air. The masticating throng were momentarily stilled.

'I'll get you one!' I rasped.

'I want it!'

Amos grinned and waggled his head from side to side to show how absolutely great the hat was. I leaned over to him, restraining the writhing and sobbing Sinead as best I could.

'Amos, darling – may she have it? I'll get another.'

'Sure.' I breathed a sigh of relief. 'In a minute.'

'Sinead,' I said, 'darling – Amos says you can have a go in a minute.'

Gulping and snuffling, Sinead climbed on to the banquette and pressed up against her brother. He shuffled sideways. She did the same. He shuffled sideways again, reached the end of the banquette and ran round to the other end. She followed.

'Sit still!' I admonished. I turned to the young women at the next table. 'Look, I wonder if I could ask you very kindly to keep an eye on these two while I'm at the counter?'

They said yeah, they would, with blank-eyed little smiles which did not inspire confidence.

'Stay there, sit still and behave!' I said once more. 'These ladies are going to keep an eye on you and they'll tell me if you're naughty. I won't be long.'

In fact it was several minutes before I returned, hot, bothered and ripped off, with a Family Fun Meal for four (you could only get it for four) and the accompanying forage caps. The crowd had eased slightly. There were now several empty tables. One of them was that of the young women I'd left in charge. Another was ours.

I gazed distractedly about. There was absolutely no sign of the children. I pounced on some gel-haired young men in suits at a nearby table.

'Did you see two children – excuse me, I'm sorry to interrupt, but my grandchildren were here – at the window table – and they're not now. Did you by any chance see where they went?'

'Sorry, only just got here,' said one of them.

'Tried the toilets?' asked another.

'No – good idea. I will.' I dumped the Family Fun Meal on our table and rushed off. I could sense the young men shaking their heads and smirking. Poor soul.

They were not in the loos. I even braved the Gents in case Amos had dragged his sister in there. It was empty, and I only succeeded in giving a nasty turn to a lad unbuttoning his 501s.

I asked at the counter. I checked all the tables. I could not believe this was happening. I felt physically sick with the horror of it. This was something you read about, something you saw on television – and it was happening to me. Those girls – had they taken them? Were they not the gossipy little retail-assistant airheads I'd taken them for but a bunch of nasty sadists? Or had someone – oh God! – lured the children out on to the pavement? My heart fluttered and my hands and face felt cold as I scoured the room. In the faces of the other people I could see some sympathy, but mostly a smug, passive accusation. I had been negligent. Their children were sitting safely beside them, properly looked after. My grandchildren had been left, and had gone.

'Hallo, I'm Barry the manager. Can I help?'

Barry was about eighteen years old in a red and green striped blazer and white trousers.

'I left my grandchildren at that window table – over there – while I ordered, and I asked the girls next door to keep an eye on them for me, but they've gone, and I can't find them!'

'Don't worry,' said Barry gently, placing his hand on my arm. 'We've never lost a customer yet.'

His kindness, and the hand on my arm, made my throat and eyes fill with tears.

'But where are they?' I asked helplessly.

'Let's look in the street, shall we?' he suggested, guiding me to the door. In retrospect he was probably intent on removing this embarrassment from the premises, but he did it so nicely that I allowed myself to be propelled out on to the pavement where we stood gazing up and down.

'See them anywhere?' he asked.

'No – no. Oh God, where on earth can they be?'

'Most runaways are found safe and well within a few hundred yards of their homes,' said Barry.

'But this isn't their home, and they may not have run away – they could have been abducted!'

'How long have they been missing?' he asked.

'God – I don't know – well – a few minutes.'

He smiled. 'They won't have gone far in a few minutes.'

My legs were shaking. To make matters worse I saw the rescue van from Bunker's Garage go by with Becca in the passenger seat and the buckled Mini in tow. Becca, who knew nothing, who believed her children to be safe and happy in their grandmother's care . . . I whimpered in panic.

'They could have gone miles in a few minutes in a fast car! I think I should call the police, is there a phone I can use?'

Beside myself and oblivious to Barry's soothings, I turned to go back into Planet Burger and almost tripped over Amos and Sinead going the same way.

'Grannee!'

I couldn't speak. Until that moment I hadn't known what relief was. It felt as though my whole body were melting down. I crouched down and hugged Sinead so hard that I could feel her small, still pliable bones through her dungarees. Amos stood staring uninterestedly and I grabbed him too, but he backed off.

'Hi, Gran.'

'Well,' said Barry. 'Another happy ending. I'll leave you all to it.'

'Did you get the burgers?' asked Amos, as I stood up and rummaged in my bag for a tissue to repair the ravages.

'Yes, I did – but where did you go? That was so *naughty* of you when I'd specially asked you to wait for me.'

'Actually,' said a voice at my shoulder, 'he was doing the right thing, coming after his little sister. She came into the newsagent's and found me, and together we found him – and then we all came back to find you. Which we did.'

I had hardly been aware of this adult in attendance, but now I turned upon him what I'm afraid was a glare of naked suspicion and hostility.

'We're fated to meet, Mrs Lewis.'

And that was how I came to meet Patrick Lynch for the second time, and how the four of us ate a replacement Family Fun Meal on the house at Planet Burger.

6

It's traditional to say one can't remember what was said at key moments in one's life. But because of the rather curious circumstances I can recall a good deal of the conversation (if you can call it that) which took place over the yellow-and-white flecked formica in Planet Burger.

Patrick was conspicuously – almost ostentatiously – out of place. Glyn in this setting would have (and indeed often had) been a food franchise operator's wet dream. He would have worn a hat, drunk a milk shake through a flavoured twirly-straw, done the colouring-in on the menu and entered for the free draw to win the holiday in Euro-Disney. He would also have checked out what the counter-staff earned, calculated the profit margin on the Inter-Galactic Megaburger, and discovered Barry's mother's maiden name. Glyn was fascinated by what people got up to.

Patrick – well, Patrick didn't. He opened the batting by putting on hornrims, inspecting his unopened paper bags and observing, 'I confess I'm a stranger on this planet.'

'I'd never have guessed.'

'No, really,' he peered into one of the bags, 'I'm a populist to my toenails, but I'm not into fast food.' This turned out to be only partly true, but at the time I was slightly embarrassed by my familiarity with the menu.

'With these two,' I explained, 'one doesn't have much option.'

Patrick glanced down at Amos, who sat next to him. I thought he was going to say something, but he was plainly uneasy with children, and after watching Amos take a huge, untidy mouthful of burger he returned his gaze to me. The after-effects of the shock and distress were getting to me in the form of an absolutely raging hunger. I put a generous handful of fries into my mouth, but became immediately self-conscious when he enquired, 'Peckish?'

I flapped a hand in front of my face, munching madly. He laughed. When I'd swallowed I said, of course, 'Sorry.'

'Don't apologize.'

'Aren't you going to eat?'

He glanced down at the paper bags again. 'I may well do . . . On the other hand I may do the decent thing and let the rest of you have my portion.'

He was wearing a sort of lumberjack's coat in drab, whiskery checks. He felt in the pocket and produced a packet of cigarettes. Tapping and turning the packet on the table, he glanced around.

'I suppose this particular form of oral gratification would be quite out of the question in here?'

'Absolutely *verboten* I'm afraid.' He sighed gustily. 'Please, don't feel you have to stay.'

'Nonsense!' he said, and put away the packet as though the point had now been made. 'I like it here. It's a new experience.'

I pulled a face. 'I'm so grateful to you for bringing the children back, but I can quite see this isn't exactly the reward of a lifetime. Do, please, go and get on with your life – but leave me your number and perhaps you'll come round and have supper or something some time.'

'Me and the wife?'

Inexplicably, I was taken aback. 'Of course.'

'Fine, if I find one I'll bring her along.'

He was fencing, something I was out of practice at, and though I found it annoying on one level, on another it was flattering.

Sinead made a gurgling-drain noise with the last of her banana-shake.

'Do you want another?' I asked.

'Yes.'

'Yes, please.'

'Yes, please.'

'Here.' I gave her mine.

'Can I?' asked Amos.

'You'd be doing me a favour,' said Patrick, sliding his across. I wished he would stop being quite so condescending about Planet Burger. It wasn't that bad.

'Thank you!' I prompted crisply.

'Thank·you,' they mumbled gloopily, round straws.

'What do you do?' I asked with just enough obvious politeness to indicate that I was making conversation. If fencing was his weapon, this was mine – the acquired skill of the long-time wife.

'I'm Professor in English at St Stephen's.'

So he really was a creature from another planet. That shut me up.

'And you?' he asked with equal politeness. 'I mean apart from bringing up a young family . . . ?'

'Ah,' I said, 'no, these are my grandchildren.'

'Right.' He had, of course, known all along. 'You never can tell these days with all the options there are available.'

'I work at the Citizens Advice Bureau.'

'In the Corn Exchange there?'

'That's right.'

'I shall definitely drop by next time my neighbours kidnap the cat.'

'Is that what they do?'

'Yes!' he exclaimed almost quizzically, eyebrows raised, as though he himself could scarcely credit it. 'They don't care for her crapping on their alpines, so periodically, not content with whingeing to me about it, they lock her in their shed. It's like clamping – I have to go and pay an extortionate fee in terms of arse-licking, accompanied by at least one bottle of decent wine, to get her out again.'

Amos glanced up admiringly at the mention of arse-licking. I quelled him with a look. Sinead, still sucking a soggy straw, burped wetly.

I said, 'I'm not an expert on the law, but I'd have thought that was cruelty.'

'There you are, you see, you've already put your finger on the central issue. But I'm happy to say it's a bit of a Pyrrhic victory for them because Peaches craps all over their shed instead.'

'Good for her.'

'Oh—' to my surprise he next took out a cigarette and began absentmindedly to light it – 'they're not so bad really. I'd miss them if they weren't there. Life's all about conflict, I find.' He inhaled with relish. 'Conflict and copulation. Don't you think?'

He leaned his elbows on the table, fingers linked before his face, and eyed me through his smoke, in a way which reminded me of someone. People were glancing disapprovingly.

'Possibly,' I said quickly, and then hissed, 'Did you forget it's no smoking in here?'

'I did actually. Had I better go and stand outside?'

'Yes.' I was embarrassed. I could see nice, helpful Barry on his way over.

'I'm sorry, sir, I'm afraid we don't allow smoking. Perhaps you missed our sign.'

'Perhaps I did.' Patrick gave Barry a wolfish grin. I prayed he wasn't going to make a scene – he seemed exactly the type to do it.

'Why don't you have an ice-cream, sir?' suggested Barry, doing everything but wring his hands in the face of the rising hostility all round. 'Instead of the cigarette?'

'You can get choc-chip,' said Amos hopefully, wielding one of the spoons from the container on the table. It was a long spoon. Perhaps we were all supping with the devil.

'Where can I get rid of this?' asked Patrick. Barry scooped up a glass containing cola dregs from the next table and proffered it. Patrick dropped it in. There was a hiss and a smell.

'Perhaps I can get you all one?' enquired Barry. He really did deserve a good conduct award for his behaviour this afternoon. What with one thing and another we had been an instant management test in Dealing with Difficult Situations.

'No, thanks, I'm quite capable of getting my own if I want one,' said Patrick, with what I considered to be quite unnecessary crustiness since he had been transparently in the wrong. My hunger had been replaced by absolute exhaustion. I needed to pass the baton of responsibility back to Becca, and return to Alderswick Avenue for ten minutes with my tights off.

'Thanks, but we must go. Come on,' I said to the kids. 'I ought to take you home.'

Five minutes later we were all out on the pavement and I wondered if the other customers would club together to buy Barry a box of chocolates, like airline passengers saved from disaster by the safe hands and cool nerve of their pilot.

Sinead leaned against me whinily, rubbing one of her crêpe soles up and down my shin.

'Don't do that darling,' I said, 'it hurts.'

'Were you in a car?' asked Patrick, glancing quickly around.

'It's on a meter along there. Can we give you a lift?'

'No, I'm only a stone's throw from here.'

'Well – thanks again.' I decided against further mention of the dinner invitation – he'd been thanked enough.

'My pleasure. I'll hope to run into you again some time.' He'd obviously reached the same conclusion. His big, veiny hand clasped mine, and then he placed the other one on top, completely engulfing it.

'Possibly – when next the cat's banged up,' I said, retrieving my hand.

'Yes!'

Sinead needed a shoelace retying, and that gave me a chance to check which direction he was going in. It turned out to be the same as ours, so I did a double bow, and the other shoe, for good measure.

Becca's house, rented with the aid of housing benefit, was in Sumatra Road, one of a network of drab roads with exotic names which made up the Smiley Meadows estate. There had been meadows, the property of the Chadderton-Smiley family, beneath the concrete and tarmac of the estate as recently as fifteen years ago. When the Chadderton-Smileys decided to cash in on the housing boom of the early eighties, the name must have seemed an absolute gift to the planners, with its suggestion of sylvan pastures in which contented people could engage in honest labour and children frolic happy as the day was long.

Now it was more like a bad joke. Bordered by the industrial estate, the municipal landfill and the bypass, Smiley Meadows was a repository for the town's rougher element, such as it was, and a sprinkling of slightly desperate young marrieds in starter homes, slumming on toasted cheese and hope while they squirrelled away their two incomes with better things in mind. And, of course, Becca.

Glyn said I was too sensitive about Smiley Meadows, that I exaggerated its awfulness, and that in fact it wasn't awful at all but colourful, with a real sense of community. By this I could only suppose he meant the Solomon Road Stores, a supermarket which sold most things, twenty-four hours a day, 365 days a year, including Christmas. I found the Stores depressing, with its assumption that bread meant flabby white slices in polythene, and its relaxed attitude to sell-by dates, but even I had been known to make use of it when there was nowhere else to go, and the owners – he Gujerati, she Basildon – were undeniably cheery and welcoming. They should have been, with their prices.

No. 10 Sumatra Road was a three-bedroom mid-terrace with a postage stamp of garden at the back. Some of the postage stamps had beaver-board fences round, but Becca's had only chicken wire, bent severely in places where her own and the neighbours' children passed to and fro. It didn't bother her. She claimed to like her neighbours and not to feel the need for privacy. I wondered if they felt the same when Becca was sitting topless on the end of the phone, arguing *molto con brio* with one of the children's fathers . . . She was a young woman whose epitaph would be: 'She didn't give a damn'.

When we arrived I thought for a moment that she wasn't around because I couldn't see the Mini, till I remembered that it was in the care of Bunker's Garage. Its normal position at the kerb was taken by Glyn's Shogun – a gleaming invitation to every scratch-happy juvenile in the area.

'Grandpa's here!' said Amos.

'Looks like it,' I agreed.

We got out, and I locked the car – trying each door, and the boot, with a mean-spirited flourish – while the kids ran to the front door and pushed it open. It was rarely locked and, owing to a deficient latch, usually not even properly shut.

I heard Glyn's irrepressible 'Hi, gang!' from within.

Glyn and Becca were in the sitting-room drinking tea. Glyn was on the sofa and Becca was sitting sideways in the armchair with her legs draped over the arm. She'd discarded the Red Indian boots. Her toenails were an immaculate carmine but her heels were grubby. She was smoking.

She was also in high good humour.

'Christ, take it easy!' she said, as the children cast themselves upon her. They worshipped her, and she did almost nothing to deserve it. 'Want some tea?' she asked me.

'No thanks, we've come from Planet Burger.'

'You are good, thanks ever so much.'

I sat down next to Glyn, and we kissed. He aimed for my mouth but I allowed him my cheek. I was rather out of sorts. Sinead climbed on to his knee and began fingering the scattering of badges on the lapel of his bomber jacket. Amos ran out into the back garden. Through the glass door I saw him clamber wincemakingly over the chicken wire into next door's patch for some serious socializing.

'So what happened with the car?' I asked.

'Oh, it's not as bad as it looks,' said Becca airily, as well she might. She bought her own petrol, but Glyn paid for tax, insurance and repairs.

'It looked terrible,' I told Glyn.

'It must have been very nasty,' he said. 'It shakes you up, that sort of thing.'

I thought of the ashen-faced driver of the Granada. 'It does, I know. So were Bunker's able to quote you a price?'

'Not really.' I could tell by her face that they had but she hadn't yet worked out a line on it.

'Who cares?' said Glyn. 'The insurance company will cough. Premium'll go up, but what the hell, it's only money. Mum and I are just pleased no one was hurt.'

There he went, my husband, saving me from myself again. I was grateful for the better light he cast on me, but a little saddened by it too. I wished I had been the one to say that. Then I remembered that of course I had, earlier in the day when Becca first rang me up – but she had been too angry then to remember, and all she would retain of this conversation would be my mention of the cost and her father's dismissal of it . . .

'I hope it won't be too long,' sighed Becca. 'I'm lost without my wheels.'

I knew exactly what Glyn would say, and he did. 'Don't worry, Bex. I'm sure we can sort something out.'

Sinead climbed on to his knee and pressed her hands into his, bouncing up and down flirtatiously.

'That's my girl,' remarked Becca indulgently. 'She loves her men, does my Sinead.'

Speaking of which, I thought. 'How are things between you and Liam at the moment?' I asked, watching Sinead with a smile to show of how little consequence it was.

'Don't try your luck, Mum. There are no "things" between Liam and me.'

'There's Sinead.'

'I don't want to talk about it.' Becca's mood was going into free-fall. She shied her cigarette into a plant-pot and scrabbled madly for another in her 'Le Sac', her face hard and set.

'Best not to discuss it just now anyway . . .' Glyn clapped Sinead's hands together.

'It has to be discussed some time,' I persisted crazily.

'Maybe,' said Glyn.

Becca got up and tried to reclaim her daughter, who immediately twisted away and ran into the garden. She flopped down again with her legs crossed, one foot tapping. There was a moment's hateful awkwardness for which I felt entirely responsible.

'I'd better get moving,' said Glyn. 'I've got someone coming round.'

'Anyone I'd know?' I asked, latching on to the change of subject

'No, but a year from now you will. Or Josh will. Terrific sound and a nice, really level-headed bunch of guys.'

'Sounds promising.' When Glyn used phrases like 'bunch of guys' I felt about a hundred. Such phrases seemed to spring quite naturally and unaffectedly to his lips.

Without looking in our direction Becca asked; 'They're local then, are they?'

'No, Watford. Not London, though, which is good.'

'What are they called?'

'Human Condition. Remember – you heard it first here.'

'No, I've heard them – they were on at the Black Hole at New Year. The lead's called Spriggs or something?'

'Griggs.' Glyn's face lit up with enthusiasm. 'So what did you think, Bex?'

Becca inhaled deeply, our pop culture consultant. 'Not bad. Bit bland, bit take-home-to-mother – but Griggs has a nice little bum.'

Glyn laughed gleefully, while I managed a faint smile. I could never quite come to terms with Becca's blatantly consumeristic approach to the opposite sex.

'They're really, really provincial English as well,' added Becca. 'A bit like Madness.'

'Yes!' Glyn raised a triumphant fist. 'Thank you, Bex! You have just described the band of my dreams.'

'Fine.' Becca shrugged and glanced over her shoulder, ostensibly to check on the kids – but I knew her mood had changed for the better again.

We got up. Becca remained seated. Glyn went over and patted her cheek, something I'd never have dared to do.

'What's that for?'

'For vindicating my judgement.'

'Any time, Grandpa.'

'See you back at the ranch,' said Glyn to me.

When the front door had – almost – closed, I said, 'Bye then, darling. Will you be okay?'

'Of course,' she said. 'Why shouldn't I be?'

It was no good. I'd been out of order and would have to do my time and take my punishment like a man. I went to the garden door and put my head out to say goodbye to the children, but they were playing on the other side of the fence and were quite oblivious to my calls and waves.

'You're wasting your time,' said Becca from her chair.

'Oh well, give them my love when they come back.'

'I'll do that.'

It occurred to me to wonder whether there were any adults in the adjoining house but I decided now was not the moment to raise these doubts. Whatever her shortcomings, Becca was doing something right, because Amos and Sinead were as well adjusted, attractive and affectionate a pair as any grandparent could wish. And I had nearly mislaid them . . . I left, quickly and quietly, before I could stir up any more hostility.

I picked up a few things at Tesco's on the way back and came upon Verity and a couple of others loading their haul into the back of a camper-van. Verity's waiflike air was misleading. She looked willowy but was actually wiry, and as strong as an ox. Large boxes containing everything from baked beans to bog paper flew from hand to hand and into the van's interior at lightning speed. The store was still open but relatively quiet in the late afternoon, awaiting the rush of singles and young working couples between six and eight. I didn't tell her about Becca's accident – it would genuinely have ruined her day.

'Want a lift home?' I asked.

'Oh, no thanks,' said Verity, as though sorry to disappoint me. 'We're staying on till closing time.'

'It looks as though you've done well.'

'People are good,' said Verity. Her face shone with appreciation. 'They're really kind. They *want* to give. We haven't heard a cross word all day – it's been brilliant, hasn't it, Seth?'

Seth confirmed that it had been magic. Someone I might have described as an elderly body (until I realized she was about my age), stoutish and dressed in a sludge-green tracksuit, appeared at the door of the van.

'That it for now?'

'For now!' said Verity. 'Shona, this is my Mum.'

'Hallo there!' beamed Shona. 'Brought something for us?'

I was embarrassed by this oversight. 'I'm awfully sorry, I haven't—'

'No worries! Another time!' Shona hopped out, closed the doors, climbed into the driver's seat and was off, barrelling over the sleeping policemen with a brisk rattle.

Verity gave me her calm, generous smile. 'See you later, Mum.'

'What time will you be back?'

'I don't know. We've got to get another load round to the centre when the store closes, and then I might go for a drink.'

'Okay.'

As I turned out of the car park I switched on the radio. Out poured the honey-and-grits of Nat King Cole, with 'When I Fall in Love'. By the time I was on the main road there were tears trickling down my cheeks. I opened the glove compartment to grab a Kleenex and there among the broken sunglasses and out of date AA manuals was the usual small polythene bag full of what looked like dried herbs.

At Aldersmick Avenue the house had lost its earlier tranquil air. Glyn was closeted in the office, presumably with Griggs of Human Condition. Josh was lying on the sofa watching children's television and drinking orange juice out of a carton. It had got past the point where I asked him about schoolwork. He was terrifyingly clever and a law unto himself, as his teachers pointed out to us with a stern, reproachful air (as though there were a thing we could do about it). Glyn's response was always to express unqualified delight and suggest that Josh would in that case in all probability make and lose several fortunes before his thirtieth birthday.

'All right?' I asked. Josh raised a hand. I advanced to the end of the sofa and stood looking down at him.

'Something I can do for you?' he asked.

'Yes, as a matter of fact. You can stop leaving dope in my car.'

'Okay.'

'It's illegal, Josh. And you've only just got your licence.'

'Jesus H!' He sat up and zapped the programme, using the remote control like a six-gun. 'That's rich coming from you, I bet you two were sprinkling it on your cornflakes in the old days. I'll move it, okay?'

'Thank you.'

Seamlessly, and in the same belligerent tone, he added, 'By the way, Collins wants to talk to you or Dad some time.'

'Does he? What about?' David Collins was the sixth form college Head of English, a subject in which Josh was expected to get either a starred A or a stiff reprimand from the examining board.

'Usual old crap – he doesn't like my coursework essay.'

'Oh dear . . . Josh!'

'Don't panic, you're as bad as he is. It's on the kitchen table. Read it yourself. Who the fuck cares what Collins thinks anyway? He's a trainspotter.'

I went into the kitchen and picked up the sheets of lined paper covered with Josh's jagged, forward-leaning handwriting.

The title, springing off the top page in heavy capitals, declared with unmistakable *braggadocio*: 'THE PUDENDA IMAGERY IN GRIMM'.

7

On a free day not long after Becca's accident, I drove into London to meet my parents for lunch. I always told myself that I was indulging them, carrying out a not very onerous filial duty by allowing them to stand me a three-course meal every few weeks, but to be honest, the pleasure was all mine. Even after more than half a century of marriage my parents retained an aura of debonair romance. They didn't have to try; it was there, effortlessly, even in their mild bickering – the soft sensual gleam of what I could only call true love.

It was their gift, to themselves, and to Glyn and me. It was what I aspired to.

Susan often interrogated me concerning the mysteries of married sex.

'You don't have to answer this, but how often do you and Glyn do it?'

Obviously the answer to this question had varied over the years, so I tended to sidestep it. 'Often enough. MYOB.'

'MYOB!' She squeaked with laughter. 'There speaks an unreconstructed Edelrat!'

One thing, we could always laugh. We both knew that she was importunate and that I was evasive. We recognized that there were great chasms of difference between us. But we were connected by such a genuine mutual fondness and admiration that her thrusts and my parries were a game, not intended to inflict real injury and only very rarely doing so.

That was how she got away with her infidelity number.

'Can you honestly look me in the eye, Laura, and say you've never been unfaithful? In all this time?'

'No, I never have.'

'Why is that? Lack of opportunity, lack of motive or just lack of energy?'

'I've never wanted to.'

'But Glyn has, of course.'

'Not as far as I know.'

'You mean you have no evidence, but of course he has. Men simply aren't monogamous.'

'I believe he is,' I said. I did believe it, but Susan's worldly generalizations still had the power to shake me.

'Do you want to know what I believe?' she asked rhetorically, lighting up. 'I believe he loves you. I believe he loves your kids. I believe he loves marriage. But I also believe he'll have had at least one fling. In fact I'd be prepared to bet on it.'

I shook my head.

'Have you ever asked him?'

'No. I've never had any reason to.'

'I mean, asked him purely as point of information. In the interests of that culture of openness you're always on about.'

'No.'

'Then you should. I bet I'm right. You forget,' she added, radiating mischief, 'I've been the other woman too often not to know.'

My parents preferred to eat in hotels – or at a pinch department stores – rather than restaurants. They liked the leisureliness, and the space to sit in comfort. At midday (they were going to a matinee) I found them in the luxurious, sugar-almond lounge of the Clarendon, well into their second drink.

Their chosen afternoon's entertainment was a much-praised tap extravaganza, one of those shows with no plot which is simply a chance for the whole cast to display their unnatural energy levels. The audience on a Wednesday afternoon in May would be mainly composed of tourists in trainers and shoppers on return tickets, but my parents were of a generation who looked smart – I should say smarter than usual – when they came up to Town. They looked on the theatre, like church, as a place where a good turnout denoted an appropriate measure of respect. My mother did in fact own some jeans (Gloria Vanderbilt, impeccably dry-cleaned with a crease down the front), and some spotless Timberlands which she wore for walking the dog in the fields, but she would never have worn either to attend a show.

Today she was softly elegant in a camel suit which looked Jaeger but was probably M&S, a blond cashmere polo-neck and tan courts. The effect, with her hair and colouring, was of honey and cream. Someone of my generation would have sharpened this look with huge gilt-and-pearl studs and heavy gold chains at the throat and wrists, but my mother wore only the tiniest and most discreet glint of earring. She made up for this in the ring department. She had big, long-fingered hands always, in spite of ceaseless gardening, immaculately manicured, and wore three on the fourth finger of her left hand and a knuckle-duster emerald on her right. My father was in an immaculate grey suit and his MCC tie.

He stood up as I approached. 'Laura – how nice. Where do you want to park yourself . . . ?'

'Mm,' said my mother as I kissed her. 'Lovely.'

'What's it to be?' asked my father. In spite of the size of the room a waiter had, as always, instantly materialized.

'A g and t?'

'A gin and tonic, the same again for us, and we might as well have the menu if you please.'

The waiter sped away. I was sure my parents were the sort of patrons who made him happy in his work.

I felt the same. They did me good. 'How are you both?' I asked. 'You're looking marvellous.'

'Thank you, darling,' said my mother. 'My hip's playing up, but I don't admit to it.'

'Bloody but unbowed,' said my father. 'Shall we enjoy this thing, do you think?'

'Oh, I'm sure you will. Everyone says it's fantastic.'

'The dancing these days is quite out of this world.' My mother rewarded the waiter with a little smile of gratitude as he brought our drinks and dishes of olives and rice crackers. 'Even what you see on the television makes the sort of thing we used to do look absolutely clodhopping. I'm expecting a real treat.'

'I just hope they keep the sound levels a little below that of the Battle of the Atlantic,' said my father, but quite equably.

'You know perfectly well they won't,' I said. 'It will be loud.'

'I never thought I'd say this but I'm beginning to get used to it,' remarked my mother, removing the swizzle from her Bloody Mary and laying it in the ashtray.

'You're fortunate enough to be going a bit deaf, darling.' My father tapped his pocket. 'Anyway, I come prepared. I have my ear plugs.'

My mother looked at me with the enraptured expression which accompanied a determined change of subject.

'We did so enjoy your party,' she said. 'It was absolutely super. We were only sorry we had to leave when we did.'

'I'm glad,' I said.

'What time did everyone stay till, in the end?'

'Oh . . . I think we poured the last ones out at about midnight.'

'Midnight!' My mother was enchanted, this was exactly the sort of talk she most enjoyed. 'Lunch until midnight – they must have had fun!'

'I think we all did.'

'We liked the fiddle-player,' said my father. 'Was that Glyn's idea?'

'No, actually, he was a present from a friend.'

'He didn't look terribly jolly but he could certainly play.'

'It was Susan Upchurch who organized it. She couldn't come herself so she sent him.'

'Do I know her?' asked my father, looking at me and then at my mother.

'Yes – well, I certainly do,' said my mother, 'she was at QE with you, wasn't she?'

'That's right. And at our wedding.' I turned to my father. 'She was the one who arrived just as we were about to walk up the aisle.'

'Oh yes, I do harbour a vague recollection – skinny in loud checks.'

My mother raised her eyebrows. 'I often wonder, Peter,' she said, 'how you used to describe me to your friends.'

Menus arrived and we chose. In this company there was no nonsense about eating lightly in the middle of the day. My parents – corned beef sandwich merchants at home – were legendary lunchers when out, working up through the courses to pudding with heroic gusto. It was just as well they were going to the ear-busting tapfest. Anything less exuberant – Hare, say, or Stoppard, let alone Chekhov or the Bard, would surely have induced slumber in no time.

There was no point in standing aloof. I had whitebait, followed by pork in cider and cream sauce with new potatoes and seasonal veg. I nearly had cheese instead of pudding, but decided that it was equally fattening and settled for crème brûlée. They had soup and rack of lamb. My father had the treacle tart, and cheese to follow. My mother saw off one of the largest dollops of trifle I'd ever seen. It was perfectly clear that our waiter was bewitched by her high-octane between-the-wars charm.

We talked about the family. Apparently Anthea had broken a finger while putting a young horse through its paces on a lungeing rein. She and David had invited the parents to join them at Reids Hotel for a week in June and they'd accepted. Jasper still didn't have a steady girlfriend but Emma had formed a liaison (my father's expression) with a game warden named Bud. Caro was thinking of moving to a flat and Steph was thinking of marrying the newsreader, so there might be a family wedding in the summer, which would be nice (opined my mother). If they did, then presumably Ros and Brian and their two would come over from Vancouver.

'*If* it takes place,' said my father, 'and I think we ought to reserve judgment on that one, I rather doubt it'll be the full white do.'

'Why ever not?' asked my mother.

'Because Stephanie is not in the first flush of youth, and that chap she has in tow doesn't look like morning dress material to me.'

'But poor Caro's been dying for another wedding, one she can really go to town on . . .'

'Since when did Caro's wishes have the slightest influence on the terrible twins?'

'You may be right,' agreed my mother. 'But anyway, there will be some sort of party I'm sure. Yum, yum,' she added with a sigh, laying down her spoon and sitting back. 'I wish I could say that I'll never do that again.'

My father turned to me. 'How was yours, Laura-lou?'

'Wonderful,' I said. I found myself wondering, as I so often did, what Susan would have made of this lunch. Too much food and not enough drink, probably. My parents were serious cocktail-takers – three stiff ones before a meal was as nothing to them, and at the average stand-up-and-shout they could have drunk anyone of my acquaintance under the table – but a second bottle of wine was less usual.

As my father selected cheese from a board like a football pitch, my mother said, 'And how's Glyn?'

'He's fine.'

'Is he ever not fine?'

I thought about this, and remembered him as I'd seen him leaving for work in Madras checks. 'No. He almost always is.'

'As far as you know,' added my mother, inclining her head in my direction with a little smile to show that this was an expression of kinship and not a criticism.

'He has a great capacity for contentment,' I said.

'What a gift!' exclaimed my mother, who shared it.

I walked with them to the theatre, which was only a few hundred yards away. The foyer was teeming.

'God Almighty,' said my father. 'Are you sure this is the right place?'

'It's a hot ticket, Pedro,' explained my mother. She turned to me. 'Darling, if we could swap our seats for three together, would you like to join us?'

'I won't, thanks. I'd like to get back before the rush.'

'Of course, you're driving – I hope we didn't give you too much to drink,' said my mother, as though I were under five and the entire responsibility for my consumption lay with them. 'It's all right for us, we swan up first-class on our old crocks' Railcard.'

'I'm fine,' I said.

We kissed each other and agreed how nice it had been. 'I suppose you'll be wanting some of the management's extortionately priced chocolates,' said my father.

'Naturally. Black Magic.'

He moved away sideways through the crush, and I felt my mother's gaze on me: fond, speculative, collusive . . . She had intuition like a laser which even her perfect tact could not completely disguise. Though I couldn't fault her behaviour, there was something premonitory about her attitude towards me today. I had no reason to feel guilty except my thoughts.

I hadn't been entirely truthful about needing to get home before the rush. I wanted to have some time to play on the way. I didn't delude myself that I was needed at home. It was a state of affairs one longed for from the baby-rice to the school run and perhaps especially through the taxi-service years when no Friday or Saturday night was complete without its accompanying crisis at midnight, with last trains missed, purses nicked and kindly police in attendance. But now this mid-life plateau was here, I sometimes felt perversely lost.

I left the car in the underground car park and took the tube to Bond Street. I couldn't lay claim to the Diana effect – that of rendering sales staff helpless with humility – but I was at least wearing my good suit, and had not seriously troubled my credit card for several months. A spirit of reckless consumerism possessed me. I wanted something new, now, and I wanted to purchase it without wondering whether it matched other things, or whether I had the shoes to go with it. Who cared? If I had no shoes to go with it, I'd darn well buy those too.

Lightheaded with retail fever, I cruised a couple of recherché designer boutiques where the stock only came in black, white and taupe, and tried on assorted tops, skirts, jackets and jodhpurs. They were all nice, but not quite nice enough for the price. If I was going to pay an arm and a leg for casual wear, then I wanted nothing less than a transformation. I left both shops with a murmured 'Thank you' and what I hoped was the vague, unimpressed smile of the internationally experienced spender.

In the third shop there was another colour, 'Sand', and having just seen my mother wearing it I was sure it was the height of fashion *savoir*. The clothes were simple and dashing. The beaming charm of the sales assistant was quite unnecessary – I already knew I was going to buy.

I didn't take long. Once seduced, I was a pushover. I came out half an hour later toting the shop's large, glossy, stiffened carrier with black rope handles. Rustling amongst tissue inside the bag was the pants-suit (I'd picked up the lingo) to die for. In the palest gold fine wool, with a jacket so long and light it was hardly there, with a single self-covered button, and long, lean, perfect trousers that fell from the waistband like water and broke over the instep. High on the easy rush of plastic credit, I had added a narrow mesh-leather belt and a cream silk T-shirt. The mere smell of the carrier bag was enough to keep me on the high all the way back to the underground car park.

On the drive home my exhilaration ebbed away. They were, after all, only clothes. I felt rather flat, but I still wasn't ready to go back to Alderswick Avenue and relegate my wild purchases to just another couple of hangers-worth in the bedroom wardrobe. I drove to the park near the river.

The park was known as the Piece, and when we first moved out of London I had always assumed, because it was overlooked by the Church of St Michael and All Angels, that this was spelt 'Peace'. Confused agnostic though I was, I'd been disappointed to find this wasn't so, and continued privately to spell it my way. It was a pleasing park, with large trees, winding paths, some reassuring civic statuary and a pool in the centre with ducks and lily pads. Even at five o'clock people didn't hurry through it, but strolled. And beside the pond, young men with briefcases and smart girls in spike heels stood and stared, perhaps remembering when they'd stood by that same pond or one like it with a bigger person, throwing bread for the ducks.

I walked, slowly, right round the perimeter of the park, and then went through the little black iron gate into the churchyard. On the far side of the church the bustle and drone of a provincial rush hour filled Bartholomew Street, but here it was quiet.

I sat down on the only seat, and gazed at Isobel's grave from a distance. We'd chosen this place because the idea of St Michael and all his angels looking after our daughter was comforting. The church had a small but faithful ageing congregation and every Saturday there was a bring-and-buy stall by the main entrance where Glyn bought homemade fudge. The vicar was a nice, ill-looking man about ten years younger than us. Glyn had told him about Isobel, something I'd never have dreamed of doing, and he now greeted us like friends.

She had a tiny, white, arched stone, with her name and the year. From where I sat it looked like one of those panto-mime milestones that proclaim 'London, 50 miles', but promise Shangri-La.

I sat and gazed. Isobel's microscopic life gave her a kind of authority over the rest of us. She had become universal, a constant. The plain white stone, which looked as though it had been placed there only yesterday, would outlast me, Glyn, her brother and sisters, and her nephew and niece. Isobel would always be there, and always keep her counsel.

An elderly couple, probably American, certainly tourists, paused by her, and the man leaned forward to read the inscription. I could see by their faces and body language that they were affected. The man laid his hand for a moment on his wife's shoulder. As they began to walk away the woman raised her hand in a small wave of farewell, and then snapped her fingers shut abruptly as if embarrassed. I half-wanted to make myself known, but I didn't want to break the spell of calm.

As the couple walked past me the man was saying, '. . . something Victorian in a small child's gravestone . . . something weird about burying a baby . . .'

At home, Verity was in the kitchen, making a vegetable hot-pot. The good smell greeted me as I came through the door and I left my jacket and bags in the hall and went through to talk to her.

'Are you okay?' she asked, putting a cup of tea in front of me.

I told her what I'd overheard. 'It made me feel as though Isobel were some sort of freak show.'

'That's nonsense,' said Verity firmly. 'And anyway, does it matter what two perfect strangers say and think? You know what's what, and so does Our Lord, and that's the important thing.'

I always felt that Our Lord had me, a miserable sinner, foisted upon him in these situations, but I consoled myself with the thought that it was wretches like myself who presumably made His job worthwhile. If everyone were like Verity there'd be nothing left to do.

She sat down opposite me and opened a small tin to reveal homemade mueslijacks. 'How were Gran and Pops?'

'In tremendous form. We had a lovely lunch at the Clarendon and then they went off to their show.'

'Gosh . . .' Verity sighed in happy wonderment. 'They are just so – sort of *glamorous* for their age.'

This seemed like my cue to flaunt a little glamour of my own. 'I bought some clothes – rather expensive ones. Would you like to see?'

'But you must put them on!'

She was the perfect audience. In spite of her own monastic attitude to possessions she positively encouraged indulgence in others. I sometimes had the unworthy notion that she was earmarking new clothes for her vagrants a few years' hence.

'That is gorgeous!' she exclaimed, as I gave her a twirl. 'You look like something out of *Vogue*!'

'They are nice, aren't they?' I agreed, looking down at myself. 'I'm afraid it's a case of you gets what you pays for.'

'Did they cost a fortune?' I gave her a rough idea. 'Wow . . . still, you deserve it.'

'Well, I don't know . . .'

'Have you shown them to Dad?'

'Where is he?'

'In the office, go on, you must.'

I went and knocked on the door.

'Come.'

Glyn was on the phone, but he made 'Wow' faces as I came in, and held out a restraining hand to keep me there.

'Okay . . . yeah . . . sure . . . no problem,' he said, leaning forward and making winding-up motions with his hand for my benefit. This was to indicate the long-windedness of the person on the other end, but I knew very well that Glyn liked nothing better than 'a good goss on the blower' as he put it, and had probably instigated the call and been talking up a storm for hours before I arrived.

'Yup, terrific. Catch you later.' He put the receiver down and held out his arms. 'Look at you!'

'Like it?'

He linked his hands behind his head. 'It's more a question of whether I can live up to it or not.'

'No chance, I sincerely hope.'

'It won't do you any good round at the CAB I can tell you. Your poor-but-honest image shot to pieces at a stroke.'

'No, well, I wasn't thinking of wearing it at the CAB, was I?'

'We've got the agency's anniversary bash in June. Boat on the Thames, jazz band – you can give it an outing then.'

I was doubtful. 'Will it be right for that?'

'Anything's right for that. Who says you've got to fit in? You can wear what you like.'

'In that case I probably will . . .'

'Pedro and Diana okay?'

'Fine. They sent their love.'

'Verity's making supper, by the way.'

'I know, I've been talking to her.'

The small change ran out. Glyn sat there with his hands behind his head, smiling, and I suddenly felt slightly silly in my finery.

'Right,' I said, 'I'd better go and get back to normal.'

I heard him pick up the phone again as I closed the door. I collected my other clothes from the sitting-room sofa and went upstairs. The faint, unmistakable scent of pot indicated Josh's presence on the floor above.

I got back to normal.

Normality reasserted itself even more brutally the following morning when Becca called at 8 a.m. to announce that Bunker's had found more damage to the Mini than they had at first thought, and that 'that dreary little man' – the driver of the Scorpio – had written to her to say that his boot had been pushed out of alignment and a new one would cost £600. What a rip-off, and there hadn't been a single mark on his bloody great car, could we believe it? We could – I especially, having witnessed the treatment he had received at our daughter's hands. Just for good measure Josh had developed a nasty flu bug and was lying red-faced and slightly smelly in the attic, unable to get his head off the pillow. Glyn was going in to London, and Verity was visiting a housebound disabled Desert Rat, so the task of succouring the sick fell to me. I escorted him, weaving slightly, down to the sitting-room, took a firm line on a change of T-shirt and boxer shorts, gave him a clean duvet cover and pillowcases and poured him a large jug of diluted orange juice. I more or less forced him to take a couple of paracetamol, and left the packet by him with instructions to repeat the dose, although I knew perfectly well he would simply lie there in a sickly stupor until he felt slightly better, and would then get up and go out to repeat the exercise next day.

In consequence of all this I was late at the CAB and my first client, Mr Prentiss, a regular, was sitting on a hard chair waiting for me when I arrived. I apologized and let him in, clutching my polystyrene cup of coffee.

'I'm sorry – would you like one?'

'No, thanks, I'm not a coffee man.'

It was hard to know what sort of man Stan Prentiss was. My lateness would probably work in my favour since it would confirm him in his sense of superiority. Having been made redundant – with several hundred others – from A&B Holdings, he had taken on the role of professional complainer. He didn't come to us for help, but to lodge these complaints. I had run out of advice long ago, together with leaflets, useful contacts, data-sheets and sympathy. Basically, Mr Prentiss couldn't come to terms with the unfairness of life. I was far from being unsympathetic to his plight, but I slightly resented being used as a repository for the mass of generalized moans which he couldn't get to stick elsewhere. Especially as his manner made it clear that he regarded all of us at the CAB as bleeding-heart time-servers protected by income and privilege from the harsh realities experienced by people like himself. Curiously, I suspected that he was also rather right-wing and would have disapproved strongly of, say, Becca's *modus vivendi*.

'What can I do for you this morning?' I asked with a somewhat steely smile. Our relationship had gone past the point where we pretended it was more than something to be got through.

'That remains to be seen,' replied Mr Prentiss.

'How's the job search going?'

He jerked his head back in a silent 'Ha!' 'How do you think?'

'I'm sorry if you haven't found anything but I'm sure you will, with your qualifications.'

'I wish I shared your optimism.'

'It's not so much optimism – it's a case of self-esteem.'

Mr Prentiss sneered. You didn't see many honest-to-goodness, gone-for-broke sneers these days, but this was one of them. He was, I estimated, in his late thirties and rather a good-looking man, but his face was becoming pinched with discontent and resentment.

'Oh, I know what I'm worth all right,' he said. 'It's just I have this little problem,' he put his finger and thumb a centimetre apart, 'persuading other people.'

I tried to steer the conversation towards more practical topics. It was what I was there for, after all.

'How are the finances?' I asked.

'We've had to cut down to one Caribbean cruise and we've let the wife's BMW go,' he replied with heavy sarcasm.

'Is your wife still working?' I knew Mrs Prentiss worked part-time in a florist's.

'Yes.' There was a 'What of it?' in the background.

I soldiered on. 'How are the children?'

This was his weakness, and I must say I liked him for it. His manner changed from abrasive truculence to something deeper and gruffer.

'They're okay. Wondering why I'm around all the time.'

'They must like seeing more of you, though. And vice versa.'

'Hm . . .' He felt in his breast-pocket and took out a wallet. I knew he was going to show me a photograph. My heart sank.

'There they are.' He handed me the photograph. 'My Rachel and little Michaela.'

I took time to study the picture. It showed two enchanting

little girls, one of about six, the other perhaps three, in what I took to be bridesmaids' dresses of blush-pink taffeta, with garlands slightly askew on their Mabel Lucy Atwell curls. The younger one was sitting on someone's lap, the older standing alongside leaning slightly. There was something Victorian about the pose, although the setting – from the glasses and bottles glimpsed in the background – was clearly a riotous party.

'My sister-in-law's wedding,' explained Prentiss. 'Last month.'

'They're absolutely beautiful,' I said. 'You must be very proud of them.'

'I am,' he said. 'I just wish they could be proud of me.' And he burst into tears.

He didn't stay long after that. Our moment of truth was swiftly followed by a regrouping on Prentiss's part as though he couldn't wait to cover his tracks and pretend it had never happened. When he'd gone I dealt with a fairly standard NIMBY query arising from care in the community and then took the opportunity to call in on Ted, my Wednesday colleague.

'I think he may be having a nervous breakdown,' I told Ted. 'And I wish I knew what the hell to do.'

Ted had been a personnel officer with British Aerospace until relatively recently and was my consultant on all things to do with man management.

'Just what you are doing,' he said. 'I think it would be pretty unwise to try and assume any expertise you haven't got, and neither would it be advisable to go behind his back.'

'Oh no,' I assured him, 'I wouldn't dream of doing that. But I feel so helpless.'

'I'm sure you do,' said Ted. 'But in my experience in these matters, less is generally more.'

We weren't very busy, and at twelve-fifteen, still rather unsettled, I went down in search of something to eat.

When the city fathers had overseen the conversion of the Corn Exchange into a community centre some twenty-five years ago they'd envisaged a stately civic pleasure dome to which the townsfolk of all ages and persuasions would be drawn for comfort, recreation and assistance. It was a fine concept which had been only partly successful in the execution. The Exchange housed a 400-seat theatre which was used by amateur groups as well as touring professional companies and bands; a twice-weekly toy library; a Senior Citizens' drop-in and luncheon club; a single parents' encounter group (to which Verity was continually urging Becca to go and which Becca regarded as the pits); assorted evening classes; Alcoholics Anonymous; and us. At the time it must have seemed a good idea to include the CAB in this mix, but we had been put on the first floor, accessible only by a back iron staircase like a fire-escape, which was difficult for the elderly, the very young, the disabled, and people with pushchairs. We had complained, and the carrot of smart new premises near the Health Centre was being dangled. Till then we suspected that many of our potential clients, who also belonged to constituencies catered for on the ground floor, got their advice on an ad hoc basis down there, and only ventured up the fire escape in extremis.

The problem was compounded by the Barley Mow Bar in the foyer, where I was now buying a glass of cider and a wholewheat pastie. The Barley Mow's competitive prices brought it a brisk lunchtime trade from the surrounding retail outlets and the market, who packed the place out and must have acted as a deterrent to any shy or nervous person wanting to venture in.

Although I was early, all the small metal tables were already taken, so I contented myself with standing by the shelf provided for the purpose which ran along the back wall. Above the shelf was a noticeboard advertising everything from aromatherapy to the local AODS production of *Cage aux Folles*. I stood with my back to the room as I munched my pastie, using the notices as the equivalent of the lone diner's open book.

His name appeared on a large pale blue advertisement for a Brains' Trust, to be recorded for regional television in the Exchange Theatre six weeks hence. He was on a panel which also included a junior minister, a well-known biographer and a trade union leader. He was described as Patrick Lynch, Professor of English at St Stephen's College, and author of *Language and Libido*.

* * *

When I went back upstairs it was to find that we were busy again, with one client in with Ted and another two people waiting on the hard chairs. One was a neat, elderly man in a green zip-up jacket and a checked cap. The other was Patrick Lynch himself.

'Hallo there!' he exclaimed, rising. 'I've already explained to this gentleman that I'm not a customer, so I won't keep him waiting.'

'Oh, well—' I transferred my attention to the old man. 'Would you like to go on in and I'll be with you in two ticks. Just take a seat.'

I pulled the door to. 'Has your cat been held hostage again?'

'What?' He furrowed his brow and then exclaimed, 'No! I thought I'd like to see you in your context.'

'I see. Well, here I am.' It certainly wasn't his context, any more than Planet Burger had been.

'Grandchildren well?' he asked. Steady on, I thought. Okay, okay.

'Yes, thanks. Look, I really ought to go in and see my client.'

'You certainly did ought.' He stretched out an arm in an after-you gesture. 'Are you still offering dinner by the way?'

His genial bluntness caught me completely off guard. 'I'm sorry, I haven't got round to – to be honest, we don't have many dinner-parties.'

'Very wise. Nor me.'

'How about a drink?' I heard myself saying. 'Let me buy you a drink. It's the least I can do.'

'Excellent.' He beamed. 'When do you finish here?'

I told him, he named a pub, and left. I sat thoughtfully in front of my client who had a sordid little property problem with his estranged middle-aged daughter, but I was only half listening. Had something happened? And if so, had Patrick Lynch made it happen? Or had I? And what was I doing even thinking in this way?

'. . . so you see,' said my client in his clipped, golf-club voice. 'I really don't know where to turn, or what to do for the best.'

*   *   *

There were plenty of all-day pubs around the market-place. When I finished at four I went to meet Patrick Lynch in one called the Tanner's Arms. I sat alone in the saloon bar for fifteen minutes before he appeared and took me through to the public.

'Hope you don't mind,' he said, 'but I prefer a bit of spit and sawdust.'

'Not at all,' I said. 'This is fine.'

'But not what you're used to,' he suggested, lighting a cigarette.

'I don't spend that much time in pubs.' It was meant to be an explanation but came out sounding prim.

'Do you not?' He raised his eyebrows. 'What do you and Mr Lewis do, then? By way of fun?'

He spoke the last word with a slight hesitation on either side of it, like a newsreader pronouncing the name of a particularly exotic foreign city.

Actually I was stumped for an answer. The quest for fun wasn't something we went in for any more, but to say that would make us sound like a sad old couple and I particularly did not wish to give that impression to Patrick Lynch.

'We go to the pictures, we see friends, we have a large family—'

'You give parties,' he reminded me kindly.

'Yes, we do sometimes give parties.'

'But not dinner-parties.'

'Well,' I said, 'we have people round to eat, but I wouldn't dignify what I provide on those occasions with the title of dinner-party.'

'I'm sure you sell yourself short. I bet you're quite the society hostess on your night.'

'I am not!' I had to laugh at this and he snorted with satisfaction. 'Ask anyone.'

'Now tell me,' Patrick asked. 'What did you say to that poor little chap with the moustache and the highly polished shoes?'

As I outlined, as far as confidentiality would allow, my conversation with the client, I reflected that for Patrick Lynch cleanliness was next to godliness and as such was probably quite beyond the pale. As he sat there with his Guinness and his fag he exuded a rich, pungent male odour. He had a way of staring as I talked, with the occasional snapping blink that was like a nod, reminding me that he was paying attention.

Whether he was or not I couldn't tell, since the moment I finished speaking he asked, 'Now tell me, what does your husband do?'

'He runs an entertainment management agency. Mostly pop singers and bands.'

'He never does,' said Patrick. 'The little devil.'

Looking back, I believe that remark, with its stain of condescension, was a turning-point. For it was then that Patrick Lynch, whether consciously or no, tweaked at the ground beneath my feet, and I lost my footing, my presence of mind, and my way.

8

When the ground has gone from under your feet you walk on air. Cartoon characters do it – it's called the plausible impossible. It's what enables Bugs Bunny to run halfway across the canyon before realization hits. When it does he looks down, panics, and plummets, arms windmilling, to the ground . . .

The following evening the phone rang while we were eating supper in the kitchen. Josh had the phone in the sitting-room with him so that he could keep in touch with his empire even on his bed of pain.

'It's for you-hoo,' he croaked.

'Which one?' asked Glyn.

'Mrs Lewis, whoever that is.'

'I'm eating!' I called. 'Ask if I can ring back.'

There was some mumbling and a pause. 'He says it's Professor Lynch and he'll be very quick!'

I'm sure something happened to my face. I didn't blush, but I felt an internal tremor of shock.

'Are you coming or what?' Josh was plaintive. 'I can't keep on yelling, my throat hurts like buggery!'

'Go on,' said Glyn, 'I'll stick your plate in the microwave.'

Josh's arm was sticking out over the end of the sofa, holding the receiver. I took it, picked up the phone, and walked into the hall. In the kitchen I could see Glyn covering my plate with another and putting it in the microwave. This domestic act accorded ill with his red 'Chicago Bulls' T-shirt and leather jeans.

'Hallo?'

'I heard what you said – sorry to disturb supper.'

'That's all right.'

'Shan't keep you long. I enjoyed talking to you yesterday. Actually, I enjoy being with you.' The change of tense was accompanied by a change of tone. There was no denying the implication. My legs felt strange and I braced my knees backwards.

'Oh,' I said. 'Really?'

'I understand you probably can't talk now.'

I was trapped, as he knew I would be, by his assumption. 'Not really, no.'

'I'd like to see you again.'

'Would you?'

Glyn had finished eating and was standing in the doorway gazing out at the garden with his hands linked behind his head. I turned away.

'As soon as possible,' said Patrick.

'I don't see any reason why not, diary permitting.'

'Je-sus H!' He spluttered mirthfully. 'Diary permitting! How about tomorrow?'

'I'll be at the Bureau at the usual time, you could call in then.'

'Good. I will. Diary permitting.'

'Cheerio, then.'

'Cheerio!' he mimicked. 'Toodle-oo. Pip-pip. I think you're gorgeous.'

I returned the telephone to Josh. I was a trembling mass of physical symptoms but when I caught sight of myself in the drawing-room mirror I looked almost unnaturally calm, if a little bright-eyed.

'Something to do with the Bureau,' I announced, returning to the table.

'Poor bugger.' Glyn retrieved my plate from the microwave and put it in front of me. 'He won't ring again in a hurry.' He sat down opposite me. 'Diary permitting – I should ko-ko.'

Verity was going to visit the shrine at Walsingham with Shona, in Shona's camper-van.

'If there's anything or anyone in particular you'd like me

to offer up to Our Lady,' she told us as she made Marmite sandwiches, 'concentrate on it between two and three when we're there, and I'll be the channel.'

'Could you see your way to giving Human Condition a mention?' asked Glyn.

'We always do.'

'No,' I said, 'you mean the band, don't you?'

'I'll certainly offer them up,' said Verity. 'Especially now Becca's going out with Griggs.'

We gawped.

'And I always pray for everyone in this family anyway,' she added, cutting two rounds in half.

'Thank goodness, sweetheart,' said Glyn. 'We could all do with a following wind.'

It was a warm, fine day and we went to a restaurant that overlooked the Peace. The restaurant had once been a cricket pavilion, and we sat out on the wooden verandah and ate Spanish omelette.

'This is the life,' said Patrick. 'Don't you think?'

'It is,' I said. 'It's lovely.' I could feel him staring at me with that look which was both a challenge and an invitation, and which did not entertain the faintest possibility of either being turned down. I've always loved food and had a hearty appetite, but I was having difficulty finishing the omelette. I could amost feel myself getting thinner as I sat there. I recognized the sensation – it was a bad case of over-excitement. I could almost hear my father saying, 'Easy does it. Deep breaths. Brave and calm.' But it was too late for that.

'Look,' I said. He tilted his head encouragingly. 'I'm married.'

'Yes, but I'm not. So that makes it your problem.'

'I shouldn't be here.'

'Having lunch?'

'You know it's not just that.'

'Isn't it? Tell me what you think it is.'

I was boxed in. 'Never mind.'

'Let me,' he suggested, suddenly laying hold of my wrist. 'I believe we have what's known as a thing going on.'

I couldn't speak. I was thrilled and appalled. His grip on my wrist was tight – I couldn't have moved without a struggle.

'Oh yes we have,' he insisted, as though I'd argued with him. 'And here we are, sitting in the sun together, both knowing it.'

'I'm forty-nine,' I said. God knows what point I was trying to make. Perhaps I thought he'd leap from the table in disgust, never to return, thus absolving me from any further awkwardness.

'Bloody hell,' he said. 'Spooky!'

'And a grandmother.'

'I know.' He kept his hand on my wrist and shovelled in the last few mouthfuls of omelette with the other. 'And if you don't watch out I'll report you to Social Services.'

'What on earth for?'

'For failing properly to safeguard your grandchildren in a public place, for allowing them to speak to strange men, and for wilfully embarking on an extra-marital affair with a chap who, you'll be dismayed to learn, is five years younger than you.'

He released my wrist and sat back, fishing his cigarettes out of his trouser-pocket.

'You can go anytime you want,' he said. 'And without a trace of damage done if you don't count my broken heart and blue balls.'

I didn't go. We sat in silence for a couple of minutes. The click of a lighter, the long first exhalation. My silence was confused and tumultuous, his placid. A youth and a girl in their late teens walked past, and he raised a hand to them.

I realized that if I wasn't going to leave, then I had to say something – anything – in self-justification.

'I really am not used to this sort of thing.' I glanced at him. He smiled enquiringly. 'Are you not?'

'Of course not.'

'On the other hand—' He gestured. 'Here you are.'

'I must be mad . . .' I said this with my head lowered, almost to myself. I knew – and it was shamingly obvious that he knew also – that this litany of feeble protest was a mere formality. Even while I spoke I was imagining what it would feel like to be in his arms, the rough skin of his face against mine, my fingers buried in his hair, his smell in my nostrils, the solid bulk of his body pressed against me. Slip-sliding away . . .

When he stood up I was buffeted by panic. 'Where are you going?'

'Back to work,' he said. 'That way. Do you want to walk?'

I walked with him to the main road. He turned to face me, hands in pockets.

'I fancy you ferociously,' he said. 'Abso-fucking-lutely ferociously.'

Later I thought that any one of hundreds of people who knew me might have been walking past at that moment, but it was a measure of my altered state that I never took my eyes off his face. I couldn't.

'Yes,' I said.

He gave a little there-you-go shrug. 'I can't make you do anything, Laura.' It was the first time he'd used my Christian name. 'As you pointed out, you're the one with the marriage.'

'Yes.'

'So.' He took a card from the inside pocket of his jacket. 'That's me. I live alone, and there's an answering-machine. Get in touch.'

In the moment that it took me to glance down at the card, he was on his way, his open-shouldered, splay-footed swagger cleaving a path through the lunch-hour crowds in Bartholomew Street.

I went back into the Peace. Beyond the trees on the far side I could see the church tower, reminding me that Isobel's quiet, trusting little stone was very near. Perhaps she'd heard every word

The church clock struck two. I closed my eyes for a second and reminded Verity, urgently, to pray for me.

After that three more days went by, during which I carried Patrick's card about with me. On several occasions I got as far as dialling his number, but then put the phone down while it was still ringing. Twice the answering-machine was on, but I didn't leave a message. It was only later that I realized he could dial the search number to find out who'd called.

In between these aborted calls I was elated. To be fancied

ferociously was nice at any time. At my age it was powerful ju-ju indeed. To be told in a crowded street that one was fancied ferociously, by a man whom one fancied ferociously in return, was very heaven.

When it came to the consultation with Mr Collins at the college, I surprised myself. Poor Josh had developed full-blown flu – head like a bucket, eye-sockets lined with sandpaper, throat full of golf balls and a temperature only intermittently dipping below scorching. His afflictions and enforced absence from the meeting (I reasoned) would cast a more sympathetic light on him.

Glyn had Cy coming up for the day. 'Sorry I can't come,' he said, 'I know how much you hate these things.'

'I don't mind,' I replied truthfully. 'I shall be fine.'

'If they want to know what I think, tell them I think Josh writes like a pro – and he's never boring, which is more than you can say for some of these dreary tracts that win prizes.'

'I'll stick up for him,' I said, 'don't worry.'

Glyn was right, I usually disliked talking to teachers. My experience of such discussions had not been happy. He and I had turned out a trio of prime teacher-baiters, from the refusenik Becca to the too-clever-by-half Josh with his intellectual brinkmanship. But today I felt clear-headed and exuberantly confident. I even managed to junk the 'good things are for best' mentality which had dogged me all my life and wore my new suit – with Patrick's card tucked into the inside jacket pocket.

I hadn't met Mr Collins before, but my preconceived notions about what a Head of English would look like led me to expect someone pear-shaped and possibly bearded, in a V-necked tanktop and a jacket with leather at the elbows. I was therefore particularly glad I'd taken care with my appearance when I met the real thing, who was only a few years older than Josh, with a carefully arrayed mop of gelled hair, a baggy dark suit and a button-down chambray shirt. I could only assume Josh's 'trainspotter' shaft referred to his taste in essays.

'Hallo there.' He held out his hand. 'Thanks for coming in. Shall we go in the interview room?'

For me this conjured up a picture from police shows on

TV, of a windowless box with a metal-frame table and chairs, lino on the floor and a seen-it-all sergeant in shirtsleeves standing against the wall. The reality, like Mr Collins himself, could not have been more different. There was a pale blue carpet, pink and blue curtains at the window overlooking the sports field, two upholstered chairs with wooden arms, and a teak table with copies of the college prospectus and the *TES*.

Mr Collins paused in the doorway. 'Would you like some coffee? I can get you a drinkable one from the staff-room.'

'No thank you.'

'Tea?'

'No thanks.'

'Right.'

He came in and we sat down in the chairs. I leaned back in mine, hands relaxed, legs crossed; he perched on the edge of his, elbows on knees.

'Now then. Josh.' His brows furrowed as though the mere mention of my son's name left him lost for words. 'How is he by the way?'

'Groggy.'

'Do give him my regards.'

'I will.'

'Fine. Umm . . .' He bent his head and combed his fingers through his hair.

I waited, for once resisting the urge to pre-empt things by offering any view of my own. It was after all he who had asked to see me and not the other way round.

Eventually he looked up. 'Did you or your husband have an opportunity to read his essay?'

'We both have.'

'What did you think of it?'

There seemed no point in being anything but truthful. 'I must say I was taken aback.'

For some reason this appeared to please Mr Collins, who brightened noticeably. 'I can understand that.'

'What did you think of it?' I asked.

'I thought it was an extraordinary piece of work.'

'So your criticism is . . . what exactly?'

'Well – obviously he was setting out to shock, and he succeeded. I can't pretend to have been especially shocked myself, but there was a challenge being thrown down there. The thing is, Josh has such an original mind, such a command of language, such persuasive powers of argument. I'd be extremely loath to squash all that.'

'That's what my husband thinks,' I said. I didn't tell him that Glyn had said that Josh's essay would make any examiner's day. 'I'm more cautious.'

'Of course, I'd expect you to be, you're quite right to be, but I wanted to talk to you in order to establish where we go from here.'

Suddenly I had the feeling that none of this mattered very much, and that I was becoming enmeshed in a discussion which was going nowhere.

'You're his teacher,' I said. 'I think that's your problem.'

He didn't break stride but I could tell I'd surprised him. 'You do regard it as a problem, then?'

'It'd be nice if he passed his exams.'

'If you read his last report you'll know that I regard him as a potential starred A.'

'And will writing about pudenda jeopardize that?'

'It might do.'

'Then I imagine it would be better if he cleaned up his act.'

'Cleaned up his act . . . yes.' Mr Collins tapped his forefingers against his upper lip. He was starting to get on my nerves. They say that with advancing years a person becomes more right-wing. I was suddenly ambushed by the unsettling and (till now) uncharacteristic notion that I was paying this young man's salary and he was expecting me to do his job for him.

'I think,' I said firmly, 'that both Glyn and I would prefer that Josh was only allowed the licence that's commensurate with him getting a good grade.'

'Okay,' agreed Mr Collins without warmth. 'That's fair enough. Have you actually spoken to him about it?'

'Not since we read it. He's got the flu.'

'Sure, sure, but it would be best if you did.'

'I dare say we will.'

I was flying. I hadn't felt so good in years. Perhaps this was the recessive gene I'd passed on to Becca asserting itself.

'Look, Mrs Lewis,' said Collins, 'let me put my cards on the table.'

'Do.'

'I like Josh. I believe he and I understand each other. He's a very bright lad, and English is his best subject—'

'I know.'

'We're all on the same side when it comes down to it, we all want him to do as well as we know he can.'

'Yes, yes.' I let the merest hint of impatience show through.

'My feeling is,' said Mr Collins, 'that if you can provide a bit of input your end it can only be helpful.'

He was in retreat, throwing up a smokescreen of teacherspeak to cover his tracks.

'Don't worry,' I said, 'when he's feeling better we'll let him know exactly what we think.'

'And you'll indicate to him the advisability of sticking to less provocative subject matter?'

'I might,' I said, 'I can't speak for my husband.'

'Your support would be very much appreciated.'

I stood up. He did the same. My expensive suit slipped smoothly into place without a crease: his had concertinaed in all the usual places.

'Thank you again for coming in to discuss this,' he said, opening the door.

I smiled tigerishly as I swept by.

As I got into the Morris I saw Mr Collins crossing the car park between buildings, jacket flapping, folders under arm. I took some satisfaction from the knowledge that he was frightened of Josh. And now, astonishingly, of me too.

I stopped at the first call-box I came to and called Glyn. Cy answered the phone.

'Hallo, sweetie,' he said. 'Do you want the old man or will I do?'

'It's about A-level English.'

'Count me out.'

'Glyn?' I said. 'I thought I'd let you know that it went really well with Mr Collins.'

'Great,' he said when I'd outlined the exchange. 'Well done. I think Josh is going to be the new Ken Tynan.'

They were laughing like a couple of schoolboys themselves as I said goodbye.

I took out Patrick's card and dialled. Even if he hadn't picked it up right away I knew, today, that I would speak to him.

'Nadgers,' he said, in an intense undertone. 'I've got sodding students.' He made it sound like an embarrassing ailment. 'How are you placed later on?'

'How about three?' I asked. I felt like a character in a play. I couldn't believe I was doing it.

'Three it is,' he said.

It was midday. I did something almost unprecedented and went to call on Susan in her office.

I say 'office', but the premises from which she and Simon ran Ideal Homes were more like a couple of elegant drawing-rooms. In spite of their longstanding, gossipy friendship they were from different planets, domestically speaking. Simon and Richard ran a full-blown fantasy country house with bunches of herbs in the kitchen, a cake always in the tin, fruit and vegetables in the garden, wood-burning stoves, and linen sheets which lay in the airing cupboard with sprigs of dried lavender. Computers, TV, fax and phones were kept out of sight as much as possible. Susan liked her technology get-atable and regarded baking bread and drying herbs as activities for which, like stuffing mushrooms, life was much too short.

The rooms where they worked reflected these differences. Simon's was opulent and chintzy with squashy cushions, swagged curtains and a Casa Pupo bowl full of fruit: Susan's inclined towards pale, sharp chic – ash-grey leather sofas, huge paintings of daunting modernity and a chrome espresso machine.

Their PA/receptionist, Fiona, occupied a small room between the two, off the hallway. Considering the grandeur of their own surroundings, I thought Simon and Susan were a bit mean with Fiona who had to pop out of her cubbyhole like a weatherman when visitors arrived. She was a nice, sensible, well-brought-up girl (as Susan was always telling me), incapable of upstaging anyone.

'Hallo, Mrs Lewis!' she greeted me. 'Hang on a mo, I'll give her a buzz.'

Two seconds later Susan burst forth. 'How lovely! God, you look amazing! Come on in and have a glass of wine.'

Fiona smiled indulgently at us as we went through. As Susan poured the wine Simon knocked on his way in.

'Laura . . .' He held me by the shoulders and kissed me. 'I thought I heard your voice. Is this a private party or can anyone join in?'

'It's private,' said Susan. 'You may have one small glass now you're here and then we're throwing you out.'

'Girl talk?' asked Simon, 'because if so, I'm better at it than anyone.'

Susan handed us our wine. 'Don't take that old queen's line with us, Simon, it won't wash.'

'Old queen?' He laid a graceful hand on his lapel. 'I'm wounded.'

Simon was sixty – his birthday had been celebrated with some state the previous September – but looked fifteen years younger. His good looks were of the Lucky Lucan variety, with luxuriant greying hair and moustache, and heavy-lidded dark eyes. A regular hundred lengths of the pool kept his tall figure slim, and perfect grooming presented it to advantage. He lacked the hint of raffishness to make him irresistible, but there was no denying he was a handsome man.

'Now, drink up and run along,' said Susan.

'Don't be so mean,' I protested, turning to Simon. 'It's good to see you. How's Richard?'

'Frantically busy in the garden – it's that time of year.' It was hard to imagine Richard being frantically anything. '*And,*' went on Simon,' he's been offered some work on television.'

'That's wonderful,' I exclaimed. 'What?'

'Some comedy or other about growing old disgracefully.' It was clear Simon was referring to one of the most popular shows on TV, but would never in a thousand years have admitted to knowing its name.

'Something you guys should know all about,' observed Susan.

'I've seen that,' I said. 'It's funny.'

'Really? Thank heavens for a trustworthy testimonial. Richard's playing the chairman of the residents' committee. A blazer-and-cravat job, but who cares?'

I raised my glass. 'So here's to Richard, and success on the box.'

Something occurred to Susan. 'They record those things in front of a studio audience, don't they? We can all go down and be the ones with the peculiar laughs.' She screeched. 'No problem in my case!'

'I'm not sure that would be a good idea. He's slightly embarrassed by the whole thing.'

'Well, give him our love, won't you?' said Susan, eyebrows raised pointedly. 'When you next see him?'

'I shall do that. Now, not another word, I'm gone. May I take this with me?'

'Do, and tell Fiona to see off all-comers, or send them to you. I'm going to be busy with my friend here.'

Simon kissed me on the way out. He smelt delicious.

'Now!' said Susan. 'I want to know everything.'

She often began conversations in this way. Generally speaking it was a device to get my small beer out of the way before moving on to the fine wine of her own news, but today I detected a genuine interest in her manner. Or maybe it was just that I had gone round there bursting with something I knew she'd want to hear.

'About what?' I asked.

Susan took a cigarette from the box on the table. 'Don't be disingenuous,' she said as she lit it. 'You and I have known each other since dinosaurs ruled the earth, remember?' She waved her lighted cigarette at me, up and down like one of those body-search devices at airports. 'Look at you.'

'It's new,' I admitted, smoothing the sleeves lovingly.

'I can see that. But it's my duty to tell you that today you could make a bodybag look good.'

'Thank you.'

'So spit it out. Otherwise I shall just make it up anyway, you know me.'

'You're bullying me, Susan—'

'*And* I shall tell everyone what I've made up.'

'For heaven's sake!' I was appalled. 'If I tell you you mustn't tell a *soul*, not a living soul!'

'I promise.' She sat back and crossed her long, wicked legs in sheer black. They seemed to snap at me like scissors, or pincers, holding me in place. 'I promise – now you've got to tell.'

'I've met this man—'

'Oh!' Susan closed her eyes and hugged herself. 'That line! That phrase! It's the best start to a story that there is! I love it!' She composed herself theatrically. 'Continue.'

'I met—'

'Where?'

'At our house – in our garden actually—'

'When?' Her eyes were still closed. She was like Sherlock Holmes mentally constructing a case.

'About . . . four weeks ago?'

'How?'

'That's what's so incredible. It was at our party.'

'I knew it!' yelped Susan. 'Do you remember what I wished you for your anniversary? Do you remember? I wished you to have an affair – and it came true! I'm the wicked fairy!'

'He wasn't supposed to be there,' I said. 'He just turned up.'

'Really? He did? More, more – I want to know every detail.'

In one way I wanted nothing more than to debrief completely, but an inner voice warned me that to do so would be akin to selling my soul.

'Younger than you?' she asked.

'I believe so.'

'Excellent. Married?'

'No. At least he said he lived alone.'

'That's good enough. It doesn't matter who's hanging around in the background as long as they're not tapping the rolling-pin every time he's out.'

I reminded her: 'I am, though. Married.'

'So? You're *long* overdue a fling. I regard it as not just desirable but *essential* that you make the beast with two backs with this chap as soon as possible – or have you done so already?'

I shook my head. I could feel my whole face fighting

with a smile, it was like trying to contain a kitten in a blanket.

'No. But—' I glanced at my watch. 'Today may well be the day.'

Susan shot to her feet and held a tightly clenched fist at shoulder-height.

'Yes!'

9

Patrick Lynch's house was in Calcutta Road, near the town centre. There were trees along the kerb, and all the houses had steps up to the front door and pointed iron railings separating them from the pavement. It was a terrace with pretensions. The basement appeared to be a separate flat, or perhaps he let it, because as I approached I saw a girl in jeans trying to squash a bag of rubbish into an already overflowing dustbin.

I rang the doorbell and there was a shout from far back in the house, indicating that he wouldn't be a moment. I stood with my back to the door, keeping the street under observation in case anyone I knew passed by.

He opened the door to me and an exquisite oriental girl stepped out, swinging a rucksack full of books over her shoulder.

'See you Thursday,' she said to him, paying me no never mind.

'Till Thursday,' he agreed. He held out his hand to me. 'Come on in.'

'Who was that?' I asked.

'Lili, one of my students.'

'She looks like a model.'

'She is lovely, isn't she? Chinese. Mind like a razor as well as all that. Come through.'

The hall had a strip of faded red carpet with a key pattern, an uncomfortable-looking throne-like chair with a threadbare tapestry seat, a mirror on the wall with a lot of notes stuck into the marquetry frame, and a large and rather gloomy teak chest carved with elephants and trees. There was also a pair of trainers with the laces done up and the backs trodden down, and one of those palm-tree stands with several coats hanging from it, including the lumberjack jacket.

The living-room was long and narrow with an arch in the centre marking what had been the dividing wall between two smaller rooms. The window was open at the top, but the air still smelled slightly used, with a trace of scent, and the far end was obviously where he'd been sitting with the Chinese girl, for there was a table strewn with books and another with a word-processor on it.

'My place,' he said, picking up a cushion off the sofa and throwing it down again. 'Do you want a drink?'

'No, thanks.'

'Shall we go upstairs, then? We don't want to frighten the horses.'

I was shocked by his directness. Even though there wasn't the slightest question about why I was there, I had somehow expected a few preliminaries, a bit of token coaxing and wooing. Instead of which my bluff was being well and truly called.

'Okay.'

Like an obedient, nervous child I followed him, shivering, up the stairs.

His bedroom was at the back of the house, quite large and with an unfinished feel. There was a nice pine chest of drawers with a spotted mirror on top, and an absolutely ghastly old wardrobe like the Cabinet of Dr Kaligari. The bed was thoroughly slept-in, the duvet slewed and the pillowcases in need of changing. There was no bedside table. A clip-on reading light was attached to the bedhead, and a slithering pile of books and magazines was on the floor. There were clothes and shoes everywhere, and the blind had been pulled up lopsidedly. I was suddenly overcome with a paralysing attack of shyness. I was old, out of practice, out of condition – what was I doing here?

'Sorry about the mess,' he said cheerfully.

'That's all right.'

'Let's have a look at you,' he went on in a tone of lively curiosity, laying hands on me. 'Let's be having you.'

He had me, yes. Susan would have been proud of me. We made the beast with two backs, and it was a wild beast – a munching, squelching, writhing, growling monster, rough and greedy and sweaty, a slavering predator that simply pounced on my shyness and consumed it. My spare-tyre-and-cellulite fears were not just unfounded, they were irrelevant. I scarcely recognized myself.

'Awesome,' said Patrick afterwards. 'Wouldn't you say?'

He heaved a huge shuddering sigh that turned into a cough, and felt beside the bed for cigarettes and lighter. I was lying with my shoulder in his armpit and my chin on his chest but he managed the lighting-up process with considerable dexterity, and exhaled a torrent of smoke over my head.

'Glad you came?' he asked.

'Yes.'

'I'm glad you did, too – I'm bloody ecstatic!' He gave me a squeeze. 'I knew, you know.'

'What?' I was monosyllabic with pleasure and shock.

'From the moment I clapped eyes on you in your back garden I knew you'd be a sensational lay.'

I could hardly believe he was talking about me, Laura Lewis, mother, grandmother and stalwart of the CAB. A sensational lay! And yet at the same time it was dawning on me with slow, warm certainty, that I had been . . . I really had.

He went on: 'You've got just the sort of figure I like. Generous, earthy—'

'Fat?' I suggested from an ingrained habit of self-deprecation.

'On the fattish side,' he conceded kindly. 'Let me have women about me who are fat . . .' He clutched a handful of the flesh on my back. 'Mmm.'

'You're carrying a few extra pounds yourself,' I reminded him.

'More than a few. A couple of stone. That's why I don't want some catwalk skeleton rattling around in my bed – I might do her a mischief.'

He stubbed out his half-smoked cigarette and turned to face me.

'Fancy the other half?'

As he came between me and the light from the window I told myself that I'd be stiff in the morning.

*   *   *

That was it. After an hour at his house I left. We made no arrangements beyond agreeing that we'd see each other again. I kept telling myself that I was 'having an affair', trying to hammer home the enormity of what had happened, but it didn't work. Somehow what I – we – had done that afternoon was both more and less than an affair. An affair was trysts and assignations and plans and elaborate deception . . . an affair was something I had always felt that I could never be bothered to have. I didn't have the energy for all that duplicity, nor the taste for a double life.

Patrick and I had made not love, but the beast. And Glyn and I did not make love, we affirmed it. We endorsed each other, and our partnership, before lying back to back, looking in our separate directions . . .

Back at Alderswick Avenue Nathan was sitting outside in his van, immediately behind Cy's red VW Scirocco. Beyond that was the rehabilitated purple Mini. The front door of the house was open and there seemed to be a lot of people about, for which I was glad. Cy, about to leave, was standing in the hall talking to Becca. Amos and Sinead were racketing about somewhere in the background. Glyn was on the phone in the office. Verity was with Josh in the sitting-room.

'Laura!' said Cy.

'I wonder—' began Becca.

'Grannee!' squealed Sinead.

Glyn put the phone down but it rang again at once. I gave them all a general wave and a smile and ran up the stairs to change.

I bore the telltale marks of treachery. My new suit smelled of cigarette smoke. All over my breasts was a fine veil of red, like a heatrash, caused by the insistent friction of the hairs on Patrick's chest. I had a love-bite, of all things, on my shoulder, and the sticky residue of Patrick's semen in my underwear. I changed as quickly as I could, hung up the suit, pushed the offending items to the bottom of the laundry basket, sprayed myself with some eau de toilette and went back downstairs.

Nobody made the slightest comment on my transformation,

they just carried on with what they had been going to say before, except that Becca was now on the phone and Glyn had taken her place in the hall, with Sinead in his arms.

'Grannee!' She leaned out and I took her.

'Laura!' said Cy again. He sniffed. 'God, you smell wonderful.'

'Doesn't she,' agreed Glyn.

'Reminds me of your lovely party,' said Cy. 'Why *is* women's perfume so evocative? Wrecks me every time.'

'It's nothing special,' I said. 'I got it in Boots.'

'I bought her something extravagant,' explained Glyn, 'but she's too mean to wear it.'

It amused him to characterize me as bit of a puritan. I leaned back slightly to glance out of the door. 'Does Becca know Nathan's here?'

'He brought her over,' said Glyn. 'I think you'll find she wants us to have the kids tonight.'

'We're sleeping here,' announced Sinead.

'Fine.'

Glyn asked, 'Cy, are you staying for supper? Verity's made one of her stand-up soups.'

'I don't know, am I?' Cy addressed this to me.

'Looks like it,' I said.

I realized I didn't need a subterfuge. The forest of thorns just naturally grew up around me the minute I got back.

While Glyn and Cy went to the kitchen for drink, I carried Sinead into the sitting-room. There was some strange music playing, an eerie, primitive wailing underscored with the ticker-tacker of an electronic tom-tom.

'Hi, Mum,' said Verity. 'All right?'

'Yes thanks,' I replied brightly, putting Sinead down. 'Dad said you made soup – thanks, love, I appreciate it.'

'My pleasure, I like making soup.' She nodded in the direction of Josh. 'He's better.'

Josh was fully dressed and sitting with Amos on the sofa playing Donkey Kong on a Gameboy. His duvet and pillows were still in place and carried the tightly creased indentation of his ill self – it reminded me of Patrick's rumpled bedroom.

'Are you really?' I asked, putting the back of my hand against his cheek, which felt cool and – unnervingly – stubbly.

'Get off. Yes.' He brushed me away.

'Good.' I kissed Amos. 'Are you two going to stay the night here?'

'Don't ask me.'

'Yes!' cried Sinead.

'I think Mummy's going out, so you probably will be.'

'I hate soup,' said Amos.

Josh, his eyes still on Donkey Kong, dug him with his elbow. 'Tough titty. Splattered him!'

'You can have chips,' suggested Verity.

'Okay.'

I left the room and crossed the hall to close the front door. Becca was now down in the road, bending over to talk to Nathan through the van's passenger window. She was wearing a denim mini-skirt and her legs in black tights looked endless beneath the jaunty tilt of her hips. A couple of boys in school blazers ogled the view and went through a pantomime of staggering and swooning before a blast on the horn from the furious Nathan sent them packing. Becca didn't move.

'Vino?' called Glyn from the kitchen.

'Thanks.' I looked in again on the sitting-room. Verity was busy putting lots of minute stringy plaits in Sinead's hair. Amos was holding the Gameboy and Josh had taken his right sock off and was examining the sole of his foot with chimp-like thoroughness.

'I scored a hit with Mr Collins,' I said. 'Did Dad tell you?'

'He mentioned it. What did you do?'

Suddenly I couldn't remember. I only knew that I had notched up some sort of victory. 'Nothing much. Anyway, he thinks you're a potential starred A.'

'I'm glad he admits it,' agreed Josh, taking off the other sock and repeating the performance.

'Do you have to do that in here?'

'No, I'll do it in the kitchen if you like. While we're eating Ver's mess of pottage.'

'Don't you dare,' said Verity.

'All the same, I think you probably ought to be a bit more circumspect in your choice of subject matter,' I said. 'It would be a pity if you missed out on a good mark because of this insane urge to shock people.'

He didn't answer, but as I crossed the hall I heard him say to Verity, 'I reckon Collins fancies her.'

Cy and Glyn were sitting at the table. There was a delicious vegetable smell. Cy picked up my glass of wine and handed it to me. 'You look very pleased with yourself.'

The front door slammed mightily. I had the feeling my self-satisfaction was going to be short-lived.

Becca came in. 'Hi, Bex,' said Glyn, 'do you and Nathan fancy a drink?'

'He's gone, but I don't mind.'

Cy looked her up and down. 'Becca, my pretty, are you going to come and show up the pop tartlets at our riverboat party?'

'I may well do.' Becca sipped her wine, one hand on her hip.

'I thought you were going out with Nathan this evening.' I looked at her.

'I was, but I'm not any more.'

'Going to join us at the groaning board then?' said Cy, patting the chair next to him invitingly.

'No, I won't, thanks, I have to go back and get ready to drive into London in' – she looked at her watch – 'one hour.'

'So where are you off to, Bex?' asked Glyn.

'I'm going to Toffs with Griggs.'

At the same time as Cy and Glyn exchanged a glance of laddish delight, I realized that Patrick Lynch wouldn't even have understood the remark. Becca turned to me.

'Is it okay then if the kids stay?' she asked, as if she'd already mentioned it.

'Of course.'

'I'll pick them up in the morning.'

'Don't be too late, I'm at the Bureau at nine-thirty.'

'Don't worry.' She drained her glass and put it on the table. Cy grabbed her hand and kissed it. She retrieved it and waggled her fingers at Glyn and me. 'I'll go and say goodnight to them.'

Glyn topped us up, shaking his head admiringly. 'That was Griggs on the phone just now. Poor old Nathan.'

We heard the front door close behind Becca. 'I liked Nathan,' I said. 'It's a pity if she's treated him badly.'

'He'll survive. He's no Sir Galahad himself,' observed Glyn. 'Remember when he put her out of the van on the A1?'

'She could do a lot worse than be Griggs's main squeeze,' said Cy to me. 'If that band haven't charted a month from now I'll eat crow. They're going to be huge.'

Glyn got up and lifted the lid on the saucepan. 'I'm absolutely starving. Do we have to wait for Verity to dish this stuff up or can we use our initiative?'

Verity dished up, having first made Amos chips – actually made them, by cutting up and deep-frying potatoes, not oven-cooking them from frozen as I would have done. Glyn and Cy got slightly drunk. Josh, grumpy and disdainful, went up to the attic to smoke and receive friends. Verity departed for the night-shelter. I oversaw the children's bathtime and read *Dr Seuss* only to have all my good work undone again by Cy who stirred them up with his repertoire of funny walks. While Glyn put them to bed, Cy became maudlin.

'They're terrific kids.'

'They have their moments,' I said briskly, keeping a tight rein on things.

'No, they are. You don't know how much I envy you and Glyn your family life. And don't think I don't know how much commitment it takes – you make it look easy, but I know different.'

He would never know how different . . . I could think of nothing to say, but Cy had more than enough for two.

'Do you know you're the only couple I know who've made twenty-five years? Correction, you're the only couple I know who've made ten—'

'I'm sure that's not true.'

'It is, I'm telling you!'

'Perhaps,' I suggested, 'we're lazy.'

'Uh-uh.' He shook his head. 'You're too modest.'

This conversation was completely surreal. All I could do was let it happen. I must say I was relieved when Glyn said Cy shouldn't be driving and saw him to the spare room. And equally relieved when we went upstairs to find Sinead snuggled like a dormouse beneath our duvet.

'Don't disturb her,' I said, 'she looks so cosy.'

Glyn turned on the TV with the sound down. They were showing a thoughtful Australian film about growing up in the boondocks.

'Just the ticket.' He was mildly insomniac, always had been, it was the reason our bedroom was like an airport lounge, full of ways to while away the night. He pulled off his shoes and lay down fully clothed on the bed next to Sinead, his hands linked behind his head, while I went to the bathroom. I was careful to put on a nightshirt with sleeves that hid my badges of shame.

I got into bed, hoisted Sinead up a bit so she wouldn't be suffocated, and picked up my book. On the TV screen the dusty grey and green of the bush gave way to a scorching red wilderness as the heroine ran away from her brutish stepfather.

'It's funny this actress hasn't done anything worth mentioning since,' said Glyn. 'She's good, and she's gorgeous, but either she's abnormally fussy or she never got the offers.' I knew this was no idle observation but a matter of consuming interest to him – he was fascinated by what got people work, the mechanics of success.

'You say that,' I answered, 'but she's probably toiling away in some experimental theatre group in Prague, blissfully starving for her artistic integrity.'

Glyn shook his head. 'Too pretty. But if that is what she's doing it's a criminal waste.' I felt him look at me. 'You're very pretty tonight as well, Laura-lou.'

'Oh, come on,' I said. 'Thanks, but really.'

I went back to my book, but I knew he was still looking. He reached across Sinead and laid his hand on my arm – a thoughtful, prolonged touch as if he were checking my temperature. It seemed incredible that he couldn't feel the emotional turbulence inside.

In the end he removed his hand and went on watching the film. I closed the book and snuggled down with my grand-daughter, breathing in the soft smell of her hair.

*   *   *

The next morning Sinead woke us up at a quarter to six having heard Verity return from the night-shelter at five-thirty. Josh announced his intention of returning to college, and Glyn said he could have a lift since it would feel like almost lunchtime by then. I had the children ready, dressed, saucered and blown for eight forty-five.

Becca arrived an hour later. A good time had clearly been had by all because she was exhausted, unmade-up and in the foulest possible mood. I got no credit whatever for her clean, smiling, well-breakfasted offspring, indeed I was made to feel somehow to blame for her hangover and the fact that I had to go out and do a job of work, leaving her to cope.

'Where's Amos's belt?' she asked, homing in unerringly on the one thing I'd overlooked.

'I'm sorry, I don't know. Don't worry, it'll come to light and you can pick it up next time.'

'I'd rather find it now if you don't mind,' she said, the east wind in her voice. Amos sat down on the stairs with a resigned air while his sister, seeing a window of opportunity, went upstairs to pester Verity.

'I'm sorry,' I said. 'I really do have to go. I'm late already.'

She was now steaming round the sitting-room, lifting and dropping cushions and moving newspapers aside with her foot. Her voice was brittle with irritation. 'Carry on. Go! No need to hang about here. Amos, don't just sit there, come and help me look.'

My hand was reaching for the front door as Glyn returned, bearing the croissants and freshly ground coffee intended to revive Cy.

'You off?' he asked. 'Bex! Come and have a coffee and tell me how my valuable property seemed to you – hallo, hotshot, fancy a buttered bun?'

I don't think they even noticed that I'd gone. But I wasn't bitter. It was a comfort, in a way, to know they didn't need me. It gave me the permission to see Patrick again. The clutch pedal in the car found out my creaky hip joint, and I reminded myself that I was a terrific lay. To prove it I crashed a red light.

*　　*　　*

Susan called me at the Bureau, something she did fairly frequently while always claiming never to do it at all, on principle.

'You know me,' she said, 'I never ring people at work, but on this occasion – can you talk, by the way?'

'Yes, at the moment.'

'I only want to ask one thing . . .'

'We did.'

'Yes!' I pictured the fist raised again, and couldn't help laughing. It was exhilarating to have told her, and to be doing something – at last – of which she so wholeheartedly approved.

'Congratulations!' she squeaked. 'I consider this a major rite of passage! And are you feeling really, really good about it?'

'Well—'

'Yes or no?'

'Yes and no.'

'Typical! That is absolutely *typical* of you, Laura.'

'And of most adulterous grandmothers, I should think.'

She gave a gusty snort of exasperation. 'Don't give me that. You are an extremely attractive mature woman of independent mind and means—'

'Means?' Now it was my turn to squeak. 'You're always telling me that what I do is slave labour. Without Glyn I'd be on the checkout at Tesco's before you could say knife!'

'Oh, to hell with all that, it's boring,' said Susan. 'What I want to know is—'

I knew what she wanted to know, but was granted a stay of execution by the arrival of a client, whose dim, patient form I could make out through the frosted-glass panel of my door.

'I'm afraid duty calls,' I said.

'Okay. How about lunch?'

'Definitely.'

'Friday at the Lotus House?'

'You're on.'

My client was Mr Barker, the elderly gent who had been having a standoff with his daughter. He was a lot more cheerful.

'I thought I should let you know that matters are much improved.'

'I'm so glad,' I said. 'Have you managed to sort things out?'

'I told my son-in-law that I was seeking legal advice,' said Mr Barker with a vengeful gleam in his eye. 'And they've both been a lot more reasonable since.'

We always advised against litigation where possible, but this appeared to be a *fait accompli*. 'Good, I'm glad to hear it.'

He leaned forward confidentially. 'I've reached the conclusion I've been a bit too soft all these years. My wife and I always believed we should put our children first – they were everything to us, our whole world. But now I think we did them a disservice. They grew up thinking the world owed them a living. It may be a bit late in the day, but my Marian needs to appreciate that I have my own life and my own difficulties. Would you agree with that?'

For a moment I was being invested with the awful power and authority of the Person Behind the Desk. My word was about to be law. I gazed reflectively at the biro I was twiddling between my fingers.

'I would, absolutely.'

'Would it be impertinent to ask whether you're a mother yourself?'

'It wouldn't, and I am.'

'There comes a time, doesn't there,' said Mr Barker, 'when your children have to accept that you're an individual, and not simply a parent?'

'There does.' He was right, of course, but that didn't stop me forming the view that Mr Barker was rather a frightful old man, and my heart was beginning to go out to the unfortunate Marian who couldn't have been much younger than me. I thought of my own father and mother and sent up a silent Hallelujah.

'I'm glad you agree with me.' He got up. 'And thank you for your time. I hope you didn't mind me dropping in to chat?'

'Not at all.' I showed him to the door. 'I'm pleased that it's all worked out.'

When he'd gone I sat at the desk and pondered for a moment. Who was I to judge prim and prissy, peppermint-scented, brilliantined, sock-suspender-wearing Mr Barker, after what I was up to?

And why, when he was so patently right and I had no leg to stand on, did I find his attitude so depressing?

Verity was the only person in when I got back at two. She was sitting in the kitchen wanly eating a bowl of porridge with golden syrup.

'You look whacked,' I said. 'You don't have to go back there tonight, do you?'

'I don't have to go at all,' she said. 'I'm called.'

There were times when I found her selflessness infuriating and when it seemed to me that Our Lord was being a bit of a bully, but I'd learnt how to frame the argument.

'If you burn yourself out you'll be no good to anyone.'

'Oh, don't worry, I'm in no danger of that,' she said, getting up and putting her bowl in the sink. 'Fancy a coffee?'

'I'll make it.'

For once she didn't insist but sat watching me. When I joined her with the coffee she said; 'You know when Shona and I went to Walsingham?'

'Yes.'

She bent her head, her curtains of ash-coloured hair falling down on either side of her cup. 'You're going to think this sounds silly.'

'I'm sure I shan't.'

'You remember I said I'd pray for everyone – I always do, but I said I'd offer up everyone to Our Lady.'

'Yes, I remember.'

'Well,' she looked up, her face damp from the steam, 'I got a really strong feeling about Dad. That I ought to pray for him. That he needed special care.'

'Really?' I felt as if my conscience were being tickled with needles. 'Why would that be, do you think?'

'I don't know,' she shrugged. 'But I wondered if you might ... if there was anything you knew about ... I mean, I'm not trying to pry, I don't want to know what it is or anything, but if you *do* know of some reason you could tell God about it ...'

She was tremendously earnest, and very nearly overcome. I put my hand on her shoulder.

'Darling,' I said, 'I don't know of anything, honestly. Perhaps it was – you know – Dad's turn to be top of the list.'

She sniffed and smiled. 'Perhaps. He does always seem the last person to pray for because he's so happy and cheerful. But that was it, in a way, I thought, what if there's something terrible I don't know . . .' The tears slipped down her cheeks. I moved my chair round next to hers and hugged her.

'There isn't, I'm sure there isn't.'

She twisted her face to look into mine. 'He hasn't got . . . some ghastly illness, has he?'

It seemed a measure of how low I'd sunk that I felt relieved. 'No!'

'If he was going to die, you would tell us?'

'Yes, but he's not.'

Verity got up and fetched a square of paper towel, blowing her nose noisily and mopping her cheeks. Even so, when she sat down again her voice had an eggshell-crack in it.

'It's just that . . . I don't know what I'd do without Dad.'

I wasn't going to ring Patrick, not this time. I found myself wondering what Susan would advise, and I was sure she would be against it. Experienced as she was, she believed strongly that the rules of the game, at which I was so dismally out of practice, did not change, and the way to play was hard to get. It was just about okay that I had played my bold, emancipated card by inviting myself the other day, because Patrick had trapped me into it and left me no option. But now was the time to be cool.

I didn't feel cool. I was hot, bothered and bewildered. To add to my confusion I'd been experiencing for the first time, and unmistakably, one or two hot flushes. Mother Nature had picked a fine time to set the alarm on the biological clock. On the women's page I read that in the States hot flushes were being dubbed 'power surges' to help menopausal women towards a better self-image. I had never felt more English in my life.

The phone took on a baleful identity. Wherever I was in the house I felt tethered to it. When it rang it tweaked my nerves so that they jangled hectically. When it was silent it seemed to be sulkily withholding what was in its power to give. I would have said it was like being young again, but I'd never really been through this before. My boyfriends prior to Glyn were not such that it had been necessary to assume indifference. And Glyn had never been a gamesplayer. In the light of Patrick, I now saw that very clearly. With Glyn the phone had rung frequently, and it was always for me. I took it for granted.

I was sure I was losing weight but was superstitious about getting on the scales. When I met Susan at the Lotus House she wasted no time in confirming my opinion.

'My God, you're a wraith!' she cried with her usual understatement as we sat down at a window table. 'House white do you? I'd ask what you've been up to if I didn't already know!'

I instinctively glanced around, but there were no familiar faces, either shocked or gleeful.

'It's anxiety, not exercise,' I told her as she laid claim to the menu and surveyed it imperiously.

'Don't be ridiculous,' she said. 'I don't want to spend ages choosing, shall we go for the special for two?'

'Fine by me.'

'But we're going to have our drinks first, there's absolutely no hurry and tons to talk about.' Susan took fun seriously and liked to establish a timetable. As she took her first long, reviving swig her eyes glistened with pleasurable anticipation above the rim of her glass.

'Shoot.'

'I'm not sure there's really anything to add . . .'

'Start big and then fill in the detail,' she advised. 'What's he like?' I opened my mouth. 'I mean, of course, in bed.'

I glanced round again. 'I know what you mean.'

'So?'

'Look . . .' I blushed with embarrassment. 'I don't have much to compare him with.'

'I'll tell Glyn that when next I see him.'

'No, no, I mean generally. I've been faithful for twenty-five years. Longer if you count the run-up.'

Susan grimaced happily. 'I can see this is going to be a two-bottle job. Mind if I smoke? It helps me concentrate.'

I entertained a bizarre picture of Susan monitoring our activities like a judge at a skating competition – 5.4 for technical merit, 5.0 for artistic impression . . . Once again I reminded myself to preserve a discreet distance. Feeling that a display of initiative might be the best form of defence, I began speaking as she lit her cigarette.

'First, I enjoyed it. I expected to be shy' – Susan's eyebrows shot up and her chin lifted in a silent laugh – 'but I wasn't. I didn't have time to be. He was extremely – to the point.'

This time the laugh wasn't silent but a peal of amiable derision. 'I've never heard it called that before! So you like a bit of manhandling, do you, Mrs Lewis?'

'He wasn't rough,' I protested, trying to be clear. 'There was no . . . *pain*. But he made no bones about wanting to get on with it. He was, sort of . . .' I sought the word as Susan grinned witchily, 'boisterous.'

'Sounds good to me. Nice body? Well hung?'

I winced and turned the wince into an anxious little smile for the benefit of the waiter come to take our order.

When he'd gone she said, 'You haven't answered the question.'

'He's not in such good shape as Glyn, but then I get the impression he doesn't care much what he looks like.'

'Arrogant sod. And there were you looking *soignée* beyond belief in that amazing new outfit. I bet he never said how nice you looked.'

'I don't think he was interested in my clothes,' I said with a certain quiet pride.

Susan looked approving. 'Right, fair enough. So he fancies you absolutely rotten.'

'Ferociously was the word he used.'

'Excellent! And you weren't shy, and you weren't put off by all this rumbustious roll-in-the-hay stuff, in fact you really went for it.'

'I didn't have time to think. I was taken over.'

'"His rough hands tore at the flimsy fabric of your blouse," etc . . .' suggested Susan.

'Not quite that, but along those lines . . .' I began to laugh again.

'I bet . . .' Susan joined in and soon we were convulsed by immature giggles. I believe I was slightly hysterical.

She did, of course, want to know more about Patrick, but I managed to stick to my guns.

'Why are you being so coy about him?' she asked. 'Is he in line for the throne or something? Are you honour-bound to discretion?'

'No, nothing like that.'

'I know, he's a world-famous movie star.'

'Definitely not.'

She leaned forward. 'Or do you think *I* might go after him?'

This hypothesis had the advantage of being a lot simpler than the truth. 'You might very well. Who knows?'

She screeched with mirth. 'Come on! For one thing I don't care for all this rough-hands-and-perspiration stuff – I'm not that desperate, yet. I still like a bit of flash. And for another, and much more importantly, you're my *friend*, I wouldn't *dream*, *ever*, of doing the dirty on you, and you ought to know that.'

'I do, of course, I was joking.'

'And now – aren't you going to ask about me?' she enquired, blithely overlooking the fact that I had scarcely been permitted a single unsolicited remark in the past hour. 'Or are you so head over heels in lust that you haven't a thought to spare for a poor lonely soul who hasn't seen winkle in months?'

'I'm sorry. How are you, Susan?'

'Bearing up, thank you. Consumed with envy, of course. But Simon and Richard are threatening a strawberry lunch on the first Sunday in July, and I've decided that might be just the occasion to begin a great new love affair.'

'Have you?' I was back in prompt-only mode.

'They give the most wonderful parties, and the great thing about them is they don't give a toss about duty or paying back – their guests are handpicked for beauty, wit and beddability. No marks awarded for long service,' she added, handily overlooking the fact that she herself had known Simon for the best part of twenty years. 'Mind you,' she added, redeeming herself at a stroke, 'that said, I'm quite sure you and Glyn will be on the guest list.'

On the way home I marvelled that Susan seemed to see no contradiction in spurring me on to adultery in one breath, and speaking kindly of my husband in the next.

As usual, my responsibilities and commitments had formed a reception committee back at Alderswick Avenue, and were waiting, lips pursed and fingers drumming.

The first to greet me was Verity, with the news that Glyn had succumbed to Josh's bug and was upstairs dying by numbers.

'I didn't know whether to call the doctor,' she said.

'Good heavens no,' I responded bracingly, 'it's only a touch of flu.'

'Older people get these things worse, though,' she reminded me, adding reproachfully, 'It's not as if Dad's ever ill. He's not exactly a hypochondriac.'

'No, he's not,' I admitted. 'I'll go up and see him right away.'

'Mum—'

'Yes?'

'Perhaps this was what the message was about . . .'

'Message?' I glanced involuntarily in the direction of the office.

'Yes, from Our Lady. About Dad.'

'Yes!' A providential straw of this size was definitely to be clutched rather than sniffed at. 'Of course – this would be it. He was probably hatching the bug at about that time.'

Verity smiled luminously. 'That's what I thought. I'm going out now if you're sure you'll be all right.'

I supposed it was natural for siblings to polarize, but watching Verity go I did wish that she and Becca could exchange a little of those qualities which each had in abundance. I knew it was an unworthy thought, but if Becca had a smidgin of Verity's humility she might not have been a single parent, and if Verity had a fraction of Becca's savvy, she might also have a man.

Glyn, red-cheeked and hollow-eyed, lay comatose in bed with the Guys 'n' Dolls address book open and face down on the duvet next to him and *Kaleidoscope* burbling unheeded from the clock-radio. By the radio on the table were a bottle of water, a packet of paracetamol and the mobile phone.

I kissed him, and he felt hot.

'Have you taken your temperature?'

'Don't need to . . . I can't remember when I last felt this doggy.'

'Poor old you. Is there anything I can get you?'

'No thanks. Ver's been doing her Florence Nightingale number.'

'She's worried about you.'

'I'm worried about me. I've got things to do.'

I got up and began changing. 'Well, just face it, you won't be doing any of them today.'

Glyn gave a small grunt of acquiescence and his eyelids dropped again. When I'd changed I asked, 'Do you want the radio on, or do you want to sleep properly?'

'Leave it on . . .'

I picked up the phone. 'I'm confiscating this.'

Another grunt. As I went out of the door he said, 'Oh . . . Liam rang.'

I felt a familiar churning in the stomach at the thought of Sinead's father, a highly strung Irishman. 'What did he say?'

'A lot. He didn't feel he could carry on – but then neither did I so I wasn't the most sympathetic audience in the world.'

'Best thing probably,' I said with fake cheeriness. 'Did you refer him to Becca?'

'He'd been trying her – she wasn't there. Surprise, surprise . . .'

Glyn smiled dozily as I went out of the door. He seemed rather to admire Becca's ability to evade those scenes which didn't suit her.

I felt sorry for Liam. Neither of Becca's children's fathers was in regular contact with his offspring, but whereas the lovely Roberto was like a child himself, only too happy to leave the rearing of Amos to someone else and to be a sporadic source of presents and treats, Liam was a confused and melancholy Celt who longed for something more.

He was honest enough to admit that it would never have worked, and he hadn't the means – he was a picture-framer

– to support a family. The trouble was that he was still in love with Becca. His emotional importunings were an acute embarrassment to both children and an annoyance to Becca, who was brutally honest about her own feelings. When an opening presented itself I always tried to put in a word on his behalf, but with marked lack of success. In fact I suspected that my well-meaning representations did more harm than good.

I went out into the garden. We needed to plant our baskets and tubs for the summer, but if Glyn, whose task this usually was, was going to be indisposed over the weekend I could see a trip to the garden centre looming. I wondered whether I could prevail on Josh to mow the lawn for a consideration. Verity would always do it for nothing, but that, I told myself, wasn't the point. It would be good for Josh's soul, as well as his wallet – an argument which would surely carry some weight with Verity herself . . . The 'Isobel' rose showed no signs of growth.

I sat down on one of the deck-chairs which had been left out overnight but had dried off in the sun. At once the phone rang. For a moment or two I ignored it, unaccustomed to there being no one but me to answer. It was only (somewhat ironically) Glyn's strangled cry from the bedroom window which finally sparked me to action.

'Okay!' I called. 'I've got it!'

'Hallo,' said Patrick. 'Just done the four-minute mile?'

My skin prickled. 'I was out in the garden.' I tried to remember whether I'd left the bedroom door open and if so how much could be heard. 'Can you hang on a moment? I haven't got a pen.'

I put the receiver down, went into Glyn's office, pushed the door to behind me and lifted the phone in there. 'Right, I'm here.'

'Are you able to talk?'

'For heaven's sake,' I protested, 'what would you have done if someone else had answered?'

'I'd have said, "May I speak to Laura Lewis, please?" And if they asked who it was I'd have said, "Patrick Lynch." I'm funny like that.'

'It makes me very nervous.'

'You could have called me. When can you come round again?'
As he spoke, the doorbell sounded.

'There's someone at the door – hang on!'

'Call me back.' He hung up without giving me time to argue.

I opened the door.

'Liam!'

He came in. 'May I come in?'

'Yes, do.'

Liam had acquired one of the least sympathetic haircuts imaginable – so savagely short that it revealed the sites of several small scars and accentuated his pale and hunted look. 'Is she here?'

'Becca?' He looked at me, not sarcastically but woefully, as if lacking the energy to speak. 'No – no, she's not. There's only me and Glyn here, and he's got some fluey thing that's going round.'

'I know, I'm sorry I dumped on him earlier but I needed to talk.'

'I'm sure you did,' I said sympathetically. 'But I don't know where Becca is.'

'With one of her many admirers, I suppose,' said Liam with savage self-pity.

'I very much doubt it at this time of day. She's more likely to be somewhere with the kids—' I realized too late that this wasn't the smartest thing to say. Liam's gaunt, sharp features seemed to blur with emotion. 'I'm sorry.'

In a gesture that was very like one of Sinead's, he put his forearm across his eyes, but I could still see his working mouth. 'Excuse me . . .'

Glyn appeared at the top of the stairs in his yellow Hong Kong happy coat.

'Go back to bed,' I said briskly. 'It's Liam.'

'Does he want to come up?'

'Of course not, you've got flu, get back into bed.'

'No, come on, we were talking earlier, it's the least I can do.'

'Liam?'

Liam lowered his arm and looked soulfully up at Glyn. His

eyes were red. 'I'm sorry . . . it's your friendly neighbourhood emotional wreck.'

'Meet your physical equivalent. Come up, why don't you, and we can compare symptoms.'

'Thanks.' Liam took the stairs two at a time with long, awkward strides. Glyn's face reappeared momentarily over the banister.

'Who was it on the phone?'

'Not for you.'

'See how I'm treated?' he said to Liam. 'It runs in the family.'

I went back into the office and dialled Patrick's number. I could hear the patter of a keyboard as he answered.

'Patrick?'

'Mm?'

'Can I come round tomorrow afternoon?'

'I'll look forward to it.'

I realized, as I put the phone down, that I could no longer think of Patrick as an aberration, an isolated incident or a one-night stand. The last minute had blown that luxury away. As I emerged into the hall I heard the faint drone of Liam's voice, telling Glyn all about his broken heart.

'Don't expect me to massage your guilt-trip,' said Susan over club sandwiches at the King James Wine Bar. 'No can do.'

'I never asked you to do any such thing,' I protested. 'And I'm not on a guilt-trip.'

'You'd like to be, though.' Susan flapped her paper napkin at me as she munched and swallowed. 'You're a bit put out that you don't feel worse about what you're doing. Especially when I'm living like a nun. Tell me, is all this extra-curricular activity having a knock-on effect on your marital relations?'

'How do you mean?'

'For better or worse – to hijack a phrase?'

'Neither – no change.'

'Now, I find that *really* interesting,' said Susan, eyes narrowing as she charged our glasses with an impertinent New Zealand chardonnay. 'I always imagined that when two people share the deep, deep peace of the double bed for as long as you two have, any outside input would make if not waves at least very noticeable ripples.'

'I'm very careful,' I said. 'Very careful.'

'I'd have thought that alone would have aroused suspicion. But I mean, don't you want to try out your newfound expertise on the old man? Doesn't he notice a certain something about you?'

'I don't believe so – I hope not.'

She scrunched up her napkin and dropped it on her plate. 'You don't ever get the urge to tell him everything?'

'No!'

'You don't feel you owe it to your husband to be honest?'

Susan went on, with one of those swift changes of tack which made me dizzy.

'On the contrary,' I said, 'I think honesty would be absolutely fatal.'

'For who?'

'All of us.'

I took a generous draught of chardonnay while she scrutinized me. 'You know,' she mused, 'it's very interesting. You surprise me, Laura, you know that? You have a real old-fashioned courtesan's mentality.'

'Oh, please!' I had to laugh. 'Hardly!'

'No, you have. I can see you now, gliding back and forth along the corridors of country houses at the turn of the century, with a long plait and a taper. All clandestine lust and public composure, the height of discretion, the nadir of hypocrisy—'

'Steady on!'

'No, it's a compliment – I think. I'm impressed by your sangfroid.'

'It's far from "froid", I assure you.' She was so quick to slap a witty label on me, and I never had time to make her understand the byzantine complexities of my life. What she saw as a dull, scrubby plain (currently enlivened by a craggy peak) was actually a savage landscape of forests, rapids, screes and ravines through which I – roped, as it were, to the rest of the family – had to negotiate a safe path on a daily basis. In many respects my visits to Calcutta Road were the equivalent of peaceful green clearings in this hazardous terrain. When I was with Patrick, I knew where I was. At home I was charting unknown territory. I had not told Susan, for instance, that although Glyn and I had not made love in weeks the sexual tension between us was almost palpable. We were holding back. It was as if our bodies, familiar to one another through a quarter of a century of marriage, recognized some sea change in the status quo and reacted accordingly.

Susan studied me, and then said quietly, 'Are you sure you haven't failed to look where you're going, and fallen in love?'

Had I?

* * *

I went home via St Michael and All Angels, and communed for a moment with Isobel, the still small voice of calm. But on this occasion she held herself aloof. The clean white stone gave nothing away.

I went through into the Peace and walked slowly round the pond. A few hopeful mallards scudded across the surface and bobbed along next to me for a while in case I should be concealing a sliced loaf about my person. One of them had a flotilla of pussy-willow ducklings in tow. They made me want to cry.

I didn't think I was in love with Patrick, and he had made no protestations other than those of desire. I sensed that every time I walked out of his door his life picked up where it had left off a couple of hours earlier, and seamlessly. Whereas I – I remembered things: like the book he was reading (Gore Vidal), and his brand of cigarettes (Marlboro) and that he put brown sugar in his tea. I knew what brand of cat food Peaches preferred, and where he kept the corkscrew, and that he put used matches back in the box. I was a married woman, after all – self-trained to notice inconsequential things in case they should ever come in useful.

I sat down on a seat near the water and remembered the day before yesterday, when I'd tried to find out more, without success.

'Have you never been married?' I'd asked. We were both dressed and downstairs in the kitchen. He was expecting me to leave.

'No, never.'

'Is that because you didn't want to or because things went wrong?'

'Never met anyone I wanted to live with.'

'So you're a sentimental old fool who believes in love,' I said, knowing it had to be completely untrue.

'Yes.' He looked rather pleased with this assessment. 'I suppose I must be.'

We were sitting at the table, which was a clutter of news-papers, loose change, pencils, opened mail and coffee mugs. I put out my hand and placed it on the back of his neck and pulled him towards me for a kiss. His own hand met my breast as he leaned forward, and I could feel my nipple start into his palm. Over recent weeks the expression 'turned on' had meant something to me. I had become an unstable substance which, when touched by Patrick, lit up. His body was completely different from my husband's, but curiously more like my own. Glyn was spare and close to the bone, he felt the cold. Patrick was fleshy and weighty, and always warm. Sex with Glyn had always been about ourselves, and who we were and the choices we had made. With Patrick it was the complete and shocking loss of self, ecstatic, but repellent and fearful too.

I read a review in the *Sunday Times* of a new biography of Oscar Wilde. In it was quoted the phrase Wilde used to describe sex with male prostitutes – 'feasting with panthers'. It resonated in my head for days.

But in love?

He had scraped his chair round and now had his other arm round me. Enclosed by his warm, quick-breathing mass, I at once flared up, like a match protected by a cupped hand. It happened every time. He allowed something in me which normally I did not allow, or even recognize.

'I'm going,' I said, and my protest was like a sleepy child's, small and without emphasis.

'I'm coming,' he grunted. 'Hold me now . . . now . . . now . . .'

Before I left I had to go and sponge my skirt and wash my hands in the small cloakroom off the hall. I had that light, tired feeling that often follows an energetic swim. My face, reflected in the mirror over the basin, was flushed, and my mouth looked as though a giant thumb had smudged its outlines. I stared back at this reflection. It was creepy, like one of those computer-generated images where one face is superimposed on another and then blended with it to create a synthesis which is at once neither and both. I remembered one Christmas when I was about three, when my father bought a half-mask, comprising only a nose, eyebrows and glasses, and sat down to lunch wearing it, for a joke. I had never been so terrified. A complete disguise, no matter how bizarre, would have been less horrific than this mutation which was recognizably my father, but horribly altered.

I slooshed the frightening face with cold water and tidied up my eye make-up. I turned the cloakroom light off without looking in the mirror again.

When I emerged into the hall Lili was there.

'Hi,' she said briefly, on her way into the sitting-room.

''Bye, Laura,' called Patrick from beyond her. 'Be in touch.'

I had not been in touch, but I knew I would. Tomorrow probably, if Patrick didn't call first. We never fixed a next time, we seemed to go in for a series of cliffhangers. There was always the possibility that this time would be the last. Childish, really.

I got up from the seat and left the Peace. I was in something with Patrick – deep in – but it wasn't love. And I was in marriage with Glyn – deep in – and I was only just beginning to know what that might be.

I got back to find Josh and three of his friends sprawled out on the grass in the garden. They were smoking dope quite openly – its evocative smell wafted in through the kitchen door – and listening to the Red Indian dance music on a portable tape-deck. There were no girls present – Josh was peculiarly ascetic in that regard – but the four of them presented a picture of complete tranquillity and contentment. Slipping out of my shoes in the kitchen, I reflected that if this was the conflict, anxiety and anger of nineties youth we could all do with some of it. I would have gone and sat out there with them if it wouldn't have ruined Josh's afternoon.

Glyn came through from the office. It was hot, and he was wearing shorts and flip-flops.

'Good day?' he asked, getting the orange juice out of the fridge. 'How was Susan?'

'Ebullient, as ever.'

'Before I forget, another of the Old Rats phoned. The plumptious Bunny.'

'Oh really?' I hadn't seen Bunny since our party. 'What did she want?'

'To talk to you. Urgently. From her tone I suspect goss of a high order. Drink?'

'Right. Thanks.'

Glyn leaned back on the sink and gave a small backward jerk of the head in the direction of the garden. 'Is that pot?'

'Can't you smell it?'

'I'll go and have a word.'

'It seems a shame,' I said. 'They look so peaceful.'

'Well, they would, wouldn't they? We remember. But the stuff's not legal and that's our garden. It only takes one neighbour to decide to be a good citizen . . . I'd better.'

Glyn surprised me sometimes. I watched as he went out into the garden. He sat down on the grass by Josh. He looked like one of them, only healthier. I took my orange juice, collected the phone from the hall and went into the sitting-room. As I sat with my feet curled up on the sofa, dialling Bunny's number, I heard Glyn come in. On his way back to the office he put his head round the door.

'Message received and understood. Let's hope Plod isn't on his way round as we speak.'

'Let's hope so,' I agreed. 'Bunny?' Glyn closed the door discreetly. 'Bunny, it's me, Laura.'

'Laura, it's so sweet of you to ring.' Her voice was strained.

'Not at all. Glyn said it was urgent.'

'Bless him. It's only urgent in the sense that I think I'm going completely mad.'

Join the club, I thought. 'Come on, Bunny, you're the sanest woman I know.'

'George and I are splitting up.'

'*What?*' I was genuinely astonished. 'But you mustn't!'

'It's not a case of mustn't. We are. We have.'

'You've separated?'

'Not formally – legally – but we're going to. I'm going to get a divorce.'

'For God's sake, Bunny, why? You had such a good relationship – it worked so well.'

'It did, didn't it?' She sounded bewildered. 'It wasn't just me that thought that, then?'

'No! We *all* thought that. You made it work.'

'Well.' There was a horrible pause during which I knew she was fighting for control. 'Looks like we didn't, after all.'

'But why?' I said again. 'What went wrong?'

'George had a secret life. That's the only way I can put it. A horrible secret life.'

Horrible? It was hard to imagine the workaholic, money-motivated George having anything as exotic or time-consuming as a single secret, let alone a whole secret life, and a horrible one at that.

I chose my words carefully, and according to what I'd heard people say in films. 'Do you want to tell me about it?'

'Not over the phone if you don't mind. I need to hold you with my glittering eye. Could we meet? Have lunch or something?'

'Of course. When?'

The day she suggested – the Friday of the following week – was the day of the Guys 'n' Dolls anniversary riverboat party. In for a penny in for a pound, I thought.

'That'd be fine. I have to be in town that evening for something else.'

'Could you bear the flat?' She had an apartment off Harley Street.

'Very easily,' I said.

'Only it's safe, and discreet,' she pleaded as though I'd raised some objection. 'And who knows, I may not have it much longer. I'll raid Marks and Sparks for something nice.'

I made pasta and Glyn and I had ours in the garden. Josh and co. refused the pasta and then came down and laid waste every source of carbohydrate in the kitchen, leaving a blizzard of crumbs, a slick of butter, an archipelago of puddled milk and two empty cereal packets.

'What was up with Bunny?' asked Glyn, leaning back in his deck-chair. 'Or aren't you allowed to say?'

'She and George have split up.'

'That's awful.'

'It is, rather.'

'I'm shocked. Why?'

'Apparently,' I said, 'he has what she described as a horrible secret life. But I won't have any details till I meet her next Friday.'

'That's our bash, remember.'

'I know. I'll go in by train and get changed somewhere.'

'You should bring her along.'

'I don't think she's on for socializing,' I said. 'She's really cut up.'

'Poor old Bunny,' said Glyn. 'Poor old George, already. Secrets are bad news all round.'

'You'll never believe who I met in Bartholomew Street this afternoon,' said Verity when she got back an hour later. We were still out in the garden, telling ourselves we had things to do but that evenings like this were sufficiently rare to put off doing them.

'Who?' asked Glyn.

'Jasper.'

'Good old Sir Jasper, nice one,' said Glyn. 'You should have brought him back to supper.'

'I did ask, but he was on his way to the station. He's not at the Barbican any more, he's working for Streetwise – the charity for the young homeless?'

'Good for him,' I said. I could just picture David and Anthea's despair at this new development. 'And is he happy in his work?'

'Very,' said Verity, looking pretty happy herself. 'He thinks he's found his vocation.'

Glyn caught my eye. 'Tiggertiggertiggertiggertigger . . .'

'Don't be mean.' Verity laughed. 'I'm sure he has. I said I'd help in any way I could.'

'For a small fee, perhaps?' I suggested unworthily, and was rewarded by a wounded look from my daughter.

'That's not the point.'

'Of course it's not,' agreed Glyn, 'the point is to amass celestial brownie points, isn't it, Ver?' He prodded her gently with his foot to show he was teasing. 'So did he have any other news? Goings-on at the Ponderosa?'

'Yes. He said Auntie Anthea's finger was better, but would always be bent—'

'All the better for summoning stablehands.'

'And Emma's coming over for the wedding in September,' added Verity, trumping us both with a piece of real news.

'So that's when it is,' I said. 'How did Jasper know?'

'He asked Steph if she'd organize some fund-raising for Streetwise—'

'And did she?'

'She was too busy, but she said the invitations were going out soon.'

'Any idea what sort of wedding it's going to be?' asked Glyn.

'Jasper said it was at the church in Ferniehurst. Uncle David and Auntie Anthea are going to do the reception at their place, so Steph and Monty decided to keep everything local.'

'And they don't mind doing that?' I asked, intrigued by the ramifications of this arrangement.

Verity looked baffled. 'No, why should they? St. Botolph's is gorgeous, and the Beeches' house is perfect.'

I rang my parents later that evening for confirmation. My father answered the phone tersely, having been dragged away from *Inspector Morse*.

'Yes, it's to be a gathering of the clans. Heaven knows what it will be costing David, but then he's as rich as Croesus so I suppose it's a mere bagatelle to him . . . mind if I pass you over to your mother?'

'We've got ours already!' said my mother. 'Caro has gone into orbit, completely. I suppose having missed out on Ros and Brian with them being so far away, this is doubly important.'

'Are they coming over?'

'Oh yes, Nadine's going to be a bridesmaid, and don't mention it just yet but I understand Steph is going to ask Sinead as well.'

'Brilliant! She'll love that.'

'I don't know what they'll be wearing, but whatever Steph's shortcomings she has good taste in clothes, so I'm sure the dresses will be perfectly bearable, and I took the opportunity of reminding Caro that Becca wouldn't be able to afford the cost involved, and she perfectly understood and promised to convey that much to Steph. I hope I wasn't out of order?'

'No, you did right.' I looked forward to observing – from a safe distance – the negotiations between Steph and Becca on this subject.

'I think it's awfully good of David to lay all this on for them,' said my mother. 'Caro's quite overwhelmed.'

'I was a bit surprised to hear about it,' I agreed cautiously. 'I shouldn't have thought Steph was the sort to want to be under that sort of obligation. Or Monty, for that matter.'

'Come on, darling,' said my mother, with one of those glints of steel which made her such good value, 'anyone with half an eye can see he's a born sponger. And rather weak, I think. You can see it all in his mouth. Anyway, David will do them proud and it'll be a *lovely* wedding. I shall just sit back and enjoy it.'

'Do you have any family?' I asked Patrick a couple of days later, the day we got the invitation. 'Any parents extant, or anything?'

'Yes,' he said. 'I do. I have a sister in Ireland.'

I hoisted myself up on my elbow. 'Tell me about her.'

'Must I?' He rolled his eyes.

'I'm interested.'

'She's ten years older than me, and she's a pharmacist in a chemist's shop in Dublin. And she's married to a bloke called Kevin. Which by the way is a good old Irish name and doesn't have the associations it has here.'

'Does she have children – are you an uncle?'

'They've got thousands of them.'

'Nice children?' I asked.

'That's a contradiction in terms.'

I was taken aback by this acerbic generalization. 'You met my grandchildren – didn't you like them?'

'Does it matter?'

'Answer the question.'

He turned his head on the pillow to look at me directly. 'I had a good reason to make the effort.'

I found myself trapped between a compliment and an attitude I found hard to like.

The fact was, I didn't like Patrick. I was addicted to him, but I didn't like him. Whether love could accommodate the lack of this bread-and-butter feeling I didn't know. You often heard, or read, people say that they loved certain of their relations, but found it hard to like them. I sometimes felt that way about my children. And yet it was the moments of real liking, no matter how rare, that made the whole experience worthwhile.

It was true I'd been charmed by Patrick on our first meeting, and swept away by his flattering directness thereafter. But in a way that charm, that directness, were the very things that made me suspicious of him – and of myself – when we were not together. Sometimes when I was with him, while he was still inside me, my imagination would hurtle with sickening speed and clarity to Alderswick Avenue and I'd see my family, all innocent and unknowing – yes, even Becca – going about their business. They didn't even think about whether they trusted me or not, they took it for granted – and they were right to do so.

The ease with which I'd deceived everyone appalled me. I had never even had to tell an outright lie. Patrick's name had been spoken freely in our house. And such was the loose weave of my relationship with Glyn that I had never yet had to justify an absence nor explain a call. Something perverse in me wanted to be a little less dispensable. A hint of suspicion, a gleam of jealousy, a whiff of unreasonable possessiveness, would not have gone amiss. But that, I supposed, was twenty-five years of marriage for you.

Becca was at Alderswick Avenue, minus the children.

'They're at a party,' she said in response to my enquiry. 'What have you and Dad been saying to Liam?'

'Nothing. Honestly,' I added, as the dishonest do. 'Why?'

'Don't lie to me,' said Becca. 'He's been round here, hasn't he?'

'Yes. He called when I was out the other day, but only because he'd tried you and you were out. And then he came round and went upstairs to talk to Glyn. It was that time when your father had the flu—'

'Where's Dad now?' asked Becca, glancing round. She was

wearing white shorts and a bikini-top but her demeanour
suggested that she had about her sparsely clad person a Colt
44, primed and loaded.

'In London.'

'Typical,' she said, as though Glyn's diary were expressly
organized in order to thwart and evade her. 'So what did
he say?'

'I haven't a clue. He was feeling extremely ropey so I don't
suppose it was anything more than a friendly chat.'

'Friendly chat?' echoed Becca venomously. 'I'm sorry but I
really take exception to either of you having any kind of chats
with Liam behind my back. Whatever Dad said it's got Liam
all stirred up. He was round asking me to marry him again
last night.'

'Oh?' I said, ever hopeful. 'What did you say?'

'I said I thought he'd never ask and fell weeping into his arms!
Mum!' Her voice was shrill with a kind of hectic sarcasm. She
flopped down abruptly on the bottom stair, further revealing a
smooth, honeyed tan with no visible tidelines, the acquisition
of which must have wrought havoc among her neighbours.

Her hands were linked on the top of her head, her forearms
covered her face. This wasn't mere strutting and fretting, she
was genuinely upset.

I went to sit next to her, but there wasn't quite room and
she didn't budge up. I was being shut out.

'I'm sorry darling,' I said.

'It's all right . . .'

'Liam was obviously in a bit of a state, and you know Dad
. . . he's a sucker for a lame duck.'

'I know, I know . . .' She looked up, with a slight toss of the
head to indicate that she'd got a grip of herself once more.
'It's okay. I'm sorry, too. It's just that Liam is such a loser.
It's the reason we broke up, he knows it as well as I do. We'd
be poison for each other. He's Sinead's dad and nothing can
alter that, but I don't love him and the more he comes round
making spaniel eyes and whimpering, the more I despise him.
And I don't *want* to despise him. I want to respect him, and
have some sort of sensible relationship with him that works,
for Sinead's sake. Not all this useless moaning about a lost

cause . . .' Her eyes met mine. 'Am I making the smallest bit of sense?'

'Perfect sense.' I wanted to hug her, but was afraid of spoiling things.

'It's such a waste of time and energy.'

'I agree.'

'And it's not good for Sinead.'

'No.'

Becca got up. To my surprise she leaned forward and dropped a light kiss on my cheek.

'I must go and pick up the kids,' she said. 'See you.'

Bunny Ionides' flat was luxurious in a way that happily did not inspire the smallest twinge of envy. It was on the first floor of a tall Regency house between Cavendish Square and Harley Street, with the sort of long windows that require a national debts-worth of curtaining, in this case ivory brocade looped back with thick gold ropes. The probable cost of those curtains alone was enough to make you think pious thoughts about Third World countries. For the rest it was like a top person's furniture showroom, all ormolu clocks, gilt scrolls and ebony elephants, and a forbidding cluster of stately armchairs with undented cushions.

Bunny was over-made-up and wearing of all things a kaftan, with a strip of ruching beneath her embonpoint which made her look like a marquee on wheels.

'I know I look awful,' she said as she poured Waterford bucketfuls of g and t in the strangely echoing kitchen. 'It's called carbo-loading for comfort. I suppose any shrink would say that I'm eating to make myself fat so I'll be ugly enough to explain what's happened to me.'

'You don't look awful,' I said. 'You look like someone who thinks they do.'

She handed me my drink and plucked ruefully at the kaftan. 'I spent a fortune on this. The trouble with clothes at this end of the size range is that there's no difference in appearance between spending a fortune and raiding the Oxfam Shop.'

'It's fine,' I said, following her billowing form into the drawing-room.

'It's ghastly,' she said. 'Like my life.'

On a circular coffee table of engraved brass was set out the promised feast – lobster salad, artichoke hearts with hollandaise sauce, strawberries and cream, camembert, misty black grapes.

'Lunch looks good though,' I observed hungrily.

Bunny collapsed into a chair with an expansive wave. 'Dig in. The more you eat the less will be left for me. The tragedy is it goes down without touching the sides. I had three peanut butter sandwiches before you even got here.'

'Thanks,' I said. 'I'll eat, you talk.'

Poor Bunny, she needed no second bidding. For the next hour she talked a blue streak, cried a river, gulped down a second bucketful of gin and started on a bottle of wine, more or less without drawing breath.

George had been purchasing sado-masochistic sex at an address in Lancaster Gate for the past several years. Bunny had found out in the most straightforward and prosaic way possible. It was one of those weeks when she was taking twenty-four hours at the flat to shop and see friends, and George was supposed to be visiting designers in Stockholm. She was driving along Clipstone Gardens on her way back from lunch in Kensington and had seen George coming out of the house. She'd stopped, cheerfully enough, to offer him a lift; his discomfiture was obvious; she asked what he was doing . . . and so it went.

If I'd read the story in the papers under one of those 'Miss Whiplash' headlines it might have struck me as pathetic and even a bit comical. 'Rag Trade to Rough Trade' or perhaps 'Would You Buy Your Kids' Clothes From This Man?' But hearing it from Bunny, I was shocked. My own secret, hovering spectrally in the background, made me all too aware of the extent of Bunny's betrayal, and of George's frightful, obsessive risk-taking.

'Do you feel it's absolutely necessary to separate?' I asked tentatively.

'How can you even ask that?' She mopped her face with a paper napkin. 'He's been lying to me for months – years!'

I stared down into my glass, uncomfortable with my role as devil's advocate. 'But it's not as if George is madly in love with someone else. What he's been doing is really no more than a solitary vice. Something he had to do, and probably felt pretty bad about—'

'Laura, Laura! How do you think *I* feel?'

I was shamed. 'Pretty terrible.'

'I don't want him near me! I don't mean sex – I mean within hailing distance! When I do see him it just reminds me that all this time I never really knew him at all.'

I remembered my strange, altered face in Patrick's mirror. 'He's still the same person he always was,' I said. But if I was hoping to glean any crumbs of comfort for myself from Bunny I had come to the wrong place.

'That's it! You've put your finger on it. This has always been part of him, but I never had the least idea. He never tried to tell me or explain – never even hinted, never suggested in the smallest way – he just went off and got on with it and put all the checks and balances in place – ugh!' She shuddered. 'It's the idea of all the thought and effort he put into it, into throwing me off the scent and making the arrangements – *that's* what disgusts me.'

'If he'd made that much effort he wouldn't have got caught,' I pointed out.

She snorted. 'And that's supposed to make me feel better?'

Bunny *was* feeling slightly better now, having got such a lot off her chest, but I was feeling notably worse. On grounds of what was polite and appropriate alone I could not confide my own situation to her, and even if I had, I realized that she would have perceived it not as a problem, but as an embarrassment of riches which it was clearly my responsibility to sort out.

'I've always thought of you as very strong,' I said. 'Both of you, but particularly you. Don't you think if this ever got out, or was in the papers, that you'd feel you wanted to stick by George?'

'If this ever got into the papers,' said Bunny, flushed and strident, 'it would be me that put it there!'

The session with Bunny cast a lurid light over that evening's party. The high-octane networking of some two hundred ego-centrics dressed to kill and without a scruple to share between them was not something I could even pretend to be part of. I contented myself with being a spectator.

Cy and Glyn had pushed the boat out in more ways than one. *The Duchess of Deptford* floated down the Thames in the hazy early evening sun, moored near Greenwich in the afterglow and returned in the warm, twinkling night. A jazz band whose name I actually knew worked up a convivial lather on the upper deck. An inferno-like disco pulsated below. In the saloon between the two, beautiful young people, their smooth bare shoulders revealed by cutaway striped waistcoats, served champagne, Guinness and a breathtaking array of seafood, with ineffable haughty grace.

Glyn was in his element and a pink bow-tie. He looked the happiest man in the room, on nothing more than orange juice and job satisfaction.

'Where's Bunny?' he wanted to know as we snatched a quick domestic debriefing by the bar.

'I didn't invite her.'

'Bad as that?'

'Worse. She's absolutely wretched and she's put on about two stone.'

'Holy cow. What about George, or aren't you allowed to say in case I join in?'

I glanced around cautiously. Glyn laughed at me. 'No one here knows George, for goodness' sake.'

'You never know. He's been indulging in a spot of s and m in Lancaster Gate for ages, apparently. Bunny caught him leaving the house when he should have been somewhere else.'

'And that's – pardon me – a hanging offence?'

'It's the lying, she says. Over such a long period.'

'Yup.' Glyn nodded. 'Fair enough.'

Cy bore down on us. 'Laura – lovely. Glyn, can I drag you away from the lady wife to come and cheer up Talia?' He referred to a New Age folk songstress from Leeds who was in the way of becoming a cult hit.

'Off you go, both of you,' I said. 'I'm perfectly happy.'

I wandered. Verity had not come – she was far happier among the soaks and derelicts of the night-shelter than with the floating attention-junkies here, though it was debatable who was more

in need of Christian charity. Josh had been given a job handing
out identity badges. He wore his striped waistcoat unbuttoned
over a black T-shirt. His eyes glittered with scornful fascination
behind his round glasses. He had an ambivalent attitude towards
Glyn's work: part of him felt a perfectly natural teenage interest
in the sheen and shimmer of showbiz; another part had nothing
but disdain for the airheads (he did not include his father) who
allowed themselves to be dazzled by it. He could be terribly
unforgiving.

His duties done, he leaned against various walls – I suppose
they should have been referred to as bulkheads – moodily
sinking Black Velvet and evincing enough smart boredom to
ensure that people took him for someone they thought they
recognized.

Becca was with Griggs. Well, I say 'with', but she had too
much pride to stay in close proximity to someone genuinely
famous in this company. I caught up with her in the disco, dancing opposite an enraptured young record company executive in
braces. When Becca danced, she got into it, attracting as she did
so a good deal of attention, envious or lascivious according to
gender. When she saw me she left the still-gyrating braces and
came over.

'Hi.'

'Shouldn't you be—'

'Dominic, this is my mother. Mum, this is Dominic from
HMV.'

'Hallo.'

'How do you do,' said Dominic enthusiastically, mopping his
brow with a handkerchief. 'I won't shake your hand in case we
get glued together—'

'Catch you later,' said Becca, and steered me firmly out of
the disco.

Poor Dominic, he probably thought being introduced to me
denoted tribal approval. Instead of which it was no more than
the pretext for a swift get-out.

'Where's Griggs?' I asked when it was safe to do so.

'Search me,' said Becca. It was just as well this was rhetorical,
because she was wearing a sprayed-on white halter-neck dress
which would have left even the most determined searcher with

nowhere to go. The narrow skirt came to mid-calf, but there
was a slit up the back which exposed most of her tanned legs
and was within centimetres of showing why, in spite of the
dress's tightness, she had no visible pantyline. Her hair was
in a Bardotesque chignon with a suggestion of bouffant on
the top, and her shoes were no more than two thongs and a
stiletto.

'How are the children?' I asked.

'Having a great time, I should think,' she said. 'They've gone
to Karen's for the night.' Karen was a friend of hers in Smiley
Meadows. She was kind, but her lifestyle redefined the term
feckless. While I was reasonably sure that the fecklessness did
not extend to actually leaving young children alone at night, I
was equally sure Amos and Sinead would be shovelling down
E-numbers in front of *Terminator* II with the resident brood while
Karen pursued her active social life elsewhere in the house.

'I might give them a ring,' I said, 'and say goodnight.'

'There's no need to check up on them, you know.'

'I wasn't going to check up.'

'Yes you were. You're just like Verity, you don't trust my
friends.'

'That's not true,' I lied.

'You have no idea how insulting that attitude is,' went
on Becca.

'It's not an attitude. And it's not what I think.'

'Verity certainly does. She even offered to give up her fix
of ritual squalor and humiliation at the dosshouse so the kids
wouldn't have to go to Karen's.'

'She loves looking after them, that's all,' I explained.

'I told her to sit on it,' said Becca. Her body language suddenly
altered in a subtle, instinctive way that made me glance over my
shoulder. 'Here's Griggs.'

'How you doing, babes?'

Griggs put his arm round her waist and was introduced. As
I asked a few token questions, based on Glyn's assessment of
Human Condition, I took in this latest conquest.

There had been so many that I'd got quite practised at
calculating the degree of Becca's interest. Griggs was not as
rugged as Nathan, nor as romantically handsome as Roberto,

but there was a dapper, entertainer's swagger about him, and a warm, knowing look in his eye that was attractive. In her spike heels Becca could've given him two inches, but he exuded a confidence that reminded me of Jimmy Mullaney all those years ago. His fair hair was very short, he wore a striped suit with a white T-shirt and plimsolls, and he had a minute gold stud in the side of his nose. I was sure that whatever appeared on the album notes, he was nearer thirty than twenty.

'I tell you what, Becca's mum,' he said in reply to one of my dull stock questions, 'I don't give a tinker's whether we make it or not. I'll still be getting up and doing it on my zimmer frame.'

'He means singing with the band,' explained Becca.

Griggs chuckled. 'She's got a filthy mind, your daughter,' he observed, letting his palm slide down over Becca's buttock. 'I like that in a woman.'

I laughed, I hoped not nervously, and left them to the throb and flicker of the disco. It was entirely possible that on this occasion Becca had met her match.

'Want to dance?' mouthed Glyn as I circumnavigated the jazz band. I shook my head and pointed in the direction of the outer deck. He began to follow me, but a group of people swallowed him up.

I went out into the mellow night and walked towards the stern where it was dark and I could watch the pale, spreading V of our wake on the water. On either side London slid twinkling by. In between, the inky quiet of the Thames wrapped around the boat like amniotic fluid. It calmed me to think that the river had flowed here according to its deep, slow rhythms for thousands of years. Beneath the babble of voices and music I felt its insistent and secretive presence.

I leaned on the rail and simply let these reflections flow through my veins. I wondered, as Glyn came to stand beside me, if this was what Verity would have called a prayer.

There were a lot of other women in Patrick's life, but then I harboured no illusions about my importance in it. I had a wife and mother's acquired humility, and the great British virtue of knowing one's place. Glyn's stable of nubile clients had made me philosophical about potential competition. It hardly seemed sporting to be squeamish when I was the one being unfaithful, and Patrick was single and fancy-free.

Apart from Lili there were three or four other girl students who came regularly to Calcutta Road for tutorials. And there was Josie, the young woman who rented the basement flat while she wrote her thesis. She was one of those permanently depressed types who was often sitting at Patrick's kitchen table clasping a coffee cup and chain-smoking. At least neither she nor the students evinced the slightest interest or curiosity in me. I might have been his cleaning lady for all the attention I received.

Then there was a largely unseen coterie of colleagues, who rang up at funny times to unburden themselves. He never asked them to call back later, nor apologized for spending ages on the phone when I had to leave in an hour, and I didn't like to remonstrate with him. It was during these phone calls that I tended to wash up, to tidy, to water plants and stack CDs – from force of cohabit, I suppose, and the ridiculous need to display tact when he was talking to someone else.

One of the colleagues was called Jane. Another was Bridget. I perceived them as more of a threat than the youthful students. These would be mature women, nearer my own age, fearsomely clever and self-assured, with manes of pre-Raphaelite hair, strong classical profiles and no eye make-up. Tigers in the sack, of course. Bluestockings in suspenders. The novels of David Lodge had left me in no doubt that academics were second only to doctors and nurses in the rampant libido stakes.

'Can I ask you something?' I said one scorching afternoon in July as Patrick padded back into the bedroom with two cans of 4X and a bag of barbecue beef crisps.

'You're about to.' He dropped one of the icy cans on to the mattress next to me and I yelped. 'Oops.'

'What will you do when you're old?'

'Christ . . .' Patrick fell heavily on to his side of the bed, leaned back on the bedhead and opened his can with a hiss. 'I don't know.'

'Think.'

'Crisp? What sort of question's that, anyway?'

'I'm serious. I wonder about single people.'

He looked at me, munching. 'Why?'

'When you're married there's a pattern – you have children, and grandchildren, a stake in the future. Someone to be old with.'

'Horrific.'

'No it's not, it's one of the comforts of marriage.'

He tapped my arm with his finger. 'One of the compensations, is what you're trying to say.'

'Don't tell me what I'm trying to say,' I protested. 'Marriage is company. It's a basic human need.'

'So why are you here?'

'You haven't answered the question.'

'Okay. When I'm old, I'll do one of two things – move back into rooms in college and sink into a gouty and protected decline, or bugger off to an apartment in the South of France and do pretty much the same thing there.'

'On your own.'

'Ah – on my own when I *want* to be.'

'But what if no one wants to be with you – when you want them to be? Old age can be querulous and smelly.'

'I'll shoot myself,' he announced, and then, when I scoffed: 'No, I mean it. As a free and independent agent I shall retain that privilege, you see. And no one will be able to say how selfish it was of me.'

'Would you ever think about going to live with your sister?'

Patrick covered his eyes with his hand, his shoulders bouncing with exaggerated mirth. 'Not even if she'd have me.'

'But she's your kin.'

'I don't share your view of the mystical potency of blood ties.'

On the local news that evening there was an item about the Heritage Minister visiting the region to open a school for the performing arts. She was entertained by a squad of all-singing, all-dancing moppets dressed in buttercup yellow with frilled socks, white patent mary-janes and hair-bunches with huge yellow butterfly bows. They were cute enough to make your teeth jump.

'Thank heaven for little girls,' I said caustically. 'I blame the mothers.'

'Get away,' protested Glyn. 'They're rather sweet.'

I looked at him, and saw that he wasn't joking. His gaze, fixed on the screen, was soft.

'But they're all the same,' I complained. 'All mass-produced and ersatz like jelly babies.'

'To blame them for that is to miss the point. They're meant to be the same, they're a chorus line. Under each of those dresses beats the heart of a trouper.'

'Glyn – you'd have died if Becca or Verity had been like that.'

Glyn put out his hand and touched my knee, without looking at me. 'No, love – you'd have died.'

The next day at the CAB I saw a schoolgirl mother with her infant daughter and her grandmother, a woman of about sixty who had acted *in loco parentis* for some years while her own daughter, the girl's mother, went out to work. I felt I was seeing all that was good and bad about modern society. The great-grandmother was forty years married, she told me, the working granny was amicably divorced with a caring boyfriend, the schoolgirl's partner – a nice enough lad but not a long-term prospect – was retaking GCSEs at college. The women formed an elaborate pattern of connections, separations and support systems.

The girl and her grandmother wanted all the information they could get on help for single parents. It was obvious they bore the baby's father no ill-will and the whole exchange was conducted in a spirit of cheerful practicality.

'We only want the best for little Jasmine,' said the older woman. ''Cause she's the apple of our eye, aren't you, sweetheart?'

I gazed at the baby. Though only four months old she had on one of those headbands with a bow attached. She was rather stout and the effect was like a Christmas pudding. It was clear she wanted for nothing. Feeling rather crabby, I had consciously to remind myself that my own daughter was raising two children at least partly on the state and that the welfare system was there to be used.

'You're quite right to come to us,' I said to the girl, 'it won't be easy on your own.'

'But she's not on her own, is she?' replied Great-Granny feistily. 'She's got us.'

This encounter and its implications reverberated in my head for the rest of the day. That afternoon the urge to communicate was strong upon me. I began by writing to Bunny.

'Dearest Bunny,' I wrote. 'Thank you so much for that wonderful lunch, and for confiding in me. I can't tell you how sad I am about what's happened to you and George. If I say I hope you'll think again it's not because I can't understand how you feel – you must be devastated – but because I honestly believe George cares about you and probably couldn't help himself.'

I tore that one up. Couldn't help himself? What was I saying? George Ionides was a millionaire international businessman whose funds and lifestyle could have afforded complete, watertight discretion. Instead of which he'd chosen to court disaster with a suicidally risky and squalid deception right on his London doorstep. There could be no excuses. I substituted a different line.

'Don't for goodness' sake go on punishing yourself for all this.

You have every right to feel miserable and betrayed, but your best defence is to get out and live your life. Don't let George run it from a distance. I hate to say this, but here goes – buy some clothes in a size smaller and lose the weight. You owe it to yourself. Whatever George got up to, it's his problem, not yours. It's no good trying to make some kind of perverted sense of it now, with hindsight. You have *nothing* to be ashamed of – quite the opposite. You're a glamorous, funny, sexy woman that any man would be proud to be seen with. George must have been potty to endanger his marriage with you, and people will think the less of him for it.'

I finished off the letter with an open invitation to Bunny to come and see us whenever she could. The irony of handing out all this spirited advice was not lost on me. When I finished writing my face was hot, and not only with a power surge.

I rang Becca who, rather to my surprise, was in, and in a sunny mood.

'Hallo, darling. Just thought I'd call.'

'I heard from Steph this morning – about the bridesmaids' dresses.'

'What are they like?'

'Nice, by the sound of it. Rose-red taffeta with cream sashes and stockings. Sinead's going to look a star.'

'She will.' I took advantage of the benign climate to ask: 'How are they both?'

'Blooming. They had a whale of a time at Karen's, her new bloke's a magician.'

'What fun.' I was only too delighted to have my fears proved groundless. 'I liked Griggs, by the way.'

For a moment I thought I might have made a remark too far – I didn't want to blight a promising relationship with the canker of parental approval – but Becca simply sidestepped the comment.

'Yeah, he's okay. That reminds me, can the kids come over on Saturday night after next? Roberto's company are at the Corn Exchange.'

My head spun. 'Will he be seeing Amos?'

'Naturally, Mum. He's taking him to the funfair on Sunday.'

'Oh, he'll enjoy that.'

'I've got it all under control,' said Becca. 'By the way, is Verity there?'

'Not at the moment. Do you want to leave a message?'

'No . . .' There was a pause. 'I was bitchy to her the other night. She brings out the beast in me sometimes. I wish she'd get a life.'

Josh came in as I was putting the phone down. 'Anyone called?'

'That was Becca.'

'I mean for me.'

'No.' I added lightly: 'Were you expecting someone?'

'Not really.'

I tested the water. 'Becca's worried about Verity. She thinks she should get a life, as she puts it.'

'She's got one.' Josh's voice retreated into the kitchen. 'With her God stuff.' The fridge door opened and closed and he reappeared, drinking orange juice from the carton. 'I mean, come on, she's never here.'

'No, but I think Becca means—'

'We all know what Becca means. She ought to butt out for five minutes. Not everyone wants to be shagging everything that moves,' said Josh with some force.

'That's a little extreme.'

'Well, for Christ's sake!' Josh wiped his mouth on the unbuttoned cuff of his shirt. 'If you want my opinion, I think Ver makes Becca feel uncomfortable, bigtime.'

This exchange made *me* feel uncomfortable. I had always assumed the role of ex officio lightning conductor. Glyn was good at saying things like, 'Let them be, they're adults now, they don't have to get on all the time, it's not our problem,' or even, as the storm raged round us, 'Isn't it interesting?' But I still clung to some notional ideal of harmony and mutual understanding which it was my job to cultivate. Things had been a lot easier, I reflected, in my parents' day, when everyone had left home and its environs at eighteen or nineteen and only returned sporadically thereafter. People bemoaned the demise of the extended family, but in Alderswick Avenue it was alive and well and giving us gyp.

*　　*　　*

About two hours into the strawberry lunch, Richard took me on a tour of what he and Simon called the grounds, though in fact the two acres surrounding Gracewell constituted no more than a very large and elegant garden.

We left the terrace and lawn beneath the leaded bay windows and strolled down the path between the herbaceous borders, and through the Elizabethan knot garden to the mere. The mere did not belong to Gracewell, but where it lapped the bank there was a small wooden boathouse and jetty built by the previous occupants. Muscovy ducks, moorhens and occasional seasonal geese glided and sculled over the still, black water. Simon and Richard had replaced the windows in the boathouse, covered the floor with polished oak and a Moroccan dhurri, put in some bentwood chairs and a folding table and created a little waterside haven for themselves.

'This is where I come to learn my lines,' said Richard.

'It's perfect.'

'Sit down, do.' Richard indicated a rustic seat near the jetty. 'Unfortunately we suffer rather from the yob element at this time of year, but then who doesn't?'

'What do they do?'

'They hire rowing boats from outside the pub, and then come down here and hold impromptu orgies under the jetty.'

'Orgies?'

'Drink, drugs . . .' sighed Richard, with an actorly wave of the hand to indicate that there was more, much more, but he would spare me.

'Really?'

'You should see what they leave behind. Even the ducks won't touch it.'

'That's horrid.'

'Pretty typical of today's young, I'm afraid.'

We sat down at either end of the bench. I liked Richard, but he was of another age. I always felt that with him a 'dear lady' was waiting in the wings for the least opportunity, and that only my familiarity kept it in its place. He had been stunningly handsome in his prime but was now rather frail and getting smaller. For the party he was wearing a well-pressed cream suit, with braces, a light blue shirt with a Savage Club tie, and moccasins.

'How's the television show going?' I asked.

'We've recorded two episodes, thank you for asking, my dear.'

'And are you enjoying it?'

'I do believe I am,' he said, his mystification conveying a multiplicity of messages. 'Not that it's true acting by any standard that I would recognize.'

'How do you mean?'

'It's just behaving for the lens.'

'Isn't that what you used to do in films?'

'Look!' said Richard, changing the subject. 'Our dear swans!'

The swans came gliding regally towards us, with two gauche cygnets in tow.

'They mate for life, you know,' Richard reminded me. 'And they nest in the same place – just round the bend on our little island – provided, of course, they can escape the attentions of the yobbery.'

We fed the swans out of a bag of dried flakes kept for the purpose in the boathouse. Then we walked slowly back to the party.

'This is a lovely place,' I said as the house came back into view. 'And what you and Simon have done with it is astonishing. It's hard to imagine anyone else living here.'

'Thank you, what a nice thing to say. We do our best. I think that between us we do have a small talent for homemaking. And we're awfully lucky, we have each other, and security. We'll see our time out together here at Gracewell.'

'Like the swans,' I suggested.

'Like the swans. And you, my dear.' Richard touched my elbow. 'And that engaging husband of yours.'

Up on the terrace Glyn was with a group that included Susan. It was she who called out at my approach.

'Where've you been with Richard? Has he been offering you madeira in the shrubbery?'

'No, we walked down to the mere.'

'Been there, done that,' said Susan. 'I know this place inside out. When they decide to throw it open to the public I'm going to offer my services as a guide.'

'What's its history?' Glyn asked.

'Haven't a clue!' said Susan. 'Who cares? I'm going to invent the entire thing, complete with madness, murder and marital disharmony. And ghosts – plenty of spectral goings-on. I could have this house on the Heritage map in no time!'

Confronted with my friend in full partygoing cry, I glanced at Glyn, but he and the other couple had drawn slightly apart during the ensuing laughter and were now talking amongst themselves. I was aware as always of the slight tension that existed when my husband and friend were in close proximity. It was as if Glyn in particular knew that there were things said between Susan and me to which he was not privy and from which he deliberately chose to distance himself.

'Now, come along, Laura,' said Susan, drawing me slightly aside, 'and tell me all about everything.'

'Nothing to tell.'

'Rubbish. Let's go and get some strawberries.'

She led the way indoors to the dining room, where huge china bowls full of homegrown strawberries were presided over by Pauline, the daughter of Simon and Richard's cleaning lady.

'Strawberries, ladies?' asked Pauline. Although only sixteen and just emerged from GCSEs at the local comprehensive, she had quickly assimilated the house style.

'Not for me,' said Susan, 'but my friend here will have them for both of us.'

'And why not,' said Pauline. 'There we go.'

'Aren't you having any?' I asked, taking delivery of a piled plateful, drowned in cream.

'You know me, I get over-excited at parties. Come through here.'

Swinging a bottle of Simon's white wine in one hand, she led the way into the next room, a library. At one end was a beautiful oak desk with a large globe standing on it. At the other was a wonderful leaded bay window with a cushioned windowseat, where Susan sat us both down.

'The perfect spot for talking behind the fan,' she said. 'About your goings-on.'

'Don't you have any secrets this time?' I asked.

'That's for me to know and you to find out . . .'

'You do!'

'How could you tell?'

'Who is it?'

'Only kidding. The only thing I've embraced is chastity.'

'It's too late for that.'

'Don't be pedantic, you know what I mean – celibacy. It's the new rock and roll, Laura. All the coolest people are doing it. Or rather not doing it.'

'If you say so,' I said doubtfully.

'I do.' As always, Susan had the ability to lend an air of chic to even the least propitious activity. 'And anyway,' she added with disarming candour, 'it's a case of needs must when the devil drives. And I'm going to Crete soon, so who knows what adventures await me?' She took my empty dish from me and refilled my glass. 'Now, tell me – how are the stolen moments going?'

Susan's thirst for updates had the effect of making me see how little there was to report. The stolen moments, hot and humid though they were, were not 'going' as she put it, anywhere.

'And don't,' she ordered, 'say fine. I will not be fobbed off.'

'I know. But there's nothing to tell you. I go there, we have sex, we talk for a while, I leave.'

'Don't you ever go out?'

'Too risky.'

'No, but I mean – do it somewhere else? A hotel? A field of clover? Back of his car?'

'I don't even know if he has a car.'

'Of course he does, everyone does.'

'Not necessarily.'

'But anyway, you don't go out?'

'No.'

'Are you in love with him? I asked you before but you never said.'

'I didn't know.'

'And now?'

I glanced anxiously towards the door. I was profoundly uncomfortable talking about Patrick with Glyn only a few yards away.

'I still don't.'

'And Glyn still doesn't know?' I shook my head. 'Don't bet on it.'

'I'm sure he doesn't.'

'He trusts you implicitly?'

'It's not even that – I don't think such a thing would even cross his mind.'

'Hm. The question is,' said Susan, 'how long can it go on for?'

'I don't know.'

As we went out again, through the dining-room and hall, I said, 'I half-thought Henry might be playing here today.'

She looked at me sharply. 'Did you? No, we've none of us seen Henry for ages. He's a dark horse.'

'Susan was in good form,' commented Glyn as I drove us home.

'She always is.'

'She's your best friend.' It was a statement uttered reflectively as though trying it on for size.

'Certainly my oldest.'

'It's a funny expression, "best friend". I mean, is it a value judgement? Or is it a case of never mind the quality feel the width? Or does it just mean the person you can never ditch because they know too much about you?'

I peered both ways at a T-junction before pulling out. 'You don't like her, do you?'

'That's not true.'

I felt oddly comfortable with this conversation. It was honest but not crucially so. 'It is. You've never liked her.'

'Whatever gave you that idea?'

'I sense it.'

'That's the last resort of the unfair accusation,' said Glyn, laughing. 'Like Ver saying you've got to have faith. I'm quite sure there's nothing in my behaviour which has given you, or Susan, the smallest grounds for complaint.'

'But you still don't like her.'

Glyn turned his face towards the open window and was silent for a moment. We were driving through a shimmering prairie of East Anglian arable land. There were no people, no

animals, and precious little traffic. A troop of pylons bestrode the
gently undulating fields. A smear of smoke rose from somewhere
beyond the horizon.

'Not that it matters,' I said. I felt I'd hurt him. It was odd I
should feel that way when the potential for a far greater injury
ticked away in our lives.

He was still looking out of the window when he replied,
'Okay, you're right in a way. I sense something – some female
conspiracy.'

'You're jealous?'

'Either that or it makes me nervous.'

His intuition was spot-on. 'Now, that is silly.'

'Yes, I know.' He gave me an apologetic smile. 'Typically
insecure nineties male feeling threatened by female bonding.'

'You've no need to be,' I lied.

The City Council had taken advantage of a fine Sunday in
mid-July to tear up part of the westbound ring road. This
hadn't affected our outward journey but now I had to follow
diversion signs. I found myself driving down Calcutta Road.
Patrick, in jeans and a T-shirt, was standing halfway up his front
steps talking to Josie from the basement. There were temporary
lights at the far end and the traffic was slow-moving. I sat with
my eyes glued to the car in front as we crawled by. Something
even less clear than my peripheral vision told me that Patrick
had seen me – us – and I couldn't risk catching his eye.

A horn blared. 'Wakey-wakey,' said Glyn. 'They're green.'

When we got back I did something ridiculously bold. I had VAT
returns to do, but instead I changed out of my smart things and
into baggy shorts and loafers, and told Glyn I was going out.

'Okay,' he said. He was sitting in the garden with the Sunday
papers. He barely looked up.

'I thought I might go and take a look round the Sunday
market,' I explained.

'Fine.' He turned a page. 'Good idea.'

'I won't be long.'

'Be as long as you like.'

'I'll be back in a couple of hours, top whack.'

'Have fun.'

I seemed to be telling him far more than he wanted to know. I left the house as free as a bird, and mindful of the roadworks in Calcutta Road, got on my ancient pushbike and pedalled across town to see Patrick.

It was the first time I'd arrived unannounced.

'Are you alone?' I asked.

He looked around. 'Seem to be. Come on in.'

I went in and as soon as the door was closed I wound my arms round his neck and clamped my mouth to his. He made a little sound of amused surprise, which excited me. So he thought he'd got my number, did he? I began plucking and dragging at his clothes, I swarmed up him like a monkey so that he staggered back against the wall, and had to clutch my buttocks to take the weight from his neck and shoulders. Still grasping me, his fingers digging in, he pushed one hand between our bodies and undid his jeans, and then my shorts. When he lifted me on to him the pleasure was so intense it was a pain. I felt a gush of liquid – mine – as he pushed up my shirt and his T-shirt and rubbed his breasts against him. My legs, astride his large bulk, ached with pressure and tension, but I was in control. I wanted to surprise and even hurt him. His eyes were slitted and his mouth open. His head was nudging the ugly mirror on the wall. I wanted the mirror to fall, and smash, and Patrick's knees to buckle so that he collapsed and cut himself. The more fierce and feral the beast, the greater its power.

The mirror didn't fall, but we slithered panting to the ground, taking two telephone directories from the nearby table with us. We were surrounded by an almost palpable stillness, intensified by the hammering of the pneumatic drill and the restless drone of log-jammed traffic outside. Peaches, tail aloft, emerged from the living-room, paused to inspect us, and floated away. The faint click of the cat-flap marked her displeasure.

The phone rang. I expected Patrick to ignore it, but he raised an arm and felt for the receiver.

'Hallo? Oh – hallo.'

As his caller spoke I stood up and adjusted my clothing. With his customary piggishness Patrick sat there unabashed, receiver to ear, jeans and boxers round his ankles. I was swept by repugnance, and went into the other room and stood by the window that overlooked the street, trying to distance myself from him, and this house, and our recent behaviour. It was the next best thing to walking out, which I couldn't do.

The telephone conversation was brief, and the caller did most of the talking. At the end of it Patrick said, 'Okay, see you.' I heard the receiver go back, and in a moment he came in, buttoning his jeans.

'I'm really glad you decided to drop in.'

I couldn't bring myself to answer.

'You never fail to surprise me.'

'I surprise myself,' I said. He came across the room and I folded my arms to shut him out. It wasn't as easy as that, because he perched on the windowsill in front of me, with his back to the road, and lit a cigarette. The first inhalation brought on a fit of coughing.

'Loss of control is an excellent thing,' he said while his eyes were still watering. There seemed no point in telling him that the desire to control was precisely what had driven me just now. I shrugged.

'Oh yes,' he went on. 'Makes you feel smutty, though, doesn't it? Makes you wish you hadn't?'

I didn't answer.

'Want a drink? I've got to go out in a minute, but there's time for a beer.'

'No. I'm going.'

He followed me into the hall. The telephone directories still lay on the floor, the mirror was crooked and there was a slick of viscous moisture where we had lain.

'I don't know,' said Patrick. 'You come storming round here on a Sunday afternoon, jump me in my own front hall, and wreck the joint in the process.' He opened the door. 'You're only after one thing.'

As I cycled past the Corn Exchange I saw the poster for the show Roberto was in next weekend – *Tango Americano*. It took not just two, I thought, but a whole network of people to tango. Life was complex. It was like one of those 'magic eye' posters, a dense and meaningless accumulation of detail that none the less contained a pattern. A pattern which, given the right angle and a relaxing of the mental muscles, it would be possible to see.

That night I couldn't sleep. The more I lay still, and closed my eyes, and tried to relax, the more the turmoil seethed in my head. I became quite rigid with the effort not to toss and turn. Glyn's breathing was deep and even. I didn't want to disturb him. He was going up to Manchester for a few days 'star-stalking' as he called it, and Cy was picking him up at 5 a.m.

At two-thirty I still hadn't slept. In only ninety minutes the windows would turn grey and the first birds would send up a tentative reveille in the poplars of Alderswick Avenue. I was quite desperate, not just with the need to rest, but for oblivion. I didn't want to keep thinking. I wanted to lay down my burden, but like the Old Man of the Sea, once wilfully taken up it clung to me with ever more demanding weight.

Suddenly Glyn slipped his arm around me, felt for my hand and linked his fingers with mine. It was a light touch without pressure, either actual or implied.

'Laura . . . ?' His voice, though quiet, was distinct. I realized with a slight shock that he had been awake for ages.

'Yes.'

'All right?' He gave my hand a light squeeze.

'Yes.'

I felt something, no more than his breath, really, as he kissed the back of my hair.

'You mustn't worry,' he said.

I didn't answer, for fear of incriminating myself, even by implication. My throat and neck strained with unshed tears.

'You know what Verity would say, don't you?'

Still I was silent. His thumb brushed the back of my hand.

'All will be well,' he said.

There had never been any danger of Roberto's being a thorn in Becca's side, not because he didn't love either her (at the time) or Amos, but because he was a child himself. He was a sweet, lovely young man with all the charm in the world and a rather feminine nature. Unlike Liam, part-time fatherhood suited him perfectly, and following their eighteen-month fling he and Becca had drifted apart without acrimony. I wasn't normally in the habit of making excuses for people, but even I could see that Roberto, cooped up with domestic responsibilities, would have gone into a decline. He lacked Becca's mental toughness, her inspired opportunism and her ability to get her own way in her own way.

Amos, as he'd got older, picked up on his mother's attitude to Roberto, which was one of light-hearted fondness. He took his father as he found him. Roberto's dark eyes often filled with tears, but whether of joy or sadness they were generally short-lived: his was a small range of emotion, intensely expressed. His goals were simple and short-term – some spending money in his pocket, an opportunity to dance, and an attractive woman upon whom to lavish his romantic attentions. In his professional life, Roberto had undoubted talent, but he needed to be told what to do. He would never be a star, but he was always the one you looked at in the chorus.

While at the Corn Exchange the company of *Tango Americano* was being put up at a small hotel on the ring road, but when not on tour Roberto occupied old-fashioned digs in West Hampstead, complete with a strict and motherly landlady and shared bathroom. We were sure this arrangement suited him down to the ground. It didn't surprise us to learn from Becca that he called the landlady 'Mama'.

It was hard to imagine Roberto growing old, and in fact we tried not to – it was almost too sad. Glyn had often painted a picture of what happened to mediocre or unsuccessful entertainers when they stopped living on hope and settled into the realization that they had failed, and that it – whatever it was – was never going to happen. A few could shrug and walk off in another direction. But most were maimed in some way by the disappointment and the frustration. A professional dancer's life was cruelly short, and Roberto showed no interest in or aptitude for choreography. So perhaps it was a good thing that he did not seem ambitious. When I suggested, *entre nous*, that he might teach, Glyn simply asked, 'Can you see him keeping order?'

Roberto and Becca came round on Sunday morning to pick up the children. Verity was cooking one of her famous post-communion brunches in the kitchen. As with clothes, so with food – Verity's vegetarianism didn't prevent her cooking a mean crispy rasher. The siren-scent of frying had brought even Josh downstairs. It was one of those rare occasions when almost all the immediate family was present – Liam being the exception.

'Good morning, Laura,' said Roberto in his comic-opera accent, kissing me three times on alternate cheeks. 'Thank you for your wonderful hospitality.'

'I haven't done anything,' I said.

'Was my Amos a good boy?'

'A very good boy. He always is.'

'Just like his father,' said Becca.

As they went through into the kitchen I looked at Roberto's taut dancer's backside in fawn chinos and wondered whether he and my daughter had slept together last night. From time to time these days I suffered from a compulsive desire to unburden myself to Becca. She more than anyone in the family was most likely to understand and least likely to judge. Perhaps, I speculated wildly, we could become pals, like those mothers and grown-up daughters who featured in the Sunday newspapers . . . But something always, thank God, stopped me.

Roberto picked up Amos and embraced him extravagantly, murmuring endearments. He suffered no embarrassment about his ambiguous position in our family. I was glad about this, but in my mind's eye I couldn't help seeing Susan, one eyebrow cocked, an expression of amused rebuke on her face, and wondered if we had done right.

Verity put an assortment of plates down on the kitchen table and began distributing rashers, chipolatas, mushrooms, fried bread and the first instalment of fried eggs.

'Nice one, Ver,' said Josh. 'Mind if I take mine upstairs?'

Glyn was leaning against the sink. 'Don't forget to bring the plate down.'

'Oh no!' Josh clapped his hand to his brow. 'I was thinking of putting it with all the others that are under the bed ankle-deep in penicillin.'

'How do you like your egg, Roberto?' asked Verity.

'As it comes,' said Becca briskly. 'He's lucky to get one at all.' She picked up a rasher, and passed it rapidly from hand to hand as she went out on to the patio and sat down in a deckchair with her face to the sun. Sinead followed and cast herself down on her mother like a rag doll.

'The man of the household must come first,' said Roberto gallantly, with an expansive gesture.

Glyn waved aside the suggestion. 'Pass. It's nearly lunchtime according to my clock.'

'How's the show going?' I asked.

Roberto sat down at the table with Amos on one knee. 'Is brilliant.'

'It is actually,' said Becca from outside. 'Incredibly sexy.'

'From the bordellos of Buenos Aires to the town halls of England,' mused Glyn. 'All those sleazy old tarts, pimps and panderers must be spinning in their paupers' graves.'

'Are there any tickets left, Roberto?'

'Not many, but if you and Mr Lewis want to go it can be arranged. I shall arrange it. One or two are always held back for the cast.'

'There are none on the door, I can tell you,' said Verity. 'We're going tonight and we got almost the last ones in the house.'

'We?' enquired Glyn.

'Me and Jasper.'

I was so determined not to be betrayed by even a flicker of surprise or amusement that all I said was: 'And are they decent ones or right behind a pillar?'

'One's restricted view but we're going to swap at half-time.'

'Verity, you must come round and have a drink with me afterwards,' said Roberto. 'And bring your boyfriend with you.'

Verity's cheek was extremely pink where her hair was hooked back, but that might have been the result of cooking brunch. Roberto, oblivious to the undercurrent, allowed Amos to gloop ketchup on to the side of his plate. I glanced out at Becca but her eyes were closed. Her hand on Sinead's back patted out the rhythm of a tune in her head.

'Well, I think we ought to go,' said Glyn. The phone began to ring and as he went out to the hall he added, 'Can you sort it for us, Roberto?'

A moment later I heard him say, 'Yes, sure, I'll get her,' and I was swept by the terrible surmise that it might be Patrick on the line.

It was Bunny.

'Laura – I did appreciate your letter.'

'That's okay, the least I can do.'

'I'm feeling rather better, actually.'

'I'm so pleased.'

'I've taken to heart what you said.'

I tried to remember exactly what it was I had said. 'Good.'

'I've begun losing weight and I'm not going to allow George's sordid goings-on to prevent me living my life.'

'That's the spirit.'

'I've spoken to the lawyers and I'm going to keep this flat while I look for something else, and it's the very least George can do. What he does with the house is his own affair – if that's not an unfortunate phrase.'

'No, no. Good idea. So you are definitely going ahead with the divorce then?'

'No question. It's underway.' She paused as if inviting comment, but I could think of nothing to say. 'And don't be disapproving, Laura, because there's no other solution.'

'I'm not disapproving.'

'You think I should be magnanimous.'

'Not should. Of course not, Bunny. But could.'

'But I couldn't!'

'Okay.'

'You don't understand.' She sounded exasperated. If she only knew! But it wasn't her fault that she didn't.

'It must be absolutely ghastly,' I said. 'I can't begin to imagine what you've been going through.'

'No, well . . . But that's not what I meant. I meant that George and I were never in the least like you and Glyn.'

'In what way?'

'You two were made for each other. Yours is a real love match. It was never like that with us.'

I looked over my shoulder towards the kitchen. Glyn was standing holding Sinead. She was nibbling a chipolata, occasionally offering him a bite. He wore a waistcoat handpainted with densely packed images of colourful parrots. It was his pride and joy, but he didn't flinch as the greasy sausage missed its mark, fell, and was trapped snugly between him and his grand-daughter. He even laughed as he prised it out.

'Laura?'

'Yes.'

'Oh, you're still there, I thought I'd lost you. I just want to impress upon you that we were never a shining example of the married state. That old thing about the secret of success being constant separation is really what we were all about.'

'Nothing the matter with that,' I said. It was odd standing here in the hall, poised, as it were, between the soulless comfort of Bunny's apartment in Harley Street and the lacerating complexities of life in Alderswick Avenue. It was even odder that Bunny should be treating me as a touchstone, and our marriage as a barometer of how marriages ought to be.

'. . . I'm not kidding myself that something beautiful's dying here,' she continued in my ear. 'And we don't have children, so that one can't be levelled against me.'

'No, you're quite right,' I said. 'I didn't mean to be preachy. Good luck to you, Bun.'

'Thanks, but you can wish me luck in person, because the

other reason I rang is that a few of the Edelrats are getting together next week – we thought we'd go to the Gondola, for old times' sake. Does that appeal?'

'Very much, in principle. What day?'

'Friday? School's out then, isn't it?'

I was about to contradict, but realized she was alluding to the adult perception of a Friday, and not the academic year which, thank God, had another ten days to run. I got my diary and wrote down the date.

'I'll look forward to it.'

In the late afternoon Jasper turned up. Glyn was mowing the grass and I was desultorily clipping edges in his wake. His appearance, with Verity, at the kitchen door was the perfect excuse to down tools.

'Hi there,' said Glyn, switching off the motor. 'Good to see you – fancy a cold drink?'

'Love one.'

I collapsed in a deck-chair and Jasper and Verity sat on the grass. There was a slight awkwardness occasioned by the new dispensation. It wasn't unpleasant and it was easily overcome. Other people's difficulties were mere flea-bites to me at the moment.

'So you're off to see Roberto doing his number,' I said. 'We're hoping to go ourselves.'

'Yes, it should be good,' said Jasper. 'I like dance. Though working at the Barbican was an eye-opener – dance is by far the least cost-effective of the arts. Without subsidy there quite literally wouldn't be any.'

'No wonder hoofers are so poorly paid,' remarked Glyn, bringing a tray with orange juice and cans of beer and putting it down on the grass. 'It's a meat market with a limited audience. And virtually no stars. We don't have a single dancer on our books.'

'But they pour in in their thousands to see things like *Starlight Express* and *42nd Street*,' pointed out Jasper. 'It's pure dance that can't pay its way . . .'

They began discussing the inequities of showbusiness, and I looked at Verity. She was pulling at the newly cut stubs of grass between her feet, but she sensed me looking at her and raised her head. I smiled. She smiled back.

I rang Susan on Monday with the intention of unburdening myself. Properly this time. I couldn't go on like this, and there was no one else to whom I could thoroughly debrief. I needed to hear what I said, in order to know what I thought.

I called her from the CAB and was astonished to be told by Fiona that she was off sick.

'But she's never ill,' I protested. 'She doesn't believe in it.'

'No, I know, but there you are,' said Fiona. 'She is now. Unless she's malingering, which is hardly likely! She did sound pretty rocky on the phone. Do you want to speak to Simon?'

'No, that's all right.'

I dialled Susan's number, let it ring a couple of times and then replaced the receiver guiltily. She was ill, for heaven's sake, an almost unheard-of circumstance, and all I could do was badger her with my own problems. It made me realize how much I depended on her. The expression 'there for me' exactly summed up Susan's position in my life. Opinionated, meddlesome and infuriating though she was, she was unwavering in her loyalty.

I was five minutes into a standard exchange about noise pollution when she called me back.

'You rang.' Her voice sounded even more gravelly than usual.

'I'm sorry, you shouldn't have bothered to call me back.'

'That's all right. It's only some fucking flu.'

'Can I catch up with you in a moment?'

'Sure.'

I despatched my client with an info-pack on the rights and responsibilities of a neighbour who wants also to be a good citizen, plus the usual admonitions about not jumping too hastily into litigation. Then I rang Susan again.

'How are you?'

'Like absolute death.'

'You must be. You could've knocked me down with a feather when Fiona told me. I've never known you take to your bed before.'

'Who said anything about bed? I'm propped up in a chair like a Proustian heroine.'

'Can I come and see you?'

'Sure. Come for lunch. And bring some lemon barley, can you? If I'm going to revert to childhood I may as well do it properly.'

I got the lemon barley, and also some prawn sandwiches, a goat's cheese and seedless grapes. When I got to Susan's I was surprised a second time by how ill she looked. The phone conversation had half-persuaded me that even if the illness were kosher she would still appear exactly the same, having subdued the virus by force of personality the way she did everything else. But she answered the door in plaid pyjamas and a large cardigan, teeth chattering, with the puffy eyes and reddened cheeks of the authentic flu-sufferer.

'How sweet of you,' she said as I put my purchases down in the kitchen. 'I couldn't swallow a solid mouthful myself, but you carry on. Just give me a squash, shaken not stirred.'

She had her duvet and pillows on the sofa in the living-room.

'I hate doing this, it's piggy, but it's preferable to staring at the bedroom walls,' she explained as I sat down with my sandwich. 'I can't begin to tell you how nice it is to see you.'

'Is there anything else you want?' I asked. 'Shopping, errands of mercy? A doctor?'

'Not unless he's Harrison Ford . . . but then what would I do with Harrison Ford in my condition?'

She collapsed on to the sofa and pulled the pillows round her neck and the duvet up to her chin. 'Yuk,' she croaked. 'I think I'm going to die.'

I brought the lemon barley. She took a few sips, eyes closed, and then laid her head back. I stared at her, worried and disconcerted.

'Are you sure you wouldn't like a doctor? This isn't like you.'

'Mm.' She swallowed wincingly round her swollen tonsils. 'I fear it is. Hubris has brought this on. It's been so long since the bacteria managed to get so much as a toehold they've decided to make the most of it.'

'Have you been taking anything? Paracetamol?'

'By the handful. I'm not due any more for two hours . . .'

She lay still, apparently dozing. I gazed round the room. It was pretty, costly and cared for. Susan was not one of those single people to whom their surroundings mean nothing, and for whom the term 'domestic' is a dirty word. She was houseproud in a way that I had never been. It was hard to imagine Susan bustling about with a J-cloth and a bottle of houshold cleaner, but she obviously did, and on a regular basis. In the sunlight the glass on her expensive pictures gleamed, smudge-free, and the paintings beneath were innocent of the freckling of thunderflies so characteristic of this time of year. The paintings, though representational, were modern, and so were the sculptures and ceramics she collected – a child's head, a leaping fish – but the inlay table on which a vase of freesias stood was antique. Above the table and opposite the window was an oval art nouveau mirror, the pewter frame made up of sinuously cavorting nymphs. Susan had a good eye, assured taste and the confidence to buy what pleased her and to place her purchases, old and new, alongside each other to great effect.

Her breathing, each intake marked by a whisper, each exhalation with a whistle, grew steady. Sure she was asleep, I got up and helped myself to a glass of white wine from the fridge – I wasn't being furtive, she would have been dismayed if I hadn't done so. Returning, I walked over to the windows of the living-room which overlooked the river, at this time of year teeming with punts and rowboats full of tourists and local teenagers, the languid students having departed for the summer. People strolled on the footpath while kids on bikes and rollerblades wove in and out of them with sickening bravado. This was the other side of town to the one I normally inhabited – our area was town, Susan's was gown, the city of the travel brochure and the weekend break, a place of spires and ancient trees and pubs abutting the river, a place where you could buy Byron or Benjamin Zefaniah on a Sunday, but might struggle to find a pint of milk on a weekday afternoon.

The flat had a small balcony, hardly more than an extended windowsill, on which Susan had clustered a continental mass of pelargoniums in purple, red and white. I slid the glass panel back and leaned out. The warm, polluted sunshine bustled round me; I heard the clop of oars, the chatter and shriek of voices, the brisk rattle of skateboards. A large group of people were playing rounders in the open space beyond the river. They'd thrown down sweatshirts and caps as bases, and were using a cricket stump as a bat. They were all different shapes and sizes, a group of perhaps two or three families, I surmised.

I wondered what it was like to be Susan, living in this delightful theatre-box of a flat, alone, with only those choices and decisions to make which directly affected her. It would have been nice to suppose that in these circumstances I too would have been as organized, as smart and as self-sufficient as Susan, but I doubted it. I should have found it peaceful for a while and then I should have descended first into inertia and then into panic. I had long since concluded that I needed the convolutions, extensions and uncertainties of my life to divert me from the grim prospect of too much self-examination. Cosmetic changes, no matter how sweeping, could not alter the nature of the beast . . .

It was as this last phrase occurred to me that I saw Patrick. It was a case of sight being quicker on the uptake than thought, for my eye followed his dawdling figure along the path for a good few seconds before my brain registered why it was doing so. And the moment it did, it was as though I'd called to him, for he stopped and glanced round.

His stopping had nothing to do with me, of course. There she was, Lili the Chinese supermodel, coming along the path behind him. She wore jeans, with a black halter-neck T-shirt, and her hair was tied back in a red scarf the ends of which trailed artlessly down her bare back. Becca with soy sauce.

I watched spellbound. They weren't all that far away but they might as well have been – they would never guess they were being watched, let alone by me, and if they did look in this direction they wouldn't be expecting to see me, and that would effectively render me invisible.

He stood and waited for her to catch up – that figured, I thought. On the other hand she didn't exactly rush to his side – full marks to her. I don't know what I'd been half-expecting, but there was no embrace, no kiss, not even the hint of a casual caress. Instead, the very absence of all these things made their body language speak louder than words. Gazing, fascinated, across the water at them as they stood with the summer-afternoon strollers parting and rejoining round them, I knew from the tilt of their heads, her hands in her hip pockets, his arms folded across his chest, the unnecessary nearness of their positions, as though they were being filmed by a television camera, that they slept together. Not once, nor in the past, nor even occasionally, but regularly, and currently.

There was no shock, more a slow, burning dawn of humiliating realization. It wasn't just that Patrick made love to that slim, youthful, unblemished body as well as to my solid, middle-aged, child-scarred one. It was that everything about this chance encounter on the bustling riverbank made it abundantly clear that Patrick colonized everything with a pulse. If I had ever succeeded in fooling myself about the truth – that Patrick slept with his glee club – I was no longer able to now.

The girl lowered her tilted head, brushing the toe of her sandal lightly back and forth on the path. Patrick swayed very slightly forward – he was speaking, she was listening. I hadn't the slightest desire to hear what they were saying; from this distance their conversation was not about words, but posture and demeanour. Patrick, still talking, actually glanced up in my direction and I froze, but he didn't see me. At the same moment Susan said, 'What's going on out there?'

'Nothing!'

She coughed painfully. 'I don't believe you. I bet the whole world and his wife are out there taking the sunshine.'

'The whole world and his wife' struck me for the first time as a curious expression. 'No.'

I turned back into the room just as Patrick looked up again. In the comparative darkness of the flat my startled reflection in the mirror confronted me like some latterday Lady of Shalott. While between it and me lay Susan, passive for once, dependent on me for news of the outside world.

'There are plenty of people about,' I said. 'You're better off in here.'

'I never for a moment doubted it.'

*   *   *

I stayed about another hour, during which Susan perked up and even accepted a glass of her own white wine. Taking it from me, she knelt up on the sofa and surveyed herself in the mirror.

'God in heaven, what do I look like?'

'Someone with the flu,' I said.

'Tomorrow I'm getting up and subjecting myself to a complete overhaul and once-over.'

'I'm sure that's a mistake,' I said. 'The advice is always to stay in bed for at least one day after the temperature's back to normal, and yours has only just gone up.'

She gave me a sidelong look of friendly contempt which persuaded me the paracetamol were taking effect. Seeing Patrick had put paid to any idea I'd had of confiding in her. The last thing I wanted at this moment was Susan's stringent advice – I was sufficiently honest with myself to know that the more apposite it was, the less I'd welcome it.

For something to say, I mentioned the Edelrats' get-together.

'Would you be interested in coming along?' I asked. 'Because if you are we could go in together.'

'I'm not in the least interested,' she said. 'But what does interest me is why you should be.'

'They're old friends. It'll be amusing.'

'That's a matter of opinion.'

'Bunny's been through a dreadful time – still going through it, actually. I regard it as a gesture of solidarity to go.'

'Oh yes . . .' Susan's eyes narrowed, betraying a glimmer of interest. 'I read about that in the paper.'

I felt suddenly protective towards Bunny. 'It's a tragedy for the people concerned.'

'Tragedy?' Her voice was thin with scorn. 'Do me a favour. It's just another sad little tale of hypocrisy and repression.'

'That's neither fair nor kind, and you know it.'

'Oh!' She closed her eyes and tipped her head back on the sofa in an attitude of despair. 'You really are the world's worst perpetrator of the double standard, Laura. Things are only terrible for Bunny, if they *are* terrible for Bunny, because George was idiotic enough to be found out.' Susan's eyes, wide open now, fixed on me with a look of chilling intransigence.

'It only requires a little imagination. A little sophistication, for God's sake. I mean – you manage it.'

I called on Becca on the way back and found her doing housework, alone and beetle-browed with discontent.

'How's it going?' I asked over the drone of the hoover.

'I'm fed up,' she announced flatly. 'And don't ask why.'

'Okay.'

'Do you want something? I've only got teabags till I've been shopping.'

'A teabag would be just the job.'

She switched the hoover off and went into the kitchen. I sat down on the sofa. Becca's living-room bore testament to an afternoon of violent and resentful subjugation. Every surface gleamed, the plants had been spray-misted and the carpet was smooth and debris-free. There was a faint smell of polish.

She came back in with the tea and handed me mine.

'Enjoying some peace and quiet?' I said.

'They're at Karen's, if that's what you mean. I don't know about the peace and quiet.'

'It's all looking very nice.'

'Makes a change.'

'That's not what I meant.'

'No, it's what I meant.'

There followed a short pause. I had the idea that Becca wanted the reason for her malaise dragged out of her, but I honestly hadn't the energy. Also, I'd learnt that the best way to handle her moods was simply to sit them out passively.

'Roberto seemed in good form,' I remarked.

'He was, yes.'

'Did Amos enjoy seeing him?'

'I think so. They're both about the same age at the moment. In a year or two Amos will be taking Roberto out.'

I took this to be a stab at black humour, and laughed. 'You're probably right.'

'Yeah.' Becca took her cigarettes off the mantelpiece and lit one with a flourish. She smoked in a way that came perilously close to reinvesting the habit with glamour. A lifelong non-smoker, when I saw her with a cigarette I almost wished to have one myself.

'Where does the show move on to?' I asked.

'Ipswich. The mind boggles.'

'I'm sure it'll go down a storm in Ipswich.'

'Possibly.'

The phone rang and it was as if she'd been subjected to several hundred volts. The barely started cigarette was stubbed out and she jumped up and went into the hall, not quite breaking into a run, and closed the door smartly behind her. I noticed that she must then have stood by the phone for a minute before picking it up, because it rang about four more times. That's my girl, I thought.

In spite of the closed door I didn't wish to be suspected of listening so I switched on the television. There was one of those typical late-afternoon quiz programmes fronted by a well-groomed man with grey hair and spectacles. The contestants were drawn from both genders, all age-groups and every conceivable walk of life. There were a lot of cardigans and several waterfall blouses. I was amazed at how much they knew. Did they sit down and read encylopaedias every evening? One man – Roger from Chorleywood – had a terrifying detailed knowledge of the life and work of Fellini and could also list Uncle Tom Cobbleigh's fellow-travellers in the correct order. It was, as Josh might have said, awesome.

Becca came back into the room a changed woman. The very air had altered. Her skin glowed, her eyes were bright, and her voice no longer grated with discontent. Yet again, knowing my subject, I didn't ask.

'What's this?' she asked, sitting down with her legs draped over the arm of the chair and lighting another cigarette. 'Oh, this thing.'

'Switch it off,' I said, embarrassed. 'I wasn't really watching.'

'I know. You were being tactful.'

'Partly.'

'You didn't have to worry. It was nothing private.'

'Oh.' I picked up the remote control and zapped the quiz. Becca gave me a sidelong look and then one of her most devastating grins.

'I know you're dying to know – it was Griggs.'

Her happiness was like a fire beyond a closed window. I could see its light and its glow, but I couldn't experience its warmth. I was cut off.

We went to see *Tango Americano* the following night. It was a wonderful over-the-top tour de force of writhing hips, smouldering machismo and haughtily stamping feet. Roberto had two solos – one as a youthful gigolo seducing, and subsequently breaking the heart of, a rich older woman; the other as a rough youth off the street who is taught to tango and subsequently outshines everyone else with his natural talent. In this role in particular he shone. Sweat flew from his dark hair as he strutted and prowled, and his face burned with a furious passion which I'd never seen there in real life.

We went round to see him afterwards. The backstage area at the Corn Exchange was a warren of small, poorly ventilated rooms with peeling paint and a pungent smell comprising years of make-up, sweat, alcohol and unwashed costumes. Roberto shared one of these with two other male dancers, small, genial men, shorter and older than their stage personae had suggested. After greeting us warmly they withdrew, leaving us alone with Roberto who opened a screwtop bottle of red wine.

'Put it there,' said Glyn, holding out a hand. 'You were plain terrific.'

'You were,' I agreed. 'We were terribly impressed.'

'I'm so glad that you came,' said Roberto. 'I appreciate it. And you really enjoyed it?'

We assured him that we had. Glyn was quite bright-eyed with the thrill of it all. I did hope he wasn't going to make some ill-advised offer. The thought of our sin-in-law's livelihood being our responsibility was a further complication I felt we could live without.

'Will you be going into the West End?'

Roberto shrugged – a real dancer's shrug that seemed to use every muscle in his body, just enough. 'We can only hope.'

'I think you'd be a sensation, all of you,' said Glyn.

'Tango isn't new.'

'No, but then new isn't necessarily box office at the moment.

What people want is a new slant on the familiar. Stuff they've seen before, but done bigger and better.'

Roberto smiled modestly. 'We shall see. I'm only pleased to have been here so that all my family could come.'

'So we're "all his family",' said Glyn on the way home. 'I never thought he saw us like that.'

'Nor me.'

'It makes you think, doesn't it?' He glanced across at me to gauge my reaction, and when there was none, laughed self-deprecatingly. 'Though I'm not quite sure what about.'

13

I had no contact with Patrick until the night before I was due to go into London to meet up with the Edelrats. He rang up quite blatantly, as usual, when we were having supper and Josh was on his way out. It was Josh who picked up the phone.

'Mum! It's for you.'

'Who is it?'

'I dunno . . . Some bloke . . .' Josh's voice faded and was cut off by the slamming of the front door.

For the first time I resorted to subterfuge: 'That'll be Colin.' Colin was one of my pickier book-keeping clients.

I lifted the receiver in the hall. 'Hi there,' said Patrick. 'I've been thinking about you.'

'Hi there,' I said loudly, 'I was expecting you to call.'

'Were you? Or is this some elaborate subterfuge?'

'I think I'll be okay for that meeting, I'll just take a look.' I replaced the hall receiver and went into Glyn's office where I knew I couldn't be heard, but leaving the door open so as not to appear secretive. When I picked the phone up I hissed, 'Why do you do this? What would you have done if Glyn had answered the phone?'

'Asked to speak to you of course.'

'Don't be so stupid – what are you trying to do?'

'Precisely nothing. Guilty behaviour engenders suspicion. Why do you think most burglaries take place in broad daylight? Because no one thinks twice about two blokes loading up a furniture van outside an open front door.'

'That's not analogous, and you know it.'

'So can you come round?' he said blandly.

'I don't know.'

'Tomorrow?'

'I can't, I'm in London.'

'Day after?'

'It's the weekend.'

'It was the weekend last time as I recall . . .'

'I'll see.'

'Monday, then?'

'Perhaps.'

'Monday it is.'

I went back into the kitchen, boiling with nervous fury. Glyn glanced at me. 'All sorted out?'

'Yes,' I said. I looked down at what remained of my salad. I could no sooner have eaten it now than flown.

'How was he?'

I felt a little cold explosion in the pit of my stomach before I regained my presence of mind.

'He was fine. You know Colin. A bit of an old woman.'

Glyn seemed to accept this. 'You're going in to carouse with the girls tomorrow, aren't you?'

'That's right.'

'I'm going into the office – fancy a lift? Then you can get really legless and travel home in comfort.'

I debated this swiftly with myself. I didn't want his generosity, I couldn't cope with it. 'I don't know when we'll be finished.'

He gave a wry smile. 'I'm sure you don't. Let's leave it that if you stagger into G and D before I leave, then the lift's there. Otherwise British Rail can have the pleasure of your patronage. At any rate, we'll go in together, shall we?' He got up and put his plate in the machine. 'Coming through? Human Condition's on Channel Four.'

They did two numbers, and came over very well. They wore suits over bare chests, and gym shoes. They were very English. Their lyrics were cryptic and full of streetwise, lower-middle-class irony. There were references to mums, and buses, and job centres, and old cars, and dogs. The tunes were downbeat but catchy. The presenter, an elder statesman of the British rock scene, his receding hairline compensated for by a generous ponytail, interviewed Griggs. He asked him if he saw himself as part of a tradition.

'Definitely,' said Griggs. 'We can trace our line right back, back to the Music Hall via David Bowie and Alma Cogan.'

'Attaboy,' said Glyn. 'I like his style.'

The presenter asked several more questions along philosophical lines, all of which Griggs fielded adeptly with laconic, Lennonish humour.

When the programme finished, Glyn switched off in high good spirits.

'Comes over a treat, doesn't he?'

'Yes,' I agreed, 'he does.'

'I have a feeling we've just been watching our meal ticket for the foreseeable future. How's the liaison with Becca going, by the way, any idea?'

'It's still on, I think.'

'No sign of the big E yet?'

'Not as far as I know.'

'That's what I like to hear,' said Glyn, bouncing up from his chair. 'I'm going to give Cy a bell in case he missed it.'

A little later, while Glyn played in the office, I gave Susan a ring at home.

'How are you? Are you better?'

'Never more so,' she said. I detected a sharpness in her tone, probably due to embarrassment over having been ill at all in the first place. Sympathetic queries had been given their marching orders.

'Good. I don't suppose you've changed your mind about tomorrow, have you? The Edelrats' lunch in town?'

'No, I haven't. Sorry, Laura, but it's not my cup of tea.'

'That's okay.'

'But give them my regards, by all means.'

'I will.'

'Where are you going?'

'The Gondola.'

'Ah, a nostalgia trip,' said Susan. 'Still, not too weighed down by suits. They should be sympathetic to all that dreadful rattling of purses that goes on with large groups of women.'

I let this completely unreasonable sally pass, not without some difficulty. She was goading me because she needed to, not because I needed it. With Susan you took the rough with the smooth.

One thing I didn't intend to do was pass on her regards. If Susan were actually to turn up, the others would have been guardedly pleased to see her, but a message would ring distinctly hollow, something she must have known as well as I did.

Quite unexpectedly, she said, 'You've got a family wedding coming up, haven't you?'

'In three weeks. It's clever of you to remember.'

'You always underestimate me, Laura.'

I sensed that this was a time and a conversation in which it would behove me to humour my friend.

'It's my cousin's,' I explained. 'Sinead's going to be a bridesmaid.'

'Nice dress?'

'Sweet. Even Becca thinks so.'

'How grateful you must be about *that*.'

'It does help, yes.'

'And what about you, what will you wear?'

'I haven't thought. I suppose I shall have to go shopping for something suitably gracious.'

'What's gracious got to do with it? You're not the fucking Queen Mother!'

'Wrong word. Perhaps I meant elegant.'

'Elegant? Gracious? Whatever happened to knockout and drop dead?'

I was awfully glad I wasn't sitting in a restaurant with her. 'They're fine, but you forget I have to turn up with two grown-up daughters both of whom will look absolutely stunning and have youth on their side.'

'That doesn't mean you have to dress like a dowager duchess.'

'I assure you I won't.'

'Hm.' There was a brief pause during which I pictured Susan taking a draught of wine, or drawing on her cigarette. 'Perhaps I'd better come on this shopping trip with you.' Her voice brightened. 'You need saving from yourself. We could bash the plastic and then have lunch.'

'I'll probably wind up wearing something I've already got.'

Susan sucked her teeth. 'What about the men?'

'What about them?'

'What will they be wearing?'

'I believe it's morning dress.'

'Nice, I approve.'

'Glyn hates it. And Josh won't wear it.'

'You'll have to whip them into line.'

'Oh, Glyn'll go along with it.'

'If you ask me,' said Susan, 'going along with things is your husband's speciality.'

She'd touched a nerve, and I flinched. 'What's that supposed to mean?'

'What it says.'

'When I want your opinion, I'll ask for it!' I snapped, and heard her chuckle as I hung up. Verity was coming down the stairs.

'Mum? What's up?'

'Oh, nothing.'

'Who was that you were giving stick to?'

'A friend.'

'Ah,' said Verity. 'Of course. I'll pray for her.'

'By all means do.' It was the best put-down for Susan at my disposal – to have her prayed for, whether she liked it or not.

It was raining next day. We needed lights on in the house as we got up, and the headlamps on as we drove into London through a haze of oily spray thrown up by the lorries on the A1. The weather and the driving conditions made me tense, but not Glyn.

'This is ghastly,' I said, 'we should have gone on the train.'

'Nonsense. There's no hurry. And it can't last all day.'

'I do hope not.'

'No worries,' said Glyn. It might have been his personal motto. 'Why don't we pull off somewhere,' he suggested, 'and have a coffee? With average luck it'll have eased off a bit by the time we get back on the road.'

'All right. If we've got time.'

He glanced at me. 'All the time in the world.'

We came off at the Hertford turning and drove for about ten minutes before coming into a village. After cruising back and forth up the main drag we established that the choice was between a dismal-looking café and a half-timbered hotel, the George, which proclaimed itself an old coaching inn with parking for patrons through the arch at the rear.

'Lovely job,' said Glyn.

Considering it was August, the George was surprisingly quiet. I suppose its location only about twenty-five miles from London made it not so much a destination as an en route stop, and we had arrived during the mid-morning lull. A girl in a waistcoat and bow-tie stood behind the reception desk, and the clink of crockery and the drone of a hoover were faintly audible. A woman in a blue overall was polishing the tables in something called the Oak Room Bar.

'Good morning, how may I help you?' asked the receptionist.

'We'd like to sit somewhere quiet and have some coffee.'

'No problem at all sir,' said the girl, dimpling. Glyn was an arresting sight in this – or indeed any – context this morning, dressed for work in a yellow shirt, brown and white brogues, white cotton trousers, and braces patterned with Sonic the Hedgehog.

She showed us to the lounge, and our arrival was the cue for another functionary – the one wielding the hoover – to melt away.

'If you'd like to make yourselves comfortable,' said the receptionist, 'I'll send someone along to take your order.'

'Just coffee for two,' said Glyn. 'And some Heritage bikkies if you've got them.'

'Heritage . . . ?'

'Those big fat ones that pretend to be homemade?'

'We'll see what we can do.'

She obviously wasn't going to be treated as a waitress, because a moment later another girl came along and Glyn repeated his request.

'Youth Opportunities heaven,' he remarked. 'Still, it's rather nice.'

It was. I'm one of those people who find hotels erotic. Even in a small place like this there was a tension between the shared amenities down here and the honeycomb of rooms upstairs, with their locked doors and clean bedlinen, and their illusory sense of privacy. And then there was the quietness of everything – the thick carpets, the doors that swung to without a sound, and the invisibility of all the usual domestic nuts and bolts. In a hotel you were both on parade and offered intimacy.

'Think of it,' said Glyn, as though reading my mind. 'Nobody knows we're here. Not a soul. And they couldn't guess, either.' He leaned towards me. 'Shall we book in for an hour?'

I fancied I caught something in his eye that was at odds with his teasing tone, but there was no time to answer before the waitress arrived with the coffee. I watched as Glyn thanked and paid her. I could see how she responded to him, and he wasn't even trying. He liked his fellow man and woman. My husband wore his heart on his sleeve. He would be terribly easy to hurt.

'Don't worry,' he said. 'I didn't mean it. Shall I be mother?'

As I watched him pour, and a watery sun began to filter through the hotel's diamond-paned window, I experienced one of those small gear-shifts of mood which only when we were back in the car was I able to identify as disappointment.

The Gondola, a cheerful, family-run Italian restaurant, was just off the Tottenham Court Road. Its charm for the Edelrats was that it had changed scarcely at all since the sixties. It was a tratt, plain and simple, with whitewashed walls, red lamps in arched niches, a tiled floor, gingham tablecloths and mandoline muzak. It was comforting to know that the breadsticks and giant peppergrinders were only an eyeblink away. I could remember my date with Glyn when I'd first eaten here. I'd worn skin-tight zip-sided pvc boots which stopped all circulation just below the knee and allowed one's feet to go slowly numb in a bog of perspiration. It was my Patti Boyd phase, and my hair hung in flat, bleached curtains on either side of the false eyelashes which clung to each eyelid like twin flue-brushes. My skirt was a black hipster, barely twelve inches from belt to hem, and my black and white shirt was from Ginger Group, with big cuffs and a rounded collar. Only two tables away there was the pomaded star of a TV sleuth show, and we were fairly sure we could see Justin de Villeneuve in the corner, with a bird who wasn't Twiggy.

The place had survived because the food was good – hearty, homely, authentic Italian cooking using fresh ingredients and served in awesome quantities. And the cosy immutability of the décor was in danger of making it fashionable again. In the hardnosed nineties the Gondola had taken on a whimsical retro charm, and business, as the noise level indicated, was booming.

There were five of us at the corner table – Bunny and I, plus Daffs, Lucilla and Mijou. Annette, apparently, would be along in half an hour. Bunny was positively febrile with the possibilities for a new life, and began addressing us on the subject almost at once.

'I simply can't believe how liberated I feel!' she announced, bright-eyed, as we stared owlishly at her over our giant menus like a quartet of attentive choirboys. 'Gloria Gaynor never sang a truer word – I will survive! It's totally brilliant. And I'm heading for a size twelve.'

'What are your plans, Bun?' asked Lucilla, unfolding a pair of minute gold Dior half-specs with a brisk snap, like a Georgian courtesan unfurling a fan.

'I'm going to go back to college, do History of Art A-level, and buy some nifty little pad in Pimlico.'

'That dates you,' said Lucilla, putting on the glasses and gazing down her nose through them at the *antipasti*. 'No one has a pad any more, and Pimlico has about as much cachet as Dorking.'

'Well, wherever!' went on Bunny, unabashed. 'Didn't Tony Armstrong-Jones come from Pimlico?'

'I don't know about "come from",' I said. 'But he was living there when it all started.'

'And now I shall be living there when it all starts!' It was nice to see Bunny on such an evident high, but also impossible not to suspect that it would all end in tears. We were well into the second bottle and the starters hadn't even arrived.

Mijou leaned forward to indicate the highly personal nature of what she was about to say – a pointless gesture in these circumstances, where there was unlikely to be a single remark that was not highly personal.

'Daffs,' she said, raising an eyebrow to the rest of us. 'Why haven't you brought Ruth? We all want to meet her, don't we, girls?'

We nodded and chorused agreement, but I thought I detected something wobbly around the edges in Daffs's expression.

'Oh well . . .' she said. She blushed absolutely scarlet, something to which she'd always been a martyr. 'Never mind.'

I was pleased when Lucilla said, 'I don't blame her for not coming. Honestly, we are the worst bunch of superannuated schoolgirls – if I were Ruth I'd pay a king's ransom to stay away from people like us.'

'Not at all,' said Mijou, loudly backed up by Bunny. 'We're concerned and interested friends.'

'How are you, Daffs, anyway?' I asked.

Daffs turned if anything an even deeper shade of red. 'A bit embattled at the mo, actually.'

'Everything all right?'

'Not really.' She had our attention now, and unlike Bunny was deeply uncomfortable with it. 'But nothing to worry about.'

'And what about Ruth?' asked Lucilla. 'Because we do all feel as if we know her.'

'Oh, she's fine. And we're absolutely grand. It's nothing time won't take care of, I'm sure.'

'You know,' said Mijou, 'not for nothing is that a tired old cliché. I never believed it when other people said that to me, but it is true. You do reach a point where you can think about certain events and people without crying. When things are at their worst it seems impossible, but it sort of creeps up on you and one day you realize you're on the mend.' Good old Mijou.

'My mother said that after Daddy died,' agreed Lucilla, lighting up without asking, another generation indicator. 'She said she suddenly found she could bear to sweep up all the good memories and collect them together to look at. In fact she actually wanted to.'

From being boorishly intrusive we had suddenly become the very soul of supportive discretion, asking no more questions, proposing a few humble remedies, drawing the emotional fire. Daffs smiled redly, bright-eyed with unexpressed feeling.

I made my own offering. 'When I lost Isobel I thought I'd die of misery. But now it makes me happy to think about her. She's one of the family, as far as we're concerned. I'm sad she's not with us, but it isn't agony any more. It doesn't hurt at all.'

My friends listened respectfully. 'I can't imagine,' said Bunny, 'how awful it must be to lose a child. I mean, I've never had children, but it's so wrong – such a violation of the natural order.'

We all agreed on that. Mijou poured more wine. 'Something I've read about from time to time is that when you lose a child you eventually become grateful that they never had to grow up – that you remember them always young, and full of hope and promise, not ageing and souring like everyone else. But I don't know,' she glanced at me, 'I don't know about you, Laura, but I feel that Jacob is somehow older than everyone else. I consult him about things. As if dying young has made him wiser and fairer.'

'Yes,' I nodded. 'I do that. Isobel never lived at all, really, but she's a source of comfort.'

We sat quietly for a second. I did hope that no one, in a fit of embarrassment, would say something like 'Gosh, what a cheery conversation!' But no one did. There was a tranquillity in our silence which was moving, and a kindly grace in our pooling of our sufferings on Daffs's behalf.

'Madam – something for you ladies.' The proprietor, Gino, appeared with a bottle of champagne in a bucket.

Bunny looked at it doubtfully. 'I didn't order any – or not yet.'

'It is a present,' said Gino. 'Would you like me to pour some now? There is a second bottle.'

'Yes please!' said Lucilla. 'It's the real McCoy! I think we should guzzle it instantly, no questions asked, before it dematerializes.'

Gino brought a clutch of champagne flutes, held in one hand like a bunch of flowers, and poured with a dexterously naff flourish.

'To unknown benefactors everywhere,' suggested Mijou, raising her glass.

'A present from who?' I asked. 'Who, Gino?'

Bunny's face was screwed up into a comical expression of dread. 'God, I do *hope* it's not George hazarding some bizarre attempt at reconciliation. I really couldn't bear it.'

'The lady's name was Miss Upchurch,' said Gino. 'She said it came with her best wishes, and you were to—' he cleared his throat to indicate quotation – 'let your hair down and talk dirty.'

With an insinuating tact he lowered his eyes and withdrew amidst our burst of uneasy laughter. For the others were uneasy, there was no doubt about that.

'She should have come along,' said Bunny. 'I never thought to ask her.'

'I did,' I said. 'She couldn't make it.'

'Of course, you see quite a bit of her, don't you? I'd forgotten that. How is she these days?'

'Fine.' It was rather hard to explain how Susan was, to anyone, let alone to this group of people who thought they knew her a little but in fact knew her even less than that. You needed to have firsthand experience of Susan, and that's all there was to it.

'Still single?' asked Daffs, glad, I daresay, to turn the spotlight on to someone else.

'Congenitally,' I replied.

'And doing incredibly well for herself, I bet,' said Lucilla rather thinly, but with good manners to the fore. 'I was never a particular buddy of hers – she was a year or two above us, wasn't she? – but I do remember that she stood out from the crowd.'

The others all agreed that this was so and sipped their Veuve Clicquot with slightly baffled appreciation. I didn't mind about their gratitude, I wanted them to like Susan.

'This is absolutely typical of her,' I said. 'She loves the grand gesture.'

'As which of us does not?' responded Bunny. 'It's a heck of a lot jollier to give than to receive.'

I decided to give up on acting as Susan's agent. Once again

her friendship was the tip of the wedge slipped between me and the rest of my life. I was left in a kind of no-man's-land, my closeness with her separating me a little from my other friends. She was tweaking my strings from a distance just as she had in the spring at our silver wedding: the perfect gift, well chosen and graciously sent, placed her presence among us while not actually requiring her to muss her gloves with the spadework of social intercourse.

Over the *antipasti* we kept the conversation fairly general – the practicalities of Bunny's move to higher education, the problems Mijou faced (and successfully concealed for eight hours a day) as a bewildered technophobe in a state-of-the-art legal office, Lucilla's youngest's failure to thrive at boarding school and whether the local comprehensive was even to be contemplated ... her financial coup at the most recent of a summer-long string of cut-throat antiques fairs ... Throughout it all Daffs remained pink, and quiet.

As the main course arrived, so did Annette. She was even bigger than I remembered. I could see now why the others had arranged it so that the spare seat awaiting her was at the end of the table – she simply would not have fitted elsewhere. Like all massively overweight people she looked painfully hot. The bare flesh of her biceps shuddered and swung as she dumped her pilot's case on the floor and aligned the centre of her gigantic beam with the pathetically small wickerwork disc which was the chair seat.

'Sorry, everyone, slapped wrist, I got locked into an argument with one of my more poisonous superiors,' she puffed. Her face was blotchy and her rather thin hair was greasy with sweat.

'Who won?' asked Mijou as I poured bubbly.

'You have to ask?' replied Annette with an almost coquettish smile. I understood the absolute accuracy of the phrase 'wedded to her work'. For some reason that I was not at all proud of, her diligence and dedication depressed me. Sitting next to Annette I could smell her, not because she was dirty, but because there was three times as much of her and her bodily juices – perspiration, saliva, vaginal secretions, earwax. It was like being next door to a vast vat where the ingredients for women bubbled and seethed.

We all offered to wait on the main course while she had her starter, but she absolutely forbade it and ordered *marinara* and olive bread, which was a relief. If she'd asked for watercress salad and a glass of mineral water I think we'd have died of embarrassment and the need to conceal it from each other.

'The champagne is a present from Susan,' explained Bunny to Annette. 'With orders to us all to talk dirty.'

'Really?' said Annette, tweaking involuntarily at the folds of material beneath her armpits. 'I'm on for that. How far have you got?'

'Not very,' said Mijou, 'but then we haven't had long.'

'Never mind,' said Annette, slurping in a stringy mouthful of squid. 'I'm here now.' She munched juicily. 'Sorry, Susan who?'

'Upchurch,' said Lucilla. 'Do you remember her? She arrived late in one of those post-closure clearing operations. She was only there for two years. And she was older than us.'

'It doesn't mean a thing to me, isn't that awful?' said Annette, 'and here I am knocking back her drink like nobody's business. But here's to Susan anyway. God bless her and all who sail in her.'

I thought how much Susan would have disliked Annette. She'd got no time at all for people who didn't make the best of themselves. Obesity on this scale would have incurred her most withering displeasure.

Quite suddenly Daffs came back to life. I could see her gathering her forces for a determined sally.

'Annette,' she said, 'you could probably give me some advice.'

'It's what I do for a living, love. I'd be very surprised if I couldn't. On the other hand I can't vouch for its quality, since I'm off duty and drinking.'

'I'm sorry,' Daffs looked around, 'this is rude, I know, but can I monopolize Annette for a mo? I don't mean to be antisocial, but—'

'No buts,' said Lucilla, 'we know when we're being asked to talk amongst ourselves.'

'Not at all, it's not that, but I don't want to impose my ramblings on absolutely everyone . . .'

'Daffs!' Bunny was imperious in her role as the quintessential great survivor. 'Witter not! Dump on Annette while you can, for goodness' sake. You should look on us as a support group.'

'The Inaugural Meeting of the Certain Age Encounter Group, South Eastern Chapter,' enlarged Mijou. 'You unburden yourself, we'll talk heavy shopping.'

I turned dutifully in Bunny's direction as she opened the batting with a description of her recent visit to an image consultant.

'Apparently I'm a rectangle,' she said. 'Which means I should favour long, lean jackets and skirts that brush the top of the knee.'

'Count yourself lucky.' Lucilla gave a dry little laugh. 'I went to one of those in Cheltenham a couple of years ago and she told me I was a classic British pear. I thought to myself what the *dickens* am I doing, forking out over a hundred quid to be insulted by this very ordinary little woman in ski-pants.'

'Ski-pants,' echoed Mijou in awed tones. 'Oh, wow.'

'Did yours come to your place afterwards?' enquired Bunny. 'To assess your wardrobe?'

Lucilla shook her head. 'You're joking. If I need my morale destroying I've got a brace of large sons who'll do it any time for free.'

'Mine came round,' said Bunny, her enthusiasm for the venture undented by Lucilla's less happy experience. 'She came round a couple of days later and went through my stuff with a fine tooth-comb. When she'd finished, no kidding, there was a pile that high – you couldn't see my bed at all.'

'Pile of what?' asked Mijou.

'Clothes I didn't need. That weren't right for me.'

'And you believed her?' Mijou was incredulous.

Lucilla scoffed. 'She'll be on a backhander from somewhere, you may be bound. Where did she recommend you replace all these unsuitable garments?'

'Nowhere!' Bunny sounded aggrieved. 'She'd brought along a few bits and pieces from her own collection—'

'You don't say.'

'Only belts and scarves and things like that. And she made the most brilliant suggestions about how to put together my own things in a different way, all of which, oh ye of little faith, I'm tremendously pleased with.'

Lucilla looked over her glasses at Bunny. 'Of course you are. She's given you a sartorial placebo, and you're as happy as Larry with it.'

Bunny bridled. 'I'm not that daft. She spoke a lot of good sense.'

Mijou looked across at me. 'You're very quiet, Laura. Have you ever been to one of these gurus?'

'No. But it sounds fun.'

'Good old Laura. Always diplomatic,' said Lucilla.

'I wasn't being diplomatic – I'd love someone to come along and chuck out half of the stuff in my wardrobe. Do you remember what Matron used to say about the benefits of a "jolly good clear-out"?'

Lucilla rolled her eyes. 'Do I ever. She was obsessed with bowels, that woman. It was years before I was able to resist the urge to put a tick in my diary to mark every motion successfully passed.'

'School casts a long shadow,' I agreed. 'After all, those were our formative years we spent there.'

'Are we all hopelessly warped and stunted?' mused Mijou. 'I often think about it.'

'Warped and stunted?' Bunny, outraged, waved a glass over her cooling *fritto misto mare*. 'Look at us! A more self-aware, upstanding, emotionally mature bunch of women it would be hard to imagine!'

Lucilla inclined her head to mine. 'That's what I love about our Bun – her charming diffidence.'

Mijou laughed, and raised her glass. 'Here's to you, Bunny. You should undergo violent changes more often – they obviously do you the world of good.'

'I tell you what,' said Lucilla with the reasonable, down-to-earth air of someone mounting a hobbyhorse, 'we may laugh now, but I reckon the Rat-house did us a power of good. If I had girls I'd send them there.'

'You wouldn't, would you?' I asked, genuinely astonished.

'For sure. I believe in boarding, and I believe in single-sex schools. And I believe in some sort of consistent moral tone.'

'Consistent with what?'

'Christian values,' said Lucilla. I liked Lucilla a lot, she was sharp and funny and staunch and one hadn't the least doubt that she would be excellent to have around in a crisis. But her attitude to Our Lord and his values was not one Verity would have recognized. She personified the theory that the Anglican Church was the Tory Party at prayer.

'No, no, no, it was education according to the Old Testament,' said Bunny. 'Judgment passed and summary retribution handed out. Do you remember what happened to Margot when she ran away that time? She was shut in a practising-room for thirty-six hours till her parents came to take her away. And our parents connived at all this.'

'I don't think they had the foggiest idea,' I said. 'I never told them anything. And it was fairly enlightened by the standards of the day.'

'Compared to where I came from,' said Mijou, 'it was paradise.'

The conversation drifted towards the less contentious areas of Middle Eastern politics and human rights, and I allowed my conversational radar to focus on the exchange taking place at my end of the table. With Daffs opposite and Annette to my right, I was ideally placed to grasp the tenor of Daffs's disclosures without appearing nosey.

'. . . afraid he'll simply never be able to come to terms with it,' she was saying.

'It's going to take him a long time,' agreed Annette. 'But he will, take my word for it. Remember he's only what, twenty-one? That's no age. He's only a kid.' So it was Timmy, doing agricultural economics at Cirencester, who was the problem.

'Julia's handling it so much better,' said Daffs, 'although she's two years younger. I've been able to talk to her about it.'

'Girls are more mature, period,' said Annette, who was not, as far as I could see, coming up with anything the rest of us couldn't have said. 'You'll have to be patient with your son. He's going to have to go through all the stages, and he can't be rushed. He will come through, but only if he's allowed to find his own way. It goes against the grain, I know, but you'll have to stand back and take the flak for the time being.'

'It's awfully hard,' said Daffs tremulously. 'Timmy and I have always been close. It was Julia I used to have the bust-ups with.'

Annette mopped vigorously at her plate with a heel of *ciabatta*. 'But that's perfectly logical, don't you see? He was close to the old you, and now he's lost her. It's a bereavement.' We were well into shrink-rap now.

'But I haven't changed!' protested Daffs. 'That's the problem. Apart from being happier, I'm exactly the same as I ever was!'

'Being happier is a big change,' said Annette. 'It's a kind of betrayal. You're saying that your old life, with your husband and children, wasn't enough to make you happy. What do you think your Timmy makes of that?'

I could see there was a kernel of truth in this argument, but its stern and unpalatable logic had brought Daffs once more to the point of tears. Unwise though it is for an eavesdropper to betray an interest, I was prompted to blurt out, 'Don't you think some of it is just embarrassment?'

They both looked at me, Daffs with an urgent need for reassurance, Annette more sharply.

'What?'

'Embarrassment. My Josh likes to think he's politically correct but he would simply die if I started shacking up with another woman.' Annette glared unblinkingly. I even seemed to have attracted some interest from the other end. I addressed Daffs. 'Timmy needs to get used to it, that's all.'

'It's a bit more than embarrassment, Laura,' said Annette in an understanding way. 'This young man has lost the mother he thought he had.'

'I bet it's not that so much as what his mates will say if they find out his mum is gay.'

'You're absolutely right,' said Daffs, looking brighter. 'He's at a farming college. It's not exactly the most liberated seat of learning in the world. He must live in dread of someone finding out.'

'Why not enlist your daughter's help – Julia?' suggested Annette. 'She'll be able to demystify it for him.'

'They've always fought like nobody's business.' Daffs sounded doubtful. 'As teenagers, if you said pass the sugar they turned it into World War Three.'

'In that case you're doing them a favour,' said Annette. 'Discussing you will be a very bonding experience.'

Based on my own experience this, at least, sounded true. Bunny leaned forward down the table.

'Are you sorted? Annette, have you come up with all kinds of wise saws and modern instances?'

'She has,' said Daffs, on fire again with all the attention she was getting. 'And Laura. It's been a real help. I'm sorry to be such a pain.'

'How's Gordon in all this?' asked Lucilla, a bit tactlessly, but going on to redeem herself somewhat by not waiting for an answer. 'If Huggers were in that position I know he'd go completely to pieces.'

The giant menus reappeared. 'Anyone for afters?' asked Bunny. 'Because I am.'

Bunny, Daffs and Annette ordered puddings, coffees for us all and – rashly – a third bottle of the Widow, on the basis that we couldn't possibly stop there, and anything less good would be a let-down. We were all a bit smashed and it was us against the world. We were starting to touch each other a lot and comment on each other's excellent qualities in a way we might well live to regret. I was as bevvied as the next woman, but there was also a small part of me – the part that was Susan's friend – which remained separate. With the exception of the transparently straightforward Daffs we were all, I suspected, hiding something. Our secrets waved beneath the surface like weed in a murky pond, invisible, but oxygenating the water.

While the others began on their pudding, Lucilla and I went to the Ladies, which was down a precipitate flight of stairs at the back of the restaurant. The facilities here were as unaltered as the rest of the Gondola. My skin remembered the icy temperature of the back extension and the strange clamminess of the black plastic seats, and the grey rubber handles on the loo chains. There were little windows high above the chipped cisterns. You could see next-door's brick wall through these mean oblong apertures. There was a smell of cooking and old drains.

'Dear oh dear,' said Lucilla as we peered hopefully at ourselves in the mirror over the basin. 'They could do with spending a bob or two down here.'

I agreed. 'It hasn't changed in nearly thirty years.'

'Wish I hadn't.' Lucilla gave her thin mouth a swipe of lipstick and smacked her lips. 'I look like the wrath of God.'

'You look wonderful.'

'I don't feel it. I feel ancient.'

'Rubbish.'

'It's not a topic for discussion, it's a fact.' She turned round and perched on the edge of the basin, staring down at her crossed ankles. She wore extremely expensive shoes on her narrow, elegant feet – I thought how my mother would have approved. She looked up suddenly. 'Laura, may I confide in you?'

'Of course.'

'I'm not happy.'

I waited, assuming she was going to expand on this, but she didn't. Instead, she repeated, 'I'm not happy.'

I resorted to platitudes. 'What's happy, after all?'

'Feeling good. Feeling positive. Glad for every new day that comes along.'

'Impossible.'

'No it's not. Look at how Bunny is. And you, for that matter.'

'Bunny's on an unnatural high.'

I prayed she wouldn't ask about me, and she didn't. 'I wish I could bottle some of that.'

'It's probably physical,' I said. 'It's our age.'

'Bollocks to that, I've been popping Prempack for over a year.'

'It'll pass.' I was running out of palliative phrases.

She pushed herself upright and wavered for a moment. 'Do you know what I hate most? Being a cliché. I hate going along to our sweet, fourteen-year-old GP and saying "Doctor, doctor, I'm tired and depressed and have no *joie de vivre*" when I can see in his eyes that the chair is still warm from the last tired, depressed, joyless housewife who sat there—'

'Lucilla, you are *not* a joyless housewife! You are one of the most glamorous people I know! Don't say these things about yourself, they're not true and they make me nervous. It's called taking the ground out from under a person's feet.' It was true. I simply could not cope with Lucilla – firm of jaw, clear of eye, cut-glass of vowel – being tired and depressed.

'What do you suggest then?' she asked.

'Pretend,' I said, God knows why, it just popped into my head. 'It's a proven physiological fact that if you make yourself smile you feel more cheerful.'

She looked at me as if I were completely mad.

'Are you completely mad?' I shrugged and opened the door into the icy stone passageway. 'Okay,' she said, tapping my midriff as she went by. 'It shall be smile city, as my Giles would say.'

As we milled out on to the pavement the rain, which had eased off a bit during the afternoon, was starting up again. After the cosy, winey camaraderie of the Gondola, the great outside with its chill workaday detail and noise was distinctly unwelcome. Various informal arrangements had been made: Mijou was going back to Harley Street with Bunny for a cup of tea and a chat about higher education. Lucilla was heading for Paddington, and was sharing a taxi with the other two. Daffs was going by tube to John Lewis to buy curtain material.

Annette said: 'What about you, Laura? Do you fancy a little stool-perching for a while? I don't have another meeting till six.'

The thought of Annette perched on a stool was too much. I didn't want to be another case history squeezed in between meetings. I didn't want to be with her at all. She depressed me. Her size, her smell, her awful neediness disguised as bonhomie – they filled me with gloom.

As I stood there I suddenly saw the Shogun on the other side of the road, with Glyn sitting reading the *Standard* in the driver's seat.

It's funny. When you see someone you know unexpectedly, and – more importantly – they don't see you, they make a fresh impression. It's like catching sight of your reflection in a shop window, except that that, in my experience, is invariably a chastening experience. Who, you ask yourself, is that trudging, careworn, overweight woman with the funny jacket and the bad hair?

With other people, the opposite is true – such surprise sightings make them appear taller, better-looking, intriguing.

Seeing Glyn before he saw me, I recognised with a shock how attractive he was. With his springy dark hair barely tipped with grey, his thin, muscular arms below the rolled-up sleeves of his yellow shirt, and his fingers tapping the cover of the paper in time to some inaudible music (the Human Condition, possibly), he was any woman's idea of a fanciable man. Even just sitting there at the wheel of his car an air of amiability and openness made him seem ten years younger than he was. The phrase 'young at heart' sprang spontaneously to mind. No one, certainly, would have taken him for a grandfather. A girl no older than Verity who was crossing the road shot him one of those swift, unselfconsciously appraising looks which are the sincerest form of flattery. I was moved, and more than a little shamed, that this was my husband . . .

Sensing my gaze on him he looked up, and lifted his chin in greeting before returning, relaxed as you please, to the paper.

'Actually,' I said to Annette, 'my meeting's earlier than that. I have to dash.'

We exchanged hurried, flurried, kisses in the rain. A taxi chugged alongside the kerb to pick up Lucilla, Bunny and Mijou. Daffs and Annette moved off in the direction of the tube. With wings on my feet I ran across the road and jumped into the car.

'Hi,' said Glyn, folding the paper and slinging it on the back seat. 'Good lunch?'

'Yes. Lovely. What are you doing here?'

'We finished early, so I thought I'd come along and meet you.'

'Have you been here hours?'

He glanced at his watch. 'Fifteen minutes.'

'I appreciate it, thanks.'

'You're more than welcome.' He started the engine, then suddenly reached an arm to the floor at the back. 'I nearly forgot.'

It was a single gardenia, wrapped in white tissue. The scent – the scent of our wedding – filled the car. Glyn gave it to me but didn't wait for my reaction. He began at once to move out into the traffic.

'Thanks,' I said. 'It's gorgeous.'

'Yes, well—' He glanced over his shoulder, raising a hand to thank a waiting cab. 'The world needs useless gestures.'

I rang Susan next morning. She behaved as if I were returning her call, and said at once, 'I wanted to tell you that I'm off to Crete at the end of next week.'

'Good, you could do with a holiday.'

'Well, as you know, I never take them,' she remarked. 'The idea of lying on a beach like a piece of Bombay Duck bores me terrifically, as the song has it. But a change is as good as a feast. And I might meet the man of my dreams.'

'You might well,' I agreed.

'The place I'm staying at is the most exclusive on the island. It's old and elegant. Like me!' The thought had obviously just struck her. The relief of hearing her screeching laugh, after what seemed an age of slightly frosty restraint, was intense. 'When are you two going to shake the domestic dust from your heels and get away?'

'End of September,' I said. 'We're going to northern Spain.'

'How long for?'

'A week.'

'Not long enough.'

'You're only going for a week.'

'But I go away so much more often, Laura. Mobility's part of my life. I don't know how you people stick it, day after day in this provincial hole – because let's face it, it may have pretensions but it is bloody provincial – it's not a wonder you're looking for kicks elsewhere.'

The inconsistency of this almost took my breath away. I had just enough left to change the subject swiftly.

'Thank you so much for the champagne. It was appreciated. In fact we bought another bottle.'

'Oh good, I'm glad I corrupted you,' she said, perfectly amiable again. 'And did the chap give you my instructions?'

'He did, and we followed them.'

'Who was there, anyone I'd know?' I told her. 'And did any of them have the remotest idea who I was?'

'Of course. Everyone remembers you.'

'What an idiot I must have been at school,' she said, but I could tell that she was pleased. She was a funny old thing sometimes.

'When are you seeing your fancy man again?' she asked. 'I'm starved of gossip.'

'Not till Monday.'

'I can't wait that long. That means I shan't know what occurred till after I get back. Couldn't you manage "something for the weekend"?'

'No.' The strangeness of this exchange, which would have been unthinkable less than a year ago, suddenly impressed itself on me.

'Did you tell the old girls all about it?' She placed the emphasis on the 'girls' rather than the 'old' which gave the phrase a different and less flattering meaning.

'Certainly not.'

'Spoilsport! What do you think my instructions were for?'

'We interpreted them each to her own. There was plenty of loose talk to go round without me coughing that one up. And anyway, I don't want people to know.'

There was one of those cigarette-and-raised-eyebrow pauses which I knew so well. 'I don't get it, Mrs Lewis. I simply don't get it.'

I was glad she didn't. It was nice, occasionally, to feel I'd wrongfooted her. After another short pause she said, 'But you don't mind confiding in *me*.'

'You're different.'

She gave a rusty squeak of delight. 'I like to think so!'

The remainder of the weekend was not without incident. Becca had a passage of arms with the local seamstress who was making Sinead's bridesmaid's dress. She called on me to arbitrate and, when I declined, waxed furious.

'For heaven's sake, I just want you to see that I'm *right*! It's not much to ask.'

'It really isn't my business, Becca.'

'Okay, if you want your grand-daughter to walk down the aisle in two weeks' time looking like a sack of pota- toes—'

'Don't be silly, how could she possibly look like that?'

'She will though, unless I can persuade this wretched woman to take the dress in all over.'

'Is it really much too loose?'

There was a heavy sigh on the other end. 'Yes! As I've been attempting to explain, it looks baggy and frightful.'

'But Mrs Arnold doesn't think so?'

'She says that's how the pattern is.'

'Maybe she's right.'

'Then the frigging pattern's wrong!'

Glyn, on his way through the hall, leaned over my shoulder. 'And a very good morning to you too, Bex.'

'And tell Dad to butt out.'

I waved him away. 'May I make a suggestion?'

'That is what I was hoping for.'

'It's not me you want, it's Steph. She bought the patterns, she ordered the dresses, she's paying. She knows how they ought to look. QED.'

'So what exactly are you suggesting I should do?' Becca's voice, though still surly, had dropped a couple of semitones in acknowledgement of the faint possibility of a solution.

'Give Steph a ring, check that she agrees with you. Then get her to call your lady and explain how the dress should be. It'll come much better from her, as the bride, and she'll be frightfully diplomatic – it's how she makes her living.'

'I suppose it's worth a try.'

'You never know. How's Amos?'

On Sunday Verity departed for a three-day International Chris- tian Youth Festival at a campsite outside Norwich. Shona came in her camper-van and picked her up at eight-thirty, pausing for tea and toast in the kitchen. There was no need for me to join them, but I was a congenital waver-off, and Shona was not a woman who provoked any worries about the age and condition of one's dressing-gown.

'How many people will be there?' I asked.

'Millions,' said Verity, her face shining. 'From all over the world.'

'Several thousand, anyway,' added Shona. 'The fellowship is incredible.'

'The music is magic, too,' enthused Verity. 'And all the worship is candlelit.'

'Well,' I said, 'I hope you're going to put in a good word upstairs for the rest of us, as usual.'

Verity said gravely, 'Of course.'

'Come along!' cried Shona, draining her tea and heading for the hall with a slab of peanut butter toast still in her hand. 'We've got others to pick up.'

''Bye, love.' I gave Verity a kiss. 'Is Jasper going?'

She shook her head. 'I asked him. But it's not his bag.'

It was a dreadfully unworthy thought, and I didn't much like myself for it, but as I stood at the front door watching the camper-van lurch up Alderswick Avenue, I wondered how much competition a young man could stand from the terrible trio – Our Lord, Our Lady and Him Upstairs.

Later that day Liam showed up. It was two-thirty, but if he was hoping to be offered the last portion of a gravy lunch it was not his lucky day. Josh was still in bed after a hard night's headbanging in some local garage and Glyn and I had just returned from a drinks party with people up the road, the proximity of which had allowed us both to get pleasantly sozzled. We were at the smart-togs-but-shoes-off stage in the back garden, eating cheese and chutney sandwiches.

Fortunately Liam was in good form.

'Thought I'd drop in,' he said, opening the can of Murphy's to which Glyn had instructed him to help himself. 'I've been to see Sinead in her bridesmaid's dress, and she looks a picture.'

'You'd think, wouldn't you,' mused Glyn, 'that brides, particularly those that are of riper years, like Steph, would go out of their way to avoid tiny bridesmaids.'

'Safer than glamorous young women, surely . . .' I said.

Glyn, eyes closed against the sun, wagged a finger. 'That's where you're wrong. With the older ones you can make sure they don't outshine you, by dressing them in something which is perfectly okay, but does them no favours. But with little girls nothing can save you because they look gorgeous in everything. Sinead will be the star of the show.' He opened his eyes and looked at Liam. 'There's a long tradition of female beauty in this family, you know.'

'I know that,' said Liam. 'And I always say, if you want to know what the child will be like as a woman, look at the mother. And the grandmother,' he added gallantly, and I inclined my head. 'Will you be sure to take some photographs for me at the wedding?'

'We will,' I said. 'I promise.'

Glyn was in Manchester again on Monday. I went into the CAB telling myself calmly that I was committed to nothing. It was over a week since I'd seen Patrick, I had not agreed to anything over the telephone. I told myself that I was an independent-minded woman who had choices to make, but this heady aura of freedom was a little unsettling too, because Susan was at that very moment heading for Stansted airport in a minicab. Her projected absence made me realize the extent of the influence she had over me. I felt – uncoupled. What a curious expression.

My first client of the morning was Stan Prentiss. 'Bet you're pleased to see me,' was how he greeted me, sitting down in the chair opposite with a glum but challenging look.

'Not at all,' I said in response to the tone rather than the content, and then corrected myself: 'I mean, I am.'

'Last time I was in,' he went on, 'I was out of order.'

'I don't remember.'

'Yeah, you do.'

'I remember your visit of course,' I said, 'but not that you did anything that could be described as out of order.'

'I lost it. Totally.'

'You were entitled to.'

He smiled bitterly. 'Mine's the file marked Serial Whinger, eh?'

'Of course not.' It was obvious this exchange of camouflaged apologies on his side and benign deflections on mine could have gone on for ever.

'So what can I do for you?' I asked, with a to-business air. As he opened his mouth to answer the phone rang.

'It's me,' said Patrick.

'Hallo – I'm afraid I have a client with me at the moment, may I call you back?'

'Are you coming this afternoon?'

'I don't know. Look, you'll have to excuse me—'

'Yes or no?'

Stan Prentiss glanced impatiently over his shoulder, his fingers drumming on the arms of his chair.

'Possibly. I'll look at my diary.'

Patrick laughed so loudly that Prentiss must have been able to hear. I put the receiver down.

'Sorry about that. Where were we?'

'You were asking what you could do?'

'Right.' I resumed my gravely questioning look.

'Nothing,' said Prentiss. 'I've got a job.'

I was surprised by how genuinely chuffed I was by this piece of news, and not only because Stan Prentiss had been a thorn in my side for the best part of a year.

'Great! That is really excellent news. Congratulations. Where?'

'It's not rocket scientist exactly. Round at Percy Radio.' He named a small local firm who did repairs on TVs, radios and personal stereos.

'They're jolly good,' I said. 'We've used them.' I realized too late how condescending this sounded. Prentiss favoured me with a look that, to his credit, was only tinged with scepticism.

'It'll do,' he said. The phone rang again but I didn't even twitch. I said, over the insistent ringing, 'Is the pay what you hoped for?'

'Beggars can't be—' He flapped a hand at the phone. 'Aren't you going to answer that?'

'Whoever it is will ring again if it's urgent.'

'Mustn't grumble.'

The ringing stopped, mercifully. Prentiss got up. 'Anyway, I'm taking up your precious time.'

'Not at all, I'm so glad you came and told me.'

'Yes – yes, I'm sure you are.' He said this so quietly that he probably thought I couldn't hear. I opened the door. On the way out he gave a nod back towards my desk. 'Better call him back.'

He was gone before I could think of a cool, clever put-down. Susan would have done it. There was a Becca-type with a toddler in bermudas sitting in the waiting-room. Well, I say she was like Becca, but that wasn't strictly true. She was a single parent but that was where the resemblance ended. I feared tears before bedtime.

'Come on in,' I said. As she trailed the toddler into my office the phone began to ring again. At moments like this I wished I had a secretary, or an answering-machine, or both.

I waved at the chair. 'Excuse me a moment.'

'You carry on.'

I picked up the receiver with my back to the girl and hissed through gritted teeth, 'Bugger off.'

'All right,' said Becca. 'I will.'

If I hadn't had to soothe Becca I probably wouldn't have gone round to Patrick's that afternoon. It was his fault. His telephoning habits had gone beyond a joke.

I rang Becca from the payphone in the foyer before leaving. 'I'm so sorry,' I said. 'I didn't know it was you.'

'You didn't sound like yourself at all,' she complained. 'It was so weird.'

'Sorry.'

'So who did you think you were speaking to?'

'A bloke who'd been pestering me all morning.'

'You mean a nuisance caller?'

'Yes.' It was the truth, after all, even if it wasn't what she meant.

'You want to report that,' she said. 'I had one of those. They can get to rule your life if you don't kick them in the balls at once.'

'I know. Don't worry, he's nothing serious.'

'Not yet,' warned Becca. 'Get a whistle and blow down the phone the moment you hear his voice. It works like a charm.'

'Maybe I will.'

I thought about this as I drove over to Calcutta Road. Patrick was arrogant and childish. But it was the same bluster and blarney that I'd fallen for. He believed he had things 'sorted', to use one of Josh's laddisms, and that made him a curiously easy target. I suspected that all of us – me, Lili, Josie from downstairs, Bridget and Jane and the rest of the bluestockings, all the members of the glee club – could have had him for breakfast, except that we were engaged in a kind of conspiracy to preserve Patrick as we'd first found him.

I walked through his front door in high dudgeon (I had graduated to a key), only to find a harassed and chastened Patrick who could scarcely remember why I was there.

'It's Peaches,' he said from his place on the sofa next to the cat, who looked the same as ever to me.

'What's the matter with her?'

'I don't know. She won't move. She won't eat or drink. I had to lift her up here.'

'She looks okay to me.'

'That's because you don't know her,' he said huffily, with intention to slight. I wasn't in the least slighted. I didn't like cats, and I liked Peaches least of all.

'Have you taken her to the vet?'

'There's no surgery till five.'

'Well, there you are then.'

'Poor Peaches,' murmured Patrick, 'poor girl. There, there . . .'

I hadn't heard the expression 'there there' since I listened to Alison Uttley at my mother's knee. On Patrick's lips it was like hearing Ian Paisley enjoining a crowd to take it easy.

'She's quite happy,' I said. 'Just leave her be and then bung her in the basket and whizz her round there.' I didn't normally use words like 'bung' and 'whizz' but gentler words stuck in my throat.

'I don't know . . .' He stroked Peaches and lowered his head to gaze into her slitted eyes. 'Her third lid's coming across. Perhaps I should give her a ring.'

Trust Patrick to have a lady vet. 'Won't she be out on her rounds?'

'We'll find out, won't we?' He got up and walked past me into the hall. I watched as he stood by the table and dialled a number.

There was clearly an answering-machine on, because he waited a moment and then embarked on a long exposition of Peaches' symptoms. I went over and crouched down by the sofa to study the cat. She didn't move a muscle. Only a tiny triangle of eye was visible. Her nose looked dry and crusty. Her breathing, which was shallow, was silent but for a tiny squeak on the inhalation. She did, in truth, look a bit groggy.

When he came back into the room, rasping a hand over his stubble, I felt a little ashamed of my lack of sympathy.

'Maybe she's got a cold,' I said. 'Her breathing's a bit wheezy.'

'Hm . . .' He gazed down at her distractedly. 'Cat flu can be fatal.'

'Aren't they immunized against that?'

'She has been . . . I'm not dead sure if I'm up to date. Fuck! I'd better look for the card . . .'

He went over to the bookcase and began pulling out assorted files and folders. Bits of paper fluttered to the ground. He kept muttering, 'Fuck . . . ! Shit. . . !' He was in a world of his own. It dawned on me that for the first time I was seeing Patrick with his guard down. He liked to give the impression that he didn't give a toss what people thought, but in fact his life was carefully orchestrated so that he presented a moving target. At this particular moment, searching frantically for his cat's vaccination record, he was considering nothing but the matter in hand.

'Yes! Feliflu!' he cried, holding aloft a folded white card. The doorbell rang. 'Get that, would you?'

Obediently I went into the hall and opened the door. It was Lili.

'Sorry, forgot my key, is Patrick there?' she asked, stepping past me. She treated me like the help – she wasn't actually rude, she just paid me no account. And I – because that's the kind of guy I am – fell in with her assessment of me.

'Yes, go on through,' I said unnecessarily, since she was already on her way, dipping for a nanosecond before the hall mirror to take in her reflection.

I closed the door and followed.

'Hi,' said Patrick absentimindedly. 'Fuck! She is out of date.'

'What on earth's the matter?' asked Lili, leaning her firm,

small derriere against the corner of the sofa and crossing her ankles.

'Six months! Fuck and double fuck!' His hair was standing on end, literally.

Lili turned to look at me. 'Any ideas?'

'The cat's not well,' I explained.

I suppose I thought that she, being younger and more beautiful than me, would also be a better person and more attuned to Patrick's feelings. This turned out not to be the case. Her perfect nose wrinkled.

'I beg your pardon?'

'Peaches.' I pointed at the invalid. 'She's poorly.'

'So get her fixed,' said Lili to Patrick. He threw down the card and clapped his hand to his brow. 'Or have her put down.'

He gave her a strange kind of half-glare, to indicate that he would have murdered her if he could be bothered. Then he turned to me. 'What do you think I should do?'

'You've left a message. If the vet doesn't call back, take her in to the surgery. It's only—' I glanced at my watch – 'an hour and a quarter till five. She won't succumb between now and then.'

'I hope not . . .' He chewed his lip. 'I really do . . .'

'Well!' Lili stood up, hands on hips. 'Are you free till then or will she need you to wipe her brow?'

'What?' asked Patrick. So he had double-booked anyway, but was far too preoccupied to pay that little problem no never mind.

'See you,' said Lili. She sounded not angry but cool and self-possessed. My own anger had dissipated in the face of Patrick's mini-crisis. Automatically I went into the hall and saw her out. On the front step she looked over her shoulder and said, 'I don't know about you, but I have better things to do.'

I made some sort of small sound intended to convey whatever was appropriate, and watched as she cantered coltishly down the steps and swung away down Calcutta Road. Then I closed the door quietly and returned to the living-room. Patrick was sitting on the sofa and had taken Peaches on to his knee. I began to pick up the folders and papers that were scattered over the floor, including the immunization record, which I placed on the seat next to him.

'She wasn't very pleased,' I said.

'Sorry?'

'Lili – I don't think she understood about the cat.'

'Never mind,' said Patrick. 'She'll get over it.' He couldn't even be bothered to make some slighting remark in his own defence.

'Shall I make some tea?' I asked.

'By all means . . .'

As I fiddled about in the kitchen I reflected that Lili and I, who had nothing in common and who had until now scarcely acknowledged each other's existence, had been fleetingly bonded in adversity. The difference between us was that while she had not wasted another calorie playing second fiddle to an ailing pet, I was still here, making tea. We had both been downloaded, but in a single bound she was free.

I stirred in the several sugars that Patrick liked, and took through the mugs. I handed him his, and sat down in an armchair on the other side of the room. My dealings with Becca had taught me how to handle this state of irritable anxiety in others – the thing to do was not to handle it, but to stand back and await developments.

Because of the need to provide a lap for the cat, Patrick sat with his legs pressed neatly together from thigh to ankle. It was an old-maidish attitude completely at variance with his tousled bulk and unshaven face. Pathetic he might be, but the bit of me that was a decent God-fearing wife, mother and grandmother rather liked him for worrying about his cat, and realized that this was the first time liking had entered into the relationship.

'Thanks for the tea,' he said, stroking with one hand and raising the mug to his lips with the other.

'My pleasure.'

'Christ!' He took a slurp and looked at me as though he'd suddenly remembered. 'Lili – she buggered off.'

'She did.'

'Shit. I was worried.'

'I know,' I said, but couldn't resist adding. 'But she'd have buggered off anyway.'

'Why's that?'

'Because I was here. You invited us both at the same time.'

'No I didn't.' He must have been feeling cheerier, because his voice was returning to normal, and regaining its customary note of robust self-confidence. 'She just turned up.'

'She seemed to be expecting you to be free.'

I was championing my rival. It was bizarre.

'She was wrong.'

'Anyway,' I said, 'I'll be off now.'

'Must you?' he asked absentmindedly. I didn't even bother to answer.

'So chances are I won't be able to come,' said Josh with the studied casualness of the man planting an explosive device.

'You must come,' I said. 'It's a family wedding.'

Josh was standing on the top landing, outside his room, leaning over the banisters. I was on the first-floor landing, carrying a plastic basket of washing and looking up at him, getting a crick in my neck. He had an unerring instinct for advantageous positioning.

'They won't miss me,' he said. 'They hardly know me. They'll be better off without me.'

'That's not the point.'

'Then what is?'

'There are only so many occasions when we all get together as a family, and this is one.'

'But it's work.'

'Only work, Josh.'

'Not so much of the "only" – double time, for crying out loud!'

We eyeballed each other, neither of us entirely sure of our ground but hoping the other would blink first. Josh had a holiday job cleaning up classic cars for some more-money-than-sense individual on the edge of town. The Saturday of Steph's wedding, he had just revealed, was the day the cars were to be moved to their new home in a motor museum in the Midlands. Not only was there double-time on offer from six in the morning to six at night, but Josh would actually get to drive some of the pampered beauties he had been cosseting, even if only to the end of the drive. It was the big payoff in every sense.

'It is tough,' I said, 'but even if Steph doesn't care, the grandparents will. It means a lot to them.'

'As a matter of fact I mentioned it to Gran,' said Josh, 'and she thought I'd be barmy to turn down the big bucks.'

Well, thanks a bunch, Mommie Dearest, I thought. 'You know perefectly well Gran will say whatever she thinks you'd like to hear.'

'You talk about your mother as if she were ga-ga. How would you like it if we talked about you like that, hm?'

'I wouldn't, of course, but that isn't what I meant. She's very far from ga-ga, but she's extremely indulgent towards you lot. That doesn't mean she wouldn't like to see you turn up at a big family occasion.'

'Second-guessing someone else is no basis for rational argument,' he said, and withdrew from the banister. The door closed behind him. The resonant patter of tom-toms and the yelps and ululations of an electronically enhanced war party signalled that the exchange was at an end.

Later in the evening Becca dropped in with the children. I knew better than to enquire about the bridesmaid's dress. Liam's remarks and the fact that she was here at all and in apparent good humour, were enough to indicate that the necessary alterations had been made. The last thing I was about to do was claim any credit.

The children went out into the garden with a bag of chipsticks, and Becca and I had a glass of wine.

'Griggs is on again this evening,' she said. 'Mind if I record it?'

'Do.'

'It's not till about ten,' she added.

'Don't worry, I'll put a tape on.'

'Where's Dad?'

'Manchester.'

'And Verity?'

'Gospel Camp.'

Becca gave me a speaking look. 'Nightmare. I mean, come on, can you imagine anything more ghastly?'

'She'll be having a wonderful time. Have you heard from Roberto?'

'He rang up. It looks as if they may get three weeks at Her Majesty's before Christmas.'

'Fantastic! How thrilling! We must all go.'

'He is cute, isn't he?' agreed Becca absentmindedly. We went and sat on the patio. Amos did death-defying things on the climbing frame while Sinead sat on the grass shovelling down the remaining chipsticks while the going was good.

'Liam came round,' I said cautiously.

'Crying?' asked Becca, entirely without sarcasm.

'Cheerful. He asked if we'd take photos of Sinead at the wedding.'

'I'll try, but I'm hopeless at remembering to take pictures.'

'Someone will.'

'Amos! I'll give you such a walloping if you do that again!' shouted Becca, barely turning her head in her son's direction. In a normal voice she added, 'He was okay the other night. Maybe Sinead's dress provided the necessary distraction, but we actually managed a whole hour without my explaining why I don't want to marry him. Or anybody else.'

I recorded Human Condition doing their spot on an arts programme, and Griggs making a good job of the subsequent interview with the thinking man's totty. It was obvious that the totty was hopelessly attracted to her subject, and her self-consciousness made her unnecessarily tart.

I'm afraid that a smile of unseemly maternal pleasure wreathed my lips as I switched off the TV and went upstairs.

I was in bed when Patrick rang. He was fully restored and up to his old tricks.

'All clear?'

'Yes. As it happens. But please don't do this.'

'Sorry about this afternoon.'

'Never mind. How's Peaches?'

'She stuck a syringe like an Exocet into her, and she's got to take three tablets a day for a week, but she'll be fine.'

'Thank goodness for that,' I said testily.

'So how about now?'

'Out of the question.'

'Why? You said the coast was clear. No obstacles, no traffic.'

'My son's upstairs. I can't think of any pretext whatever on which to get up, get dressed and leave the house at eleven-thirty at night.'

'He won't even notice.'

'He will, believe me. And he'll ask.'

'Tell him you're going to succour a distressed friend,' suggested Patrick. 'You have no idea how much I want you to come.'

'I'll see,' I said, and hung up.

I went to the bedroom door and listened. Josh had been out with a couple of cronies and was now back, but the Red Indians were still in full cry. I decided to take the initiative and brazen it out. I put on a track-suit – easy to get on and off – went up the stairs to his landing, and knocked on the door.

'Josh – I'm popping out.'

'What?'

'Open up.'

He appeared at the door, wearing only his boxer shorts and glasses, and carrying the Penguin Classics edition of *The Mayor of Casterbridge*.

'What?'

'I'm popping out.'

'Fine.' He was completely uninterested.

'I thought I ought to let you know.'

'Okay, fine.'

'A friend of mine just rang.' I considered this to be especially plausible, since he might well have heard the phone ring. 'Susan Upchurch – you know?' Josh stared back uncomprehendingly but I blundered on. 'She's feeling awfully down so as Dad's not here I'm going to pop over and offer a bit of shoulder.'

'Right. Fine.'

'I shan't be more than a couple of hours.'

'Okay.'

Unsurprisingly he looked baffled by this unwarranted flood of information. It was quite obvious he wanted me to cut along as soon as possible. Which I did.

I got back to Alderswick Avenue at 3 a.m. All was quiet, and dark. I decided with a certain pride in my own decadence that

I'd have a lie-in the next day. I was tired, but I felt light and airy as a leaf.

Because of the hour and the near-emptiness of the house, my return wasn't attended by the usual sense of my roles and responsibilities baying at me like a pack of hounds. I poured myself a long glass of orange juice and mineral water and went slowly up the stairs.

There was a note on my pillow, in Josh's handwriting.

Susan Upchurch called from Crete about five minutes after you left. I think she was pissed. She said to tell you she's thinking of you. The night has a thousand eyes, according to her. She'll call again.

Josh was up before me, to go to work on the classic cars. He appeared in the bedroom doorway.

'Get my message?'

'Yes, thanks.'

'How was your friend?'

'Okay.'

'See you.'

He didn't have to labour the point. I could tell, by the cantering rhythm of his feet on the stairs, that he reckoned his chances of double-time on the day of the wedding had improved immeasurably.

15

Glyn was due back on the Wednesday. I went into London during the day to egg my mother on as she bought something to wear at the wedding. She was a great one for dress exchanges, and had recently found a new one in South Molton Street at which top people's castoffs changed hands at relatively silly prices. She explained why this particular one had commended itself to her.

'There's another female giant somewhere,' she told me as we strode along the pavement to the fancifully named Almost Paradise, 'a rich one, and she brings her mistakes here. It's incredible how often I've found the very thing in the right size. I feel as if I know this woman!'

We went in. The girl in charge was American and greeted my mother like the second coming.

'Mrs Beech, hi, great, you couldn't have come at a better moment. I have just a million things that will drive you crazy.'

'Truly?' said my mother. 'Lead me to them.'

It was restful shopping with my mother because she was so good at it. For a start, she brought out the best in shop assistants. This may not have been so applicable to the American girl, who was the type to be up for Employee of the Month wherever she went, but even in post offices my mother elicited the very best attention.

These circumstances were her spiritual home. Given chic clothes at time-warp prices, a saleswoman for whom nothing was too much trouble, a congenial companion and an upholstered chair just in case, she was in her element.

'What do you think?' she asked me after the shortlist of

three had been tried on and we were drinking coffee while the American served someone else.

'They're all nice. The yellow's stunning.'

'It is, isn't it – terribly jolly! But I'm not sure that my desiccated old cortex can stand up to it. I don't want to look any more tortoiselike than I can help.'

In anyone but my mother the remark could have been construed as shameless fishing for compliments, but she had a genuinely robust attitude to the effects of ageing and a healthy desire to look as good as possible. She was a beauty, but a practical one. I agreed that looking tortoiselike was to be avoided at all costs.

Having discounted the yellow we were left with a choice between tailored french navy with white piping, and a shift and matching pleated coat in aquamarine silk. My mother – I could have written the script – talked her way into the crisp navy and white, and then at the last moment followed the dictates of her heart and went with the coat and dress.

'Shall I be mutton dressed as lamb?' she enquired of the shop at large. There was a murmur of dissent from the two lean and well-heeled Sloane matrons cruising the racks, and an explosion of approbation from the assistant.

'Mrs Beech, it's perfect. Not everyone can wear really romantic clothes, but you definitely can. Don't you agree?' She turned her wide, toothy smile and shining eyes in my direction. There was a look of more penetrating enquiry on my mother's face.

'Yes, Laura. What do you think?'

'It's lovely. Really.'

We took charge of the aquamarine outfit and then set off to the nearest branch of a well-known chainstore to look for a hat.

'I am not,' said my mother, 'on this occasion, going to make my usual mistake of spending more on the accessories than on the outfit itself.'

She was as good as her word. She found a plain cream picture hat and some wide grosgrain ribbon that matched the dress and coat. The most expensive part of the hat was a signature cream silk tea rose to sew on to the side.

'Gloves? Handbag?' I asked weakly.

'Got 'em,' she said, to my huge relief. 'Or got what will do perfectly well. Shall we go in search of lunch? My treat.'

Having graciously taken control, my mother conveyed us by taxi to Rules for a meal hedonistically loaded with saturated fats. 'A very successful morning!' she declared over the g and t's when we'd ordered. 'Thank you so much for your moral support, darling, it makes such a difference.'

'My pleasure,' I said truthfully.

'Peter's never enjoyed shopping. But then I'm not sure I'd want to be married to one of these men who like to tell their wives what to wear.'

'Nor me. Like being a kept woman.'

'Exactly.' She laughed. 'Though that's what I've been all my life when you come to think of it.'

'You could say the same of a lot of married women of your generation.'

'Perhaps you could.' She thought about this. 'Perhaps.' I thought she was going to add something, but she didn't. Instead she exclaimed ecstatically over the arrival of her potted shrimps and peered curiously at my warm salad with bacon and avocado. 'Remind me . . .' she said. I told her. 'It's a sign of advancing decrepitude, but I still see a warm salad as a contradiction in terms.'

'It's nice.' I gave my plate a push. 'Have a mouthful, go on.'

'May I?' She swooped her fork over and back and munched reflectively. 'Oh dear, I shall write out "Must be more adventurous" a hundred times.'

From there we talked about food, and restaurants, and the catering for the wedding. My mother was full of it.

'The works, Anthea tells me. A hundred and fifty people, all seated. I shudder to think what that must cost. I remember Pedro and I had spam sandwiches and a cake made with dried egg in an RAF nissen hut . . . I danced with a man called Tony Thrace who must have been six inches shorter than me, he did terribly well not to nuzzle my cleavage the entire time . . . I wonder what happened to all those people? Steph's having dancing too – they've got some people called the Tuney Loons, do you know them?' I confessed that I didn't. 'Anthea and David don't either, but Steph says they're the absolute thing for this kind of do. Perhaps Glyn would have heard of them?'

'He might,' I said doubtfully, 'but if they're purely on the dinner-dance circuit it's unlikely.'

'Of course, of course.' My mother waved aside her own foolishness. 'He has bigger fish to fry.'

'Did I tell you Becca was going out with one of his clients?'

'You didn't – how exciting. Is it anyone I'd know?'

'I don't suppose you will have done, but he's in the process of becoming quite famous. He's the lead singer with a band called Human Condition.'

'That's where you're wrong,' said my mother. 'We saw Griggs on one of those chat-shows the other evening. I remember because we used to know someone called Griggs when Peter was in Basingtstoke and we wondered whether he might be a son or something. He wasn't, no,' she added in response to my unspoken query, 'but your father and I rather liked him. He kept his end up awfully well, we thought, with that smart-alec lady presenter – most people look like complete idiots.'

'Yes, he's bright,' I said. 'And don't say I told you, but I think Becca's in love with him.'

'That is such good news.' My mother sat back as her plate was removed, and enslaved the waiter with a winning smile of gratitude. 'She needs a strong man, and I can imagine that chap being able to give as good as he got.'

'Did Anthea say anything about Jasper?' I asked.

'She said he'd got some new job or other working for a charity. She wasn't happy about it, but then she never is. She cannot resign herself to his not being a national hunt jockey or a tea planter or something.' The disparity in these two sample occupations was a striking indication of how well my mother understood her daughter-in-law.

'She didn't mention a new girlfriend?' I asked.

'Heavens, no. I don't know about new girlfriend, *any* girlfriend would cheer them up. Of course you know what their greatest fear is, don't you? And it matters to them dreadfully, far more than it should in this day and age . . .'

'They shouldn't worry,' I said. 'He's going out with Verity.'

'No! How lovely!' My mother was a wonderful audience, her

response to this titbit was wide-screen and technicolour. 'That is a turn-up for the books – I wonder if first cousins are legal?'

We moved on to cover the holiday with David and Anthea in Madeira. It wasn't till coffee – accompanied in my mother's case by a Tia Maria – that I ventured the smallest hint of censure.

'I gather you spoke to Josh recently.'

'I did, yes. I rang to ask you about coming up today and you weren't there so I had a chinwag with him.'

'Then you know he wants to work instead of coming to the wedding.'

'He said, and I must say I'm absolutely on his side.'

'Well, I'm not. I think he ought to make the effort and turn up. It's not as if he's asked to do anything very much, ever. He suits himself virtually the whole time . . .' I continued for a couple of minutes in the same vein, the parent from hell. My mother listened, wearing a deeply sympathetic expression. It was clear she was going to disagree with me. When I'd finished, she said, 'It's a difficult one, isn't it? But I don't suppose Steph cares a fig either way, and it is work, after all. I mean he's not just refusing to come because it would bore him to tears. Which it probably would. But he's not doing that, he's being frightfully conscientious.'

'Come on, Mum, he wants the money! He goes back to college the following week and he wants to squeeze every last buck out of this fat cat he's working for.'

My mother laughed merrily. 'But that's what it's like at seventeen, Laura! Independence is everything, and money provides it. You remember. *I* remember! It does seem incredible, but at his age I was a chorus girl, working in Paris, being eyed by men old enough to be my father, some of them card-carrying Nazis. I'm hardly in a position to preach to younger generations. As a matter of fact I think your children are wonderful, the way they go along with all these family events. They were so sweet at your anniversary party. At their age I was never at home, and my own parents didn't know the half of it! I admire all the straight talking that goes on these days, even if it does make life more complicated.'

She took her last sip of Tia Maria. Her eyes sparkled with mischievous *joie de vivre*. It was hopeless.

* * *

After lunch she suggested a show, but I pointed out that it was already quarter to four.

'Oh well,' she sighed, 'I'd better hightail it back to Dullsville.'

I watched her stalk along the station platform with her carrier bags, with only a trace of a limp, attracting glances as she went. I wondered where on earth she picked up her vocabulary – but wherever Diana was could never be Dullsville.

Notes seemed to be the order of the day in my life at that moment. I got back soon after five-thirty to find that Glyn had been in and gone out again. He had left a sheet of A4, secured by a trainer, in the centre of the hall carpet so that I couldn't miss it.

'Simon was in touch – Richard died, huge stroke. Gone over to see what can be done. XX – Glyn.'

I was quite dazed for a moment. I took the note through into the kitchen and dropped it on the table. There was some post there – last chance to buy cheap coal, a plumber's bill, and a postcard from Verity who was due back next day. She said that she and Shona were having a wonderful time and she felt completely regenerated. Then I went back into Glyn's office and checked the answering-machine. There was one from Cy, back in London, for Glyn. And there was another from Jasper for Verity, under the impression that she was already home.

I went back into the kitchen and picked up the note again. There it was – 'Richard died'. Plain and simple and shocking. I thought of Richard as I'd last seen him, walking beside the mere, a thoroughly contented man.

The phone rang. I ran into the hall to pick it up and Glyn's recorded voice began to speak over mine because the machine was still on. It was a confusing world.

'Hang on,' I shouted, and went into the office and switched Glyn off, only to hear the real thing.

'Hallo, it's me. Did you get my message?'

'Yes – awful.'

'Not as awful as it might have been. He went out like a light apparently, after a day at the TV studio – died with his boots on. Simon's absolutely brilliant.'

'Where are you?'

'I'm on my way back, on the Mutchfield road, I've just left

Simon. His housekeeper's there and a couple of other friends turned up a few minutes ago.'

'Is there anything I could do?'

'I tell you what – you could track down Susan and tell her. Simon thinks she'd want to know.'

'She's in Crete,' I said stupidly.

'I know, but if anyone can contact her you can. And Simon's running out of steam.'

'Okay, I'll try.'

'Funeral's the day after tomorrow.'

'That's so quick!'

'Well . . . to put it brutally, not so many people die in the summer and Simon wants to get back to normal quickly.'

I sat down in Glyn's chair. The nodding flower on the desk still trembled slightly from the sound of my voice a moment ago. On the wall facing me was the photo-collage, a silent hubbub of smiling faces – groups, individuals, places, seasons and settings jumbled together in bewildering profusion. Glyn carrying Becca as a baby, in Queen's Park, his sideburns down to below his earlobes; me with all three children in the parents' garden; Verity and Becca as Laurel and Hardy; Josh as one of the Three Kings; Amos, newborn, wrapped like a chrysalis in his perspex hospital cot; and with his first birthday cake – had I really constructed it to look like Thomas the Tank Engine?; Roberto hanging out from the side of the climbing frame like a star; Liam and Sinead drawing at the kitchen table; Josh doing his James Dean impression on the bonnet of the car; Christmas at my parents' house . . . Christmas here . . . our silver wedding . . .

I got up and went to look more closely at these, taken by Verity. I hadn't even been aware that anyone was taking pictures. There were several of the grandchildren, and my parents, and one of Cy with my mother. Then there was one of us being given our present by Becca and Josh, holding the album between us, our faces creased up with delight and surprise. And there was one of us together, not smiling, but dreaming – listening to Henry play his fiddle. Glyn had his arm round me, and my hand covered his hand. We stood together, but not looking at one another: joined, but lost in our separate reflections.

*   *   *

The front door banged and Josh appeared in the hall, fresh from the workface, hot and grubby and pleased with himself.

'Howdy.'

'Hallo.'

'Looking out the life insurance policy?'

'Sorry?'

'Never mind.'

He disappeared in the direction of the kitchen and I heard the poop and blare of the radio being retuned to the local independent station. To my surprise he reappeared in the doorway of the office.

'Still here – want some tea? You okay?'

'Yes, why?'

'You look funny. But then you always do.'

I came out into the hall. 'Richard Fawcett died,' I explained. Josh looked blank. 'He's an actor – was. He used to be a rather big film star at one time, and he just landed a part in a television comedy, which makes it even sadder. He was such a nice man.'

'Bummer,' said Josh.

'Yes,' I agreed. 'It is.'

That evening I didn't do well on tracking down Susan. Her message on the answering-machine had been wiped, and it was too soon to have received a postcard, so there were no clues. Glyn had to ring Cy as soon as he got in, and this call spawned about half a dozen others which peppered the evening and rendered him no help at all and the phone largely out of commission. In the end I reconciled myself to contacting her next day.

'Try the travel agent,' said Glyn. 'In fact any travel agent. I mean, how many hotels can there be on Crete?'

'Thousands,' I said gloomily.

'I mean that Susan would stay in?'

'You're right, that cuts it down.'

Next morning I remembered her 'old and elegant' comment, and mentioned it when I called Worldwise Travel.

'Oh yes,' said Michelle, having asked in what way she could help me. 'That has to be the Porphyrie. It's much more of a Heritage package.'

I filed this description away to tell Susan. 'I don't suppose you could give me the phone number.'

'No problem, no problem at all,' chimed Michelle.

They spoke English at the Porphyrie, and in response to my insistence that it was urgent, said that although Ms Upchurch was not in her room they would ensure that she called me back as soon as possible.

In fact it was lunchtime before she did so. She spent the first five minutes describing a visit to a riveting Minoan palace with the smuttiest wall mosaics she had ever seen. It did not appear to cross her mind that I wanted to do anything but hear about her holiday.

I was left with no option but to interrupt and break the news far more brutally than I would like to have done.

'Susan!'

'Yes?'

'I'm so sorry – Richard's dead.'

'Oh God.' The change in her voice was quite shocking. 'Poor Simon.'

'I am sorry. You knew him much better than we did. But Glyn went over—'

'Glyn did?'

'Yes—'

'Why Glyn?' she asked sharply.

'I think Simon called, and I was in London, so he thought he'd see if he could help. Anyway, he particularly wanted to let you know as soon as possible – Susan, does it matter?'

'Not really.' I was left in no doubt that it did. It occurred to me that she was jealous. 'Poor Simon,' she repeated, as though the digression had never happened. 'When's the funeral?'

'Tomorrow, I'm afraid. It was in the paper today.'

'That looks like almost indecent haste. Still, the luvvies will doubtless turn up in their droves – what else have they got to do all day? I'll have a word with Simon.'

She sounded so abrasive that I had to resist the temptation to remind her that Simon had just lost his partner of nearly thirty years. Fortunately for us both, I kept my mouth shut.

'I'm sorry to have to tell you this when you're on a well-deserved holiday,' I said.

'Holiday, schmoliday,' she replied. 'Who needs 'em?'

Richard's funeral at the parish church in Mutchfield was simple and unfussy. It was, as Susan had predicted, well attended, but the congregation was pensive and restrained. There was little if any 'mwah-mwah' or luvviedom of any kind. Faces were grim and voices lowered. Simon, and even Glyn, looked austere and dignified in dark suits.

The weather was fine, but that Friday was the first day of September and there was an edge in the air, as though a collective awareness of impending autumn had wrought a change in the temperature which suited people's funeral clothes, dug out from the back of wardrobes.

Glyn and I sat discreetly at the back, conscious of the delicate hierarchy of grief. Simon was unbelievably composed, greeting and seating people, including a whole row of plain, solid, elderly relatives – Richard's family, probably – with a couple of miserably embarrassed youngsters.

We sang 'Lead us, heavenly Father, lead us' and 'Praise my soul the King of Heaven', and Simon delivered the eulogy with dry eyes and a ringing voice. He said it was just like Richard to go when there were two thousand bulbs to be planted. He mentioned Richard's love of the mere, and the birds that lived there, and finished on an elegiac note: '". . . And after many a summer dies the swan."'

The rector, hard-pressed shepherd of a flock dispersed over five parishes, was reduced to the role of master of ceremonies, and had the good sense to accept it. All he said, outside the beautiful, sonorous phrases of the service, was that Gracewell was the best monument Richard could have, and that anyone who wished to go back there was welcome.

We weren't sure whether to or not. We weren't close friends, and there were obviously a lot of people there who'd travelled miles. The thought of partaking hospitality, no matter how freely and generously given, where we'd availed ourselves of it in happier circumstances only a few weeks earlier, made us uncomfortable.

'Let's just go and leave this for Simon,' I said, 'and come away.'

I'd bought a magnolia tree for him to plant. It was Susan's rose for Isobel that had given me the idea, and I half-expected to see Susan herself standing tall, black-clad and dramatic among the graves when we emerged for the burial, but there was no sign of her. Glyn must have caught my glance around because he inclined his head to mine.

'She hasn't made it, then.'

'No . . .'

'Sad.'

'Yes.'

Suddenly I was, terribly sad. Sad for all of us, with our confusion and uncertainty and lack of character. Richard's coffin, being lowered waveringly into its narrow, green baize-lined resting place, seemed to carry with it the last traces of dignity, order and discretion in a world half-crazed with the desire for self-fulfilment, whatever that might mean. Glyn tucked my arm through his and chafed my hand between both of his as though it were cold.

'Tell you what,' he said quietly, not looking at my quivering, melting face. 'Old Richard's happy.'

We took our time leaving the churchyard, and ours was the last car to pull away in the lane outside. Looking over my shoulder, I could see the bright scar of the newly dug grave, the pile of earth, the flash of snooker-table green. I told myself sternly that Richard wasn't lonely, because he was dead. He wasn't there in that carefully husbanded and measured slot – he was with Our Lord.

'I could do with Verity right now,' I said. 'To say the properly uplifting thing.'

'She's good at that,' agreed Glyn.

'I suppose those were all relations sitting at the front.'

'They looked suitably out of place,' Glyn smiled, 'so they must have been.'

When we got to Gracewell Glyn opted to stay in the car, and I got out, rather self-consciously carrying the magnolia in its gift-wrapped tub. There was a short queue at the front door – Simon was obviously welcoming people in the hall. I decided to go and leave our present somewhere on the terrace overlooking the garden.

As I walked round, with the warm mossy bricks of the house on one side and the daisied lawn stretching down to the mere on the other, I heard music. I stopped at the foot of the steps. Henry was standing near the stone balustrade, wearing the same drab clothes he had worn in the spring, playing his violin. His eyes were closed, he leaned slightly with the instrument like a thin tree trained by a prevailing wind. The tune he was playing was 'Someone to watch over me'.

I put the magnolia on the top step and stood to listen. 'Won't you tell him please to put on some speed, follow my lead, oh how I need, someone . . .'

I listened for a moment, dizzy with confused melancholy and the sweetness of the tune. It was as I turned back towards the front of the house that I noticed a figure sitting on the seat by the edge of the mere, near the boathouse where Richard and I had walked. The figure was very still and upright. Even at this distance I sensed her unhappiness, and knew that it was Susan.

'Are you sure it was her?' asked Glyn as we rejoined the main road.

'Positive.'

'Didn't you want to stay and talk to her? There was no hurry.'

'No – it's all right.'

It was difficult to explain that just as I knew it was Susan, I knew she was too broken up to approach. She was like one of those unbelievers who vaunt their atheism but want other people, in the face of their scorn, to attend church and do the spiritual spadework on their behalf. The mere thought of marriage made her lip curl and her eyes glitter, but she needed to have happy marriages about her to show that it could be done, and that her single state was one of choice and not self-preservation or cowardice. And Richard's and Simon's was arguably the most successful marriage to touch her life.

Glyn said, without looking at me, 'It's funny, I hardly knew the bloke but I feel as if a piece has gone from the jigsaw.'

'Me too.'

'I suppose we all lose something when someone dies that we like. We acquire a kind of stake in that person's survival, and when they go part of us goes too.'

'Yes.'

'Good old Richard,' said Glyn.

It was not so much that he'd agreed with me – I had said nothing to agree with – but that he'd articulated what I'd been thinking. Was that symbiosis? I had read so often that a symbiotic relationship was unhealthy, but I wasn't so sure. I glanced at my husband as he drove. His separateness, his difference was what continually surprised me. We had come together, but our roots were apart. Where we touched and empathized, we became instantly one. It was more mysterious, I thought, looking out of the window, than the typical shorthand of marriage. There was something which defied analysis and eluded understanding. I acknowledged its ineluctable, visceral power over us both.

Susan rang up later that evening and was entirely herself. I knew that she wouldn't mention Richard, and she didn't.

'I'm back!'

'I know.'

'Where were you?'

'We decided against the funeral bakemeats – we didn't think it appropriate.'

She sighed gustily. 'You should have come. I couldn't make the church.'

'Well,' I said, 'it was a fair division of labour.'

'It was a nice party – I called Henry from the airport, and he came.'

'Yes, as a matter of fact I saw him.'

'I thought you said you weren't there?'

'I dropped by to leave a small present for Simon, and Henry was playing out on the terrace.'

I could hear the smile in her voice as she said, 'Wasn't he wonderful?'

'Wonderful – it made me cry. He was playing one of my favourite tunes.'

'Which is that?' I told her, and she squeaked appreciatively. 'You're a sentimental old fool, Mrs Lewis. Did you get a chance to talk to him?'

'No – he didn't even see me.' There was a tiny, dead pause, and I thought we'd been cut off. 'Susan?'

'Present.'

'Are you going back – to Crete?'

'Good Lord no, I can't be bothered. If I ever see another mosaic it'll be too soon. But we must have lunch, I've got a present for you.'

'You shouldn't have.'

'I know, I know, but that's the kind of guy I am. Let's go and guzzle ribs at that Old Orleans place and play havoc with our cholesterol levels.'

'You're on,' I said. We fixed the time for next week. When I put the phone down I felt a current of happy anticipation run through me because Susan was back.

16

The Old Orleans in Charity Court was a rootin'-tootin', down-home, good-ol'-boy, have-a-nice-day American mish-mash, broadly Southern in tone. There was piped Cajun music, wood panelling, smoking griddles, hunky cooks with bandannas tied round their heads, waitresses in Li'l Abner dungarees, and framed photographs of the Civil War. The food was as big as all outdoors (one soon cottoned on to the lingo) and calico napkins the size of tablecloths came as standard and were (unless you were very quick and very firm) tied round your neck by a beaming food facilitator. Getting grease on your chin and relish on your fingers was a must. The message was 'Abandon couth all ye who enter here' or perhaps, 'Come on you tight-arsed Brits, and let us show you what real eating's about'.

At any rate, we liked it.

We always had the gumbo to start with, then the rib platter with potato salad and deep-fried onions. Then we generally said we'd never eat again before changing our minds and having the double chocolate, chocolate-chip ice-cream or its calorific equivalent. We generally kicked off with a gin and tonic and went on to American bottled beer.

Orders out of the way, Susan produced a parcel, beautifully wrapped in Japanese paper with a blue and gold paper butterfly perched on the outside.

'From me, to you and Isobel,' she said.

I stroked the butterfly's wings with my finger. 'How lovely . . . where did you find this?'

'I had it lying around. Now open.'

I opened it carefully, to preserve the paper and not damage the butterfly. Inside was a picture frame, about eight by ten inches. It was made of carved wood. To begin with I thought the carving, which was dense and elaborate, was of flowers, but on a closer look I could see that it was hands, a profusion of them, clenched in fists, intertwined, outspread, clasped in prayer – hands of all shapes and sizes and textures.

'Do you like it?' she asked, minding more than she let on. 'I just happened to spot it.'

'I couldn't possibly like it more,' I said truthfully, and leaned across to peck her on the cheek, but she was rummaging in her bag for cigarettes. 'Thank you very, very much.'

'My pleasure.' She lit up and beamed at me, glass in hand. 'I knew you'd appreciate the symbolism. As soon as my eye fell on it I thought, that is so Laura.'

'And Isobel,' I reminded her.

'Yes!' She put the glass down and took the frame from me. 'What I want you to do is this. I want you to have a beautiful picture taken of your children and your grandchildren – none of those unmarried fathers, they don't count – near Isobel's white rose. Wouldn't that be nice?'

'It would,' I said. 'I shall definitely do it.'

'I know it's schmaltzy,' she went on as though I'd demurred, 'but I feel schmaltzy at the moment. And I want to be a good godmother to my only godchild.'

'I absolutely love it.'

'You know what it made me think of?' she asked. 'It reminded me of your life.'

'Why's that?'

'It's a kind of muddle. An overcrowded, complicated muddle. I mean, look at all the conflicting messages in that carving. There are fights and prayers and hugs and greetings and goodbyes and promises. Whatever is one supposed to make of it?'

'I don't know ...' I felt a bit crestfallen. 'What did you make of it?'

'I thought – that's a pretty thing. Then I looked closely and thought, Jesus, it's like Hieronymous Bosch. I feared for the sanity – not to mention the eyesight – of the person who made it. Then I stepped back again and thought, it's a muddle, but it's all of a piece – just like Laura.' She handed me back the frame and must have read my expression correctly, because she added, 'And if you're wondering how to take that, it's a compliment.'

'I'm awfully glad you told me.'

'Put it away, put it away,' she ordered. 'Here comes the Mississippi sludge.'

'Alrighty . . .' said the waitress. 'Gumbo. Enjoy, ladies!'

The soup came in great brown, glazed crocks the shape of Ali Baba jars. 'God, but I adore this stuff.' Susan closed her eyes and inhaled the steam deeply. 'Mm – ambrosian whiff!'

'How was your holiday,' I asked, 'what there was of it?'

Susan smacked her lips over the first mouthful. 'Great. The hotel was gracious and crumbling, and the staff were sweet. I don't think there was a microchip in the place. There was a frog in the swimming-pool.'

'Is that good?' I asked uncertainly.

'I thought so. I'd much rather have Kermit sharing the pool and ironed linen sheets every day than . . . whatever the alternative is.'

'You could have both.'

'True, but the fact that they didn't added greatly to their charm – and coincidentally showed they had their priorities right.'

We wrangled affably about what hotels should and shouldn't provide until well into the ribs, when I asked, 'How's Simon?'

Susan licked her fingers. 'How should he be? Sad, lonely.'

'Back at work?'

'He never left. Fiona says the only days he missed were Richard's death, the day after, and the one of the funeral.'

'He must be devastated. They had such a good life together.'

'Do you know what I think?' Susan took a swig from her Budweiser, sliding me a sideways look past the bottle. I shook my head. She removed the bottle from her lips with a slight pop. 'I think people are far more devastated when they didn't have a good life with the person who's gone.'

I thought I understood what she meant. 'Go on.'

'It's remorse that sends people into a decline. Even if they don't recognize it as such. Remorse, and regret about all the things that weren't right, that they didn't say or do, that they didn't bother to put right because they thought they'd have the opportunity in the future, and now that option's been taken away. So – my theory is, the closer the couple the quicker the recovery.'

I thought about this. I remembered my grandmother dying, and my grandfather's subsequent withdrawal from life, a man defeated by grief. Did Susan's theory mean that their marriage had been sixty years of grim, collusive misery? It was too dreadful to contemplate.

'It's one way of looking at it,' I said. 'But it doesn't allow for the difference in individual responses. Some people are simply more resilient.'

'Of course they are,' replied Susan. 'But I have my reputation for sweeping generalizations to consider.'

She didn't often send herself up, but when she did she was spot on.

Having amassed a spot of credit, she continued unabashed. 'So it follows that Simon will recover well and move on into this new phase of his life with his chin well up. Anyway, I've told him to, so wilting is not an option.'

I felt a pang of sympathy for Simon in the face of this abrasive philosophy. But I also knew that it was not without self-interest. Simon was Susan's pal, as I was – she needed him to flourish.

We polished off the ribs, and the platters of sticky red bones, enough to make Verity faint, were borne away. Susan sighed contentedly.

'I shall have a digestive ciggy before choosing a pud . . .' She tilted the packet towards me briefly. 'Sure you won't?'

'You know perfectly well I never have. Ever.'

She lit up, squinting wickedly at me through the smoke. 'I'd accuse you of being tiresomely clean-living only I know different.'

'Thank you.'

'I love the autumn,' she went on, exhaling reflectively in the general direction of the window. 'I hate the spring. But I love the autumn.'

'We're still in summer, really,' I pointed out. I sounded pedantic, but I didn't mean to be. Usually I, too, liked the autumn, but this year it made me feel uneasy. I dreaded the short days and dark evenings, the hurrying through the cold, the pained coughing of the ancient Morris, the ever-lengthening 'run-up' to Christmas . . . Why it was known as a run-up was beyond me, since it was more like a slow and arduous assault on K2 without oxygen. Everyone would converge on Alderswick Avenue, expecting Glyn and I to work some kind of seasonal magic that would lift them, for the best part of two days, on to another plane of existence, where angels sang and children frolicked and Santa gave everyone exactly what they wanted without incurring the disfavour of the bank manager. We almost always nearly managed it. But the failure of the great family Christmas to be perfect made me feel it was a disaster. One passage of arms, one slammed door, one picky phone call – or no phone call at all – and the dream was soured, and it would feel like my fault. And this year, of all years, I wasn't sure I could face being the focus of so much expectation.

'. . . the point is,' Susan was saying, 'that September's the beginning of the academic year. At school we hated it, but now that we're nearly grown-up we can enjoy sharpening our pencils and cleaning our rubbers. I think this is the time to make good resolutions.'

'I agree,' I said fervently. 'I'm going to be a better person, more hardworking, and more truthful.'

'Ah!' Susan looked along her finger at me as though it were the barrel of a gun. 'Let's define our terms. Do you mean more truthful, or more honest?'

'They're the same thing.'

'Of course they're not. Truthful is like priggish little George Washington saying "I cannot tell a lie". Honesty's a state of mind.'

'That's ducking the issue,' I said.

'No, no, no. Look.' She leaned forward on her folded arms, staring intently into my face. 'Truthful is when your friend asks, "Do I look okay?" and you say, "No, you look fat and vulgar and like mutton dressed as lamb."'

'That's a death wish!'

'Well, okay, it's an extreme example, but truthfulness is extreme. Honest is saying, "It's okay but it does nothing for you. You're wasted in that." See?'

'That's being tactful.' She'd blown it now – how many times had she said something like the second and possibly meant the first? 'It's a false distinction,' I insisted. 'And anyway, we're straying from the point here. I just want to be an all-round better person.'

'Much too vague,' said Susan. 'Too non-specific. You won't even start, let alone make any progress.'

'Gosh, thanks for the encouragement, I really appreciate it.'

'It's true though! When it comes to self-improvement, manageable targets are the thing. Better to say I will only drink gin on a Monday and stick to it, than to take the pledge and be plunged into misery and self-loathing because you get beat.'

There was no arguing with this. 'So what's yours?'

'Simple,' replied Susan, picking up the dessert menu, 'I'm going to devote myself to the fun principle. For instance, I'm going to dispense with the usual empty show of unwillingness and go straight for the pecan pie with whipped cream.'

I jeered. 'That's not resolve, that's complete and utter spinelessness!'

'And what about you?'

'I'll have a fudge sundae,' I said, determined to match her pud for pud.

'See? It's easy.'

'But it won't do us any good, quite the reverse.'

'I disagree. Banishing guilt will do us good. As well as having fun, I'm going to take a leaf out of your book, Mrs Lewis, and have lots and lots of commitment-free sex.'

'Who with?' I asked.

'That's not very polite!' she shrieked delightedly. 'Are you implying that I can't rustle up a bit of zipless bonking on my own account? How dare you!' She was in terrifically good spirits.

'What I meant was, has Mr Wonderful showed up?'

'No, but he's about to. I feel it in my water. He could be right here, now, in this restaurant, scribbling a note for the waiter to bring over.' We both involuntarily glanced round. 'Never mind. I'm completely optimistic. He's out there somewhere – buying socks, clinching deals, sitting in the car wash, hung like a jackass—' I flinched – 'and steadily, inexorably, making his way towards me.'

'Here's to him.' I raised my glass.

The waitress came over. 'Some dessert for you, ladies.' She

pronounced this as a statement, as though she were serving us as she spoke. She had a pencil tied with blue tape to her belt, and she did something nifty with it, flicking it into the air and catching it. Susan was enchanted.

'You betcha – a double fudge sundae and pecan pie with whipped cream.'

The girl, a wag, turned to me. 'And you, ma'am?'

'She'll have what I'm having,' said Susan.

'Coming right up.'

'I hope to God she doesn't take us literally,' I murmured doubtfully as the girl strode away, ponytail swinging.

She called our bluff nicely by bringing us each two half-helpings, with a supremely confident 'There you go – have a good one.'

Conversation ground to a halt under the sheer weight of food. We were both defeated before we'd cleared our plates. Susan groaned.

'Remember those eating competitions we used to have at school?'

'I do – disgusting.'

'Weren't they? Because the food was so repulsive. How could we have done it?'

'It all goes to show,' I said, 'the indomitable spirit of the average British schoolgirl.'

'The spirit that built an Empire.'

'The spirit that brought cricket to the world.'

'The bulldog breed.'

'True Brit!'

'Bullshit!' squeaked Susan. We giggled. We'd had a lot of beer.

By the time we got up to leave we were feeling very little pain. Perhaps that was why I drew no inference from an exchange we had downstairs in the Ladies. I was leaning across the basin to the mirror, reapplying eyeliner with the meticulous care and steady hand of the nicely tipsy. Susan was still behind closed doors.

'I bet you were astonished to see Henry at the wake,' she said.

'Yes,' I said, 'I was rather. But it was a lovely idea.'

'I'm a terrible old romantic. And you say he didn't see you?'

'No. He was in a world of his own.'

Susan's laugh was drowned by the sound of the lavatory flushing, but as she emerged the broad grin was still on her face.

'You are a funny pair!'

I laughed with her as she joined me at the mirror. She pushed her glasses up on top of her head and squinted at her reflection.

'That's another thing,' she said. 'I think I'm going to put on some weight.'

'You mean you intend to?'

'Yes. Today was the first step on the road to my re-invention.'

'Why on earth would you want to do that?' I turned round and leaned against the basin, watching her tilt her face this way and that.

'Because it's bad to be thin as one gets older. It makes a person wrinkly. Very soon I'll look like a knock-kneed chicken.'

'To my bow-legged hen.'

She snorted with mirth and botched her lipstick. 'Now look what you've done!'

It was only on the way home that I wondered what she'd meant about me and Henry being a funny pair. But I was in no fit state to give it too much thought. I concluded rather fuzzily as I indulged in half an hour on the bed with my shoes off, that she was just being affectionate.

Josh tapped on the door and put his head round. 'You okay?'

'Absolutely.'

'Been out?'

What a little pig he was at heart. I'd heard that insinuating 'Good lunch?' line from a hundred London cabbies. 'None of your business.'

'Fair enough.' He leaned on the door jamb, arms folded, and adjusted his glasses with a penetrating look that reminded me of my father.

'So it's okay if I go to work that Saturday.' This was pitched somewhere between a question and a statement, but whatever it was it brooked no argument. I remembered his victorious air the night of my visit to Patrick and Susan's call from Crete and concluded that it was in my own interests, and those of consistency, not to cave in completely.

I rubbed my face and yawned. 'In my opinion, no.'

'What's that supposed to mean?'

'I can't stop you, and I can't make you come to your cousin's wedding.'

'True.'

'On the other hand it would be nice to think that you yourself might see why it was a good thing to be there.'

'Which I don't.'

'Apparently not.'

'Fine.' He pushed himself away from the door and disppeared, only to reappear almost instantly. 'So you're going to let me do what I want but you're going to be a martyr about it.'

'That's about the size of it.'

'Bloody hell!' He disappeared, this time for good.

Becca called to see if I'd have the kids the following night so she could go out with Griggs. I said yes – it was a wonderfully stabilizing and humbling thing to have one's grandchildren around, I found – but when I mentioned this to Glyn he told me I couldn't.

'Why not?'

'We've got the city fathers' bash, remember? I mean, we could get out of it, but you gave me the impression that this was the first step on your road to an OBE.'

It pleased Glyn to pretend that I was only involved in the CAB in order to get a mention in some future honours list.

'Are you sure it's tomorrow?'

He nodded in the direction of the pin-board. 'It's up there with "Yes" written on it in your handwriting.'

It was. The Mayor and Lady Mayoress requested the pleasure of our company at the City Hall tomorrow evening at what was described as a 'community reception' with wine and refreshments. This was an annual event, intended to promote good relations between commerce, council and town. It was the first time the CAB had been represented and the first time I'd seen myself not as some earnest, unskilled part-timer but as a serious person who contributed to the social fabric of the town. I was pitifully flattered and keen.

'Damn,' I said.

'You want to go, don't you?' asked Glyn.

'In a way . . .'

'Of course you do. But they don't need me there. I'll sit the kids, you cut along to the Mayor's parlour and put yourself about.'

I was feeling a shade touchy and overhung and decided against letting him get away with this perfectly well-meaning characterization of my motives.

'No, no, we'll both go.'

'Want me to call Becca?'

'I'm perfectly capable of calling her, thanks.'

'George Cross job, that . . .'

Becca's reaction didn't disappoint. 'But you said you could! And it's short notice – who else am I supposed to ask?'

'I don't know.'

'Where's Verity?'

'You mean now, or tomorrow night?'

'Either – both. Now.'

'She's upstairs at the moment. But tomorrow's her night at the shelter.'

'I thought charity was supposed to begin at home!'

'Look, darling, don't bluster at me about it—'

'Who else am I suppose to bluster at when you said you could do it and let me down at the last moment!'

'I am sorry, really.'

'I want to speak to Verity,' she said, like a chief inspector flashing his identity card – objections were out of the question.

I went halfway up the stairs and called. Irritation with Becca made me brusque, but if anyone was equipped to turn the other cheek, it was Verity.

'Becca, for you,' I said curtly as she appeared. A faint whiff of sandalwood accompanied the opening of the door. Her cheeks were pink and her hair dragged back in a scrunchy. She was obviously in the middle of something.

'What does she want?' This unprecedented querying of her sister's summons should have alerted me to a change in the prevailing wind, but I suppose I was too cross to notice.

'You'd better ask her.'

Verity followed me down the stairs and I returned to the sitting-room, where Glyn was looking at an old copy of *Viz* and occasionally helping himself to black olives out of an opened tin. He rolled his eyes up at me and tweaked one side of his mouth in an 'I told you so' expression.

'Sorry,' said Verity, out in the hall. 'I'm afraid I can't.'

We were both absolutely riveted.

'I have to be at the shelter,' she said in response to the inevitable question on the other end, and then, 'It is crucial, actually. There aren't that many of us and dependability's very important.'

I peeped out into the hall. Verity was standing with one hand resting on the banister, gazing out towards the garden, listening. And listening. Becca obviously had plenty to say.

'Can't you ask that friend of yours? You know – Karen? Oh no . . . oh, poor thing . . . I see, no, of course not.'

There was another long pause. Verity suddenly turned my way and I got up like a scalded cat and sat at the other end of the sofa, ignoring Glyn's suppressed hilarity.

'I tell you what,' suggested Verity, 'ask Griggs to come and visit you at home. If he's that crazy about you he'll come. He'd probably like to. With all the glitz and stuff he has to put up with I should think he'd enjoy a night in with a bacon butty and the telly.'

It was clear that whatever Griggs's likely preferences, Becca herself did not favour such an evening.

'I'm really sorry I can't help,' said Verity. There wasn't a trace of harshness or sarcasm in her voice – she was genuinely sorry – but she was also firm. 'They need me at the shelter. Hope you find someone. 'Bye.'

We listened to her footsteps go back up the stairs. Attuned as I was to such things, I could tell that her light, steady tread was neither weighed down by care nor propelled by rage. Having been caught out once, we didn't even look at each other again until we heard Verity's door close behind her.

'Has she been to assertiveness classes?' asked Glyn.

'Not that I know of.'

'Poor old Bex.'

'Good for Verity.'

'Absolutely. Have an olive. Anyway,' he said, 'it's not our problem.'

We heard no more from Becca on the subject. The following evening we left for the Mayor's bash while Verity was still eating her early-evening cornflakes in front of an Australian soap.

'You two look nice,' she said.

'What would you expect,' replied Glyn, 'when we're off to be fêted by the Mayor and Corporation?' He was wearing a buttermilk-coloured suit and a white button-down shirt with no tie. I considered this altogether too much of a fashion statement, and said so.

'It's not a fashion statement, it's a heat statement,' he told me. 'It's warm out, it'll be hot as hell in the town hall, so when I undo my top button I'll look smartly casual.'

I wasn't sure about this. 'They might not even let you in without a tie.'

'So? It's your body they're after, Laura-lou.' He interposed himself between Verity and Summer Bay and asked, 'What's your view on the no-tie issue, Ver?'

She looked him up and down. 'Trendy.'

'Trendy!' Not sure whether to be flattered, he grimaced over her head at me. 'A word reserved for the oldest swinger in town.'

Verity leaned sideways. 'You're a better door than a window, Dad.'

As we were about to get into the car, Josh came slouching back from the bus stop.

'Where are you off to like pox doctor's clerks?' I told him. He watched us get in and then leaned down to speak through the open window to Glyn. 'If this is your bid for civic respectability, you want to put a tie on. That look's sending all the wrong messages.'

'Get out of it,' said Glyn. But as we drove down Alderswick Avenue he craned to look at himself in the mirror. 'What's that supposed to mean?'

I couldn't resist it. 'Remember Jimmy Mullaney?'

'Jimmy who?' He drove another couple of hundred yards. 'Really? Shit a brick.'

* * *

Any notions we had about attracting attention, favourable or otherwise, were instantly dispelled on arrival. The place was packed. Our names were proclaimed, above the unheeding hubbub, by a perspiring flunkey. We had been given ID badges with our names on, mine with the qualification 'Citizens Advice' – there was no room for the 'Bureau' – and Glyn's just with 'Guest'. We could not see the Mayor or the Lady Mayoress – at least, we couldn't see any heavy-duty chains of office and we wouldn't have known these dignitaries from Adam. There was no one else we knew either. It was going to be a case of looking at badges and, as the invitation had suggested, networking.

There was red or white wine or orange juice, all being served at body temperature.

'Oh God,' I moaned through a polite half-smile, 'we should never have come!'

'Rubbish!' said Glyn, playing, as so often, Ratty to my Mole. 'It's absolutely classic. I love it. And—' he put his arm round my waist – 'we're the smartest couple here.'

'That's not saying much.' We were surrounded by more easy-care cotton-mix two-pieces and chainstore suits than you could shake a stick at.

'Let's circulate. You take the right flank, I'll cover the left.'

He was already on his way, studying closely the left breast of a Ms June Harrod, educational psychologist, and telling her that we needed her services to sort out our son who was a disturbed genius. I knew that he was enjoying himself, and that his interest in Ms Harrod, who was trim and politely startled, was completely unfeigned. He was, as the phrase went, 'into it'.

I set off doggedly in the opposite direction. This was supposed to be my evening, after all, but there were no prizes for guessing which of us would have the most fun. I had imagined being greeted at the door with a warm mayoral handshake and borne off at once to be introduced to extraordinarily interesting people whose approval would validate my twelve hours a week at the CAB. It would have been nice to demonstrate a real identity among my peers, as Glyn had been able to do, effortlessly, at the Guys 'n' Dolls riverboat party.

I did come across one familiar face, near the finger-buffet.

'Shona . . . ?'

'Mrs Lewis, hi there!' Shona was my age, but her friendship with Verity seemed to have persuaded her that she was of Verity's generation and should accord me some sort of respect.

I looked at her label. 'Oh, the night-shelter.'

'That's right. I debated long and hard whether to come, but Verity said I might meet some people with cash connections, and she and Jasper could cope—'

'Jasper?'

'Her chap, you know? He helps us out from time to time now. I suspect his motives are not entirely altruistic, but who cares?'

'No one,' I agreed. This brief conversation explained so much. I glanced across the room for Glyn and saw him wielding a bottle – how had he got it? – over the glasses of a merry group.

'It's a bit of a bear-garden, isn't it?' asked Shona.

'It is rather. I had no idea there'd be so many people.'

'Oh yes,' said Shona, displaying an unexpected streak of world-weariness, 'it's just a PR exercise for His Worship when you come to think of it. Pack as many bods in as you possibly can, which reduces the cost per capita, and let them get on with it.'

'I suppose so,' I agreed forlornly.

'I wish I had even ten per cent of what they forked out on this for our shelter. Still,' she smiled wistfully, 'mustn't complain. It's lovely to see you. And we all think the world of your Verity.'

'We do, too.'

'She's a real doer,' enthused Shona. 'We all know who to ask if we want something done.'

I reflected that as of yesterday evening Becca would not have agreed with this. I had a strong sense of the old order changing, and shifting sands beneath my feet.

'Where is the Mayor?' I asked.

Shona took my shoulder, turned me to face into the room, and pointed discreetly. 'Over there. I've already had a word, and he's not a bad chap at all actually. Why don't you go and introduce yourself? Nothing ventured, nothing gained.'

Councillor Ian Shepherd was not as old as I'd expected, or perhaps it was another function of getting older oneself that the mayors, like the policemen, got younger. I put him in his late thirties, a smooth, go-getting type with a snappy handshake.

He was also a whizz with the peripheral vision, because before I'd opened my mouth, and without even appearing to glance at my badge, he said, 'Mrs Lewis – we haven't forgotten about your new premises.'

'You understand our difficulty,' I said.

'It's my job to understand people's difficulties, or try to. I imagine that if we were able to move the Bureau on to the ground floor that would help? You have no objection to the Corn Exchange as a site, *per se*?'

I realized this was my opportunity to do some serious lobbying. This was what I was here for.

'The Corn Exchange is marvellous,' I said, 'but I think people feel rather exposed coming to see us there. You know, the bar, and everything else that goes on there . . .'

'You don't think they might find all that helpful?' asked Councillor Shepherd, furrowing his brow in an expression of concerned and penetrating enquiry. 'Perhaps a buzzy, vital place is more inviting. And while I appreciate the point that's been made about the stairs, the Exchange is central and accessible.'

I persevered. 'Seeking advice and help isn't a social activity. The kind of people who come to us are very often the ones who most want quiet and privacy – the elderly, the badly-off, single parents—'

'Ah, single parents,' said Shepherd. 'I must say that when it comes to the family I'm old-fashioned.'

I had the impression that he confided this to me in the expectation that I, too, would be old-fashioned, and would heartily agree with him. I couldn't remember when I'd instinctively disliked someone so much.

'Really?' I asked. 'In what way?'

'I feel we should give all the help we can to those who need it, naturally, but that shouldn't prevent us from aiming to re-establish the family unit.'

'Which family unit is that?'

'The conventional one. The one on which society is based and which the Christian religion advocates as the ideal way for men and women to conduct their lives and bring up their children.'

That did it. Verity was my touchstone in matters spiritual, and I was quite sure she wouldn't have given houseroom to Shepherd's smug, paternalistic views. I sensed that I was talking to someone completely devoid of ordinary human charity – a careerist. As he beamed interestedly into my face I was sure he was using that preternaturally developed peripheral vision to spot other, more susceptible and less contentious guests within his ambit. Becca, I thought, would have made mincemeat of him. But she wasn't here, so I'd have to do.

'Oh dear,' I said with a teasing smile. 'You are old-fashioned, aren't you? Never mind. You're young. You'll learn.'

I touched his wrist forgivingly and turned away. I hadn't a clue where I was headed, only that I mustn't hesitate. Mercifully I saw Glyn's backview over by one of the open windows that overlooked the market square. The person he was talking to was perched on the windowsill. I sidled my way through the crowd.

'Help,' I muttered, 'I've just been rude to the Mayor.'

'No harm in that,' said Glyn. 'The vital thing is to make an impression. By the way, do you know the Prof here?'

Patrick got up off the windowsill.

'As a matter of fact we do know each other, yes.'

'Yes,' I repeated stupidly. I had broken out in a flop sweat and could feel my silk shirt sticking where it touched.

'I knew it,' said Glyn happily. 'Networking, you see.'

Patrick folded his arms. He was wearing the usual shapeless jacket and cords. 'I bet your wife hasn't told you that I gatecrashed your party in the spring.'

'She didn't, no. She doesn't tell me a thing – she protects me from all life's little unpleasantnesses.' Glyn was clearly delighted with the whole thing, but I was panic-stricken. Patrick might say anything – he was a loose cannon. My helplessness was terrifying. If Glyn had to find out this would be the most brutal, farcical, unforgivable way possible. My heart thundered in my ears. I couldn't look at either of them – I gazed out of the window.

'I was lured in by your pied piper,' went on Patrick. 'Fairy fiddler, I should say.'

'Great, wasn't he?' agreed Glyn. 'We can't take any credit, he was a present from a friend. So what was your cover story, or didn't you bother?'

'Didn't need one. I came in at your back gate. Your wife was there. She handled the whole thing with perfect grace and tact.'

'Hear that?' Glyn tapped my arm. 'You can do it when you try.' I suppose I must have smiled or something, because he went on, 'You should have brought the Prof in for a drink.'

'She asked me,' said Patrick. 'But I declined. I have my standards.'

Glyn laughed – they both did – at this, and I could feel Patrick looking at me.

'I've called her up a few times since,' he went on chattily, 'to try and persuade her to take part in one of our Info-fairs at the college, but without success.' I realized he was not going to say anything really dangerous, simply to play with the situation like a cat with a baby bird. I breathed a little easier, but my fear was beginning to be superseded by anger. How dare he?

'What's an Info-fair when it's at home?' Glyn was asking, though he couldn't have known it, for both of us.

'It's an evening we have each term, not confined to the students and academic staff, but for anyone who wants to drop in. Began as a kind of exercise in bridging the town – gown gap. It's a completely different kettle of fish to this farrago.' He nodded round disparagingly at the assembled company. 'People who come have the opportunity to set up stands, do presentations, give out literature—'

'Patrick's problem,' I said to Glyn, 'is that he thinks I'm a serious, sensible person.'

'Bad mistake,' agreed Glyn, happy to play along. 'You're barking up the wrong tree, Prof.'

'What about you?' asked Patrick, whose expression told me he was the tiniest bit rattled. 'Aren't you in showbusiness?'

'Did Laura tell you that? No, not really. Those who can, do. Those who can't take their ten per cent.'

'I'm sure you're too modest,' said Patrick condescendingly.

'He is,' I said. 'Much too modest.'

It ended there, thank God. At that moment a handsome, deep-voiced woman with a scarf round her head put her arm through Patrick's and said, 'Mind if I steal him?'

'Do, we've finished with him,' said Glyn, adding as they disappeared, 'Great chap. Good value.'

We completed our separate circuits of the room. The meeting with Patrick had left me so limp that I was unable to make any effort and simply had to wait for people to come up to me. I met two senior traffic wardens, the coach of the local football club, a flock of librarians and the deputy head of a primary school. At one point I was standing back to back with Patrick as he talked to the Lady Mayoress, so close that I could feel his heat and the vibration of his voice as he spoke.

When Glyn and I eventually caught up with one another again I said, 'I've had enough, let's go.'

'Suits me.'

It was a quarter to eight, the evening blurring into dusk. The air in the market square was fresh after the heat and noise of the party. Never mind that there were a couple of winos sharing a flagon of cider on the steps of the drinking fountain, nor that an arrow-faced mongrel was defecating amongst the scattered litter of the empty stalls. A clattering handful of pigeons burst from the church tower to our left and wheeled away over Marks and Spencer and the central library. A group of young teenagers in baggy shirts horsed around and smoked death-defyingly on the corner by Barclays Bank.

'Shall we find something to eat?' asked Glyn.

'I'm not hungry.'

'Walk?'

I didn't answer, but we began to walk anyway. Glyn strolled hands in pockets, I paced more purposefully. Still, we both knew that it was he who led and I who followed.

We went round the edge of the square. On the far side by the Rivoli Italian restaurant I glanced back at the town hall and saw that someone had opened the bottom of the long windows and in one of them Patrick sat, sideways on, glass in hand, watching our progress – or so I thought. Seeing me, he appeared to raise the glass slightly.

On the far side of the square Glyn turned down a paved, pedestrianized lane that led into Bartholomew Street. We were going to cross Bartholomew Street and walk round the Peace.

We'd come back through St Michael and All Angels, past Isobel's white stone, and we'd slow down but not stop. And then back to the car, and home, as the soft glove of early autumn darkness slipped over the town. It was nice to be taken, not to have to decide. That's how it would be.

Halfway along the lane was Pizza Parade, where Susan and I sometimes had lunch. The chefs made the pizzas, Italian-style, in full view of customers and passers-by. It was pure street theatre. We stopped for a moment to watch them slapping and pummelling and sliding and sprinkling, and juggling the great soft clocks of pizza dough from hand to hand.

In one of the window tables, also watching, were Becca, Griggs, Amos and Sinead. Sinead was standing on her seat, with Becca's arm round her waist to steady her. Amos was slewed round in his, with his chin resting on the back. Griggs, who wore a baseball cap, was also turned away from us, watching. If the cap was meant as a disguise it didn't work, for one of the waitresses detached herself from the group in the corner and came over with a menu to ask for his autograph. He obliged, and then turned back and gazed at Becca. Her hair was in a plait and she wore a white T-shirt and droopy old cardigan. Sinead laughed and pointed at the chefs. Amos stood on his seat. Becca tweaked the seat of his jeans to make him sit down. Griggs gazed.

We walked on, to say goodnight to Isobel.

17

There was nothing, on the morning of Steph's wedding, to presage ill fortune. No shattered mirror, no change in the weather, no bad news in the post. In the end, Josh didn't even come home the night before. He left a message with Verity that he was going to stay over with Mad Max (the car collector) because of the early start, and he hoped we'd all have a good day. I chose to interpret this behaviour as conciliatory – a sign that Josh felt at least a little shamefaced about not attending the wedding.

'Look at it this way,' said Glyn, 'he'll be able to pay me back the twenty quid he's owed me since March.'

Verity was generous. 'He underestimates himself – I think Steph will be sorry he's not there.'

Becca – whom, with the children, we picked up en route – was predictably scathing. 'The little toe-rag – why do you let him get away with it?'

'What could I do?' I protested. 'He's well past the age or the size when I make him do anything he doesn't want to.'

'You'd never have let us get away with it,' pointed out Becca.

'You'd never have tried it on, Bex,' said Glyn teasingly. 'You were always far too work-shy.' I held my breath but Becca wore her I-shan't-stoop-to-answer-that expression.

'Do you think I'll feel sick?' enquired Amos.

'No,' said Becca. 'you've taken a pill.'

'I will,' said Sinead emphatically.

'Bridesmaids are never sick,' said Glyn, glancing at his grand-daughter in the rear-view mirror. 'Didn't you know?'

Sinead nodded. 'Yes, I did.'

It was a squeeze in the Shogun, particularly with all our glad-rags festooned in the rear windows and in the boot, but this arrangement permitted Becca to have a drink, and relieved us of the anxiety attendant on her hurtling down to Ferniehurst in the Mini with the kids on the back seat.

We'd been invited to shepherd's pie and bubbly at the Ponderosa beforehand. The guest annexe was to be handed over to the bridesmaids and their mothers for prenuptial titivation, and the rest of us would get changed and head for the church in advance of the bridal party.

The day, as I say, was fine, and Josh's backsliding had a pleasantly bonding effect on the rest of us. Or most of the rest of us.

'Where's Josh?' asked Amos.

'Working,' replied his mother curtly.

'Cleaning cars?'

'So he tells us.'

'Your Uncle Josh,' said Glyn, 'would rather work than have fun like the rest of us—' here Becca snorted – 'he'll go far.'

Amos gazed out of the window with a furrowed brow, considering this latest example of adult doubletalk, and how to pull it apart. Verity put her arm round Sinead.

'Are you looking forward to being a bridesmaid?'

'Yes.'

'You know you'll have some beautiful flowers to carry.'

'Yes.'

'Just so long as they're not one of those pom-poms on a string,' said Becca. 'That I couldn't stand.' She spoke like a woman who had put up with everything a capricious middle-aged bride could throw at her but had reached her limit.

'I can't think Steph's a pom-pom kind of person,' I said soothingly.

'I want a pom-pom,' said Sinead.

'No you don't,' said Becca.

Amos had a thought. 'Do I have to come?'

'Yes you do.'

We laughed about the Ponderosa, but it was pretty damn smooth.

Glyn and I told ourselves we couldn't possibly have lived in a place like it, but of course we could have done, and very easily. It looked like a cross between a ranch and a golf club. Built in the thirties by a millionaire shoe manufacturer, it was pleasingly proportioned and many-windowed, with a verandah running round two sides. Extending from the back, northerly wall, was what had been the staff quarters and was now the guest annexe. What was now the stables had been garages for the mogul's fleet of expensive cars – a reversal of the usual situation – and a large part of the park where he had grandiosely kept a herd of rare deer was divided into grazing and paddocks with immaculately maintained post-and-rail fencing, five-bar gates and jumps. The roof of the house was a whimsical melange of angles and gables and chimneys, and crenellations and a weathercock. It was as though up there the mogul's imagination had burst forth in a riot of romanticism that could be seen for miles around.

David had organized signs – 'Parking', 'Exit', 'Reception' – all of which Glyn ignored and pulled up the Shogun by the front door. Jasper was the first person we encountered, coming out to greet us carrying a box of lightbulbs and a plastic bag full of toilet rolls.

'Welcome to the house of fun,' he said with a rueful smile.

'All will be well,' said Glyn, taking an armful of clothes from the back. 'Isn't that right, Ver?'

'Absolutely.'

Jasper kissed us in his nice, unaffected way, took Verity's hand and led the party into the house.

'What are you doing with those?' asked Amos.

'Checking lightbulbs,' replied Jasper. 'And loo paper. Mum's reached the compulsive-obsessive stage,' he explained over his shoulder. 'Come on in and have a coffee.'

'Who's here?' asked Becca, lifting and carrying the suddenly shy Sinead. I knew she needed to prepare a persona for the asembled company. She was more sensitive about her marital status – or lack of it – than she let on.

'Everybody. More relatives than you ever knew you had.'

'Great,' said Glyn. 'I do love a knees-up.'

Amos skipped backwards in front of Jasper. 'Can I help?'

'Let me show everyone where to go first and you can. You can be in charge of bog rolls.'

The hall of the house ran from front to back. It was darker than usual, in spite of the weather, because an awning had been set up leading from the drawing-room to the marquee, which sat like a stranded UFO on the croquet lawn.

'Everyone's out at the back,' explained Jasper, 'because the caterers are taking over the world.'

We went through the dining-room, with its equine portraits and cabinets full of trophies, and into the kitchen which was, as Jasper had predicted, a requisitioned zone, full of piles of gold-rimmed plates and sealed caskets of food. Anthea had centred her domestic catering operation on the secondary kitchen, once the scullery, which was nowadays the preserve of the stable staff. It had a second cooker and fridge, a stone sink, a set of Homeworld formica units, and a folding table and chairs which this morning had been moved out to join a loose scrum of garden furniture on the – also secondary – patio, where the family were taking their ease, but watchfully, like any troop of primates alert to the possibility of disturbance. On the table was a tray with mugs, spoons, a large cafetiere and a milk bottle, and another with plastic tumblers, a two-litre bottle of Coke and a slab of Heinekens, already breached. More mugs and beakers were scattered about, along with two sideplates being used as ashtrays, and what remained of a jumbo bag of crisps and a packet of Kit-Kats. I thought, as we emerged into the sunshine to a chorus of greeting, that this was what money bought you: fall-back positions. Cash meant never having to say sorry about the mess.

David rose up from a deck-chair, cigar in hand, my father and Brian (the Canadian geologist) following suit. 'Hallo, hallo! Welcome! Make yourselves at home!'

This injunction, though warmly spoken and sincerely meant, and accompanied by much shoulder-squeezing and cheek-pressing, was not that easy to comply with. Or not for me – Glyn dived in like a kid at a funfair. I reflected how much easier it was to handle relatives other than one's own.

'What a gathering!' exclaimed my mother, ensconced in the only upholstered chair. 'Isn't this the greatest fun? Glyn, darling, come and sit by me, how are you?'

I sat down on a kitchen chair, appreciating the small height advantage that it gave me. Jasper, accompanied by Amos, retreated back into the house with his box of lightbulbs. Verity went to help Anthea with fresh supplies of coffee. Becca stood to one side with Sinead clinging bashfully to one leg.

My father leaned towards his great-grand-daughter, patting his knee. 'Want to sit with me?'

'I doubt it,' said Becca, 'she's being clingy.'

This shaft ensured that Sinead (ever her mother's daughter) went to sit with my father, and Becca lit a cigarette. 'Who do I have to sleep with to get a beer?'

'Help yourself for goodness sake, child,' said Anthea with her usual brusque, horsey tolerance, 'and see who else wants one.'

Ros said, 'I can't believe these are your grandchildren, Laura! And you look exactly the same. Do you remember Brian?'

'Yes, hallo,' I said. Brian was tall and hefty with a low forehead and a beard. The rest of his features, clustered together between two bushy growths of hair, were like those of a shy wild creature peering from its lair.

'Hi there.' His huge paw enveloped my hand but gave it a dismayingly limp, damp shake.

'Those are ours,' said Ros, indicating two well-scrubbed teenagers sitting on the grass with Anthea's basset hound, Percy. 'They do adore that dog!'

She had picked up a slight transatlantic inflection. Of the two of them, she was the twin who was more like Caro – the wildness of her hair, though obviously recently subjected to a 'do', was beginning to reassert itself, and her large, slightly watery eyes had a surprised look.

'We must introduce the two bridesmaids,' she said. 'How old is Sinead?'

'Three and a half.'

'Nadine is twelve. She's the youngest, so I tend to think of her as my baby, but she'll be a teenager in November – hey-ho.'

'Where's Steph?' I asked, looking round. 'And Aunt Caro?'

'Upstairs putting slices of cucumber on their eyelids.' She made it sound as though mother and daughter were enjoying an exchange of girlish confidences. 'Tell me, does your little one like the dress?'

'She's not mine – she's Becca's.' I glanced brightly across at my daughter, who didn't return my smile. Undeterred, Ros got up and went over to her.

'Brian,' I said, 'will you excuse me? I'm going to pop up and say hallo to the bride.'

'Sure, you go right ahead,' said Brian, helping himself to another beer.

I went into the house and across the hall. Caro was coming down the stairs. She was wearing a royal blue track-suit with horizontal white stripes on the top half. She fell on my neck.

'Laura! Were you going up to see Steph? I wish you would, I've been thrown out.'

'Is she okay?'

'She's in a filthy temper. Nothing I do is right. And you ought to see her dress, it's the most beautiful thing you've ever seen. Do go, it'll do her so much good to see you.'

I couldn't imagine why this should be so, but anyway I went on up and followed directions to the guest bedroom. A cistern flushed and Emma emerged into the corridor.

'Emma!'

'Aunt Laura!'

The effect of not seeing a relative for a while is always to profess, on meeting them again, more affection than is really the case. We embraced warmly and then stood back to drink each other in. Emma had only half her brother's looks, but twice his confidence. She was wrapped in a towelling robe, but wore a red and black hat like a flattened toadstool fastened to a frighteningly disciplined coiffure. Her tan was darker than was fashionable, almost weatherbeaten, but her nails were red and her teeth had been expensively capped since I'd last seen her. She was still rather chubby and chinless but she had put on the armour of fight, and I found myself admiring her. Like Anthea, she pushed relentlessly on without wasting valuable energy on what her mother would have called navel-contemplation.

'Going to see the condemned woman?'

'Is that what she is?'

'Let's put it this way, I wouldn't want to be in her shoes. Ugh!' She shuddered.

'Why on earth would a successful, attractive, independent, middle-aged woman like Steph want to get married?'

I tried to address the question, and not be sidetracked by its implications.

'She's in love with him, I suppose . . .'

'What's love got to do with it?' asked Emma rhetorically. 'I adore Bud, but I don't want his hairs in my bath. Have you met this guy?'

'She brought him to a party in the summer. He seems pleasant enough.'

'Oh well, that's all right then!' She honked with laughter. 'Don't get me wrong, I wish her well, I really do. Better go and be sociable.' From this I inferred, correctly, that she was going to go down to the garden exactly as she was. 'By the way,' she added, 'there's enough bog paper in there to wipe the backsides of the entire Home Counties!'

I continued along the corridor and knocked on Steph's door.

'Come.'

My cousin was lying on the bed in her petticoat, reading one of the guest-bedroom books, a Sherlock Holmes omnibus. She didn't look half as ready for her wedding as Emma did. But then, she was always smart and well groomed, so perhaps it was just that she looked the same as usual.

'I thought I'd come and say hallo.'

'That's nice of you. I'm sorry not to be down there doing my bit, but I really can't face it.'

'I don't blame you.'

'How is everyone?'

I sat down on the dressing-table stool. 'Raring to go.'

She closed the book and tossed it to the end of the bed. 'My mother is driving me absolutely crackers.'

'I gathered.'

'Oh God, did you meet her? Was she tearful?'

'No, not at all. But she did imply that you were a bit scratchy.'

'May I be frank?' I spread my hands in invitation. 'You got the better deal, mother-wise. Diana is so savvy, so clued up. She really is a dream. But my mother is *such* a stupid woman.'

'I'm terribly fond of her,' I said.

'Oh yes!' Steph moaned and closed her eyes. 'Yes, you would be. Everyone is. What a dear, what a sweetie – what an idiot!'

She opened her eyes again and hoisted herself up against the bedhead. 'People are fond of idiots. They're such a comfort to the rest of us.'

'You're being awfully hard on her.'

'I'm speaking as I find, for once, Laura. What I can't tolerate is her coming on like the doting mother of a tremulous virgin just because I finally decided to tie the knot.'

'It's hardly surprising,' I suggested. 'She missed out on Ros's wedding, and she wants to make the most of this one.'

'Christ, I tell you . . .' Steph came over to where I was sitting, opened her handbag and fished out cigarettes and lighter. 'You don't, do you? I'm beginning to wish I'd opted for small, streamlined and secular.'

'We're all terribly glad you didn't. This is the social highlight of our year.'

'Hmm . . .' She took a deep, contemplative drag. 'Want to see the dress?'

'I thought you'd never ask.'

It was beautiful – a waterfall of shot silk and beading, elegant and ageless, with long, graceful sleeves and a little round, beaded cap, with no veil.

Steph held the skirt out with one hand, and let it fall with a swish. 'Not too girlish?'

'Not in the least. I adore it. You're going to knock everyone's socks off.'

'Monty's too?'

'Monty's specially.'

She sighed. 'Laura, may I be honest?'

'I hope so.'

'What the hell am I doing?'

'Getting married to the man you love. Because you want to.'

'I don't know if I do.'

A lot, I felt, rested on the tenor of my response. Why me? I thought. Me of all people? Anyone less equipped for the part of Wise Woman of the Wedding would at that moment have been hard to find.

'Of course you do,' I said briskly. 'You're sensible to have taken your time, lived plenty of life – it's a mature decision.'

'I don't even know if I love Monty.'

'Oh.' I took this as my cue to leave. I was halfway to the door when she asked: 'You've been a long time wed – can you recommend it?'

I think it was the only time in my life when, called upon for an aphorism, I managed to come up with one.

'Marriage,' I said, 'is for the bloody-minded.'

At one o'clock Anthea dished up the shepherd's pie and David cracked open the bubbly. Steph came down, briefly, and allowed herself to be made much of. Then Becca, Ros and the bridesmaids trooped off to the annexe and the rest of us went upstairs to change.

I was wearing the expensive suit I'd bought back in the spring, with a white hat with a turned-up brim and a bow at the back. Glyn put on the hired morning dress in which he looked terribly handsome. He caught me looking at him and flashed me a quick shrug of a smile.

'Do you think we'll be able to take jackets off later?' he asked.

'Perhaps. Much later.'

'How was Steph when you spoke to her?'

'Nervous.'

'Who wouldn't be, taking the plunge at her time of life?' He was concentrating on his tie in the mirror. 'The time to marry is when you're young and ignorant. Like we were.'

There were a couple of dull-eyed news photographers outside the church, and the church itself was packed. Anthea, Caro and Anthea's crack team of flower ladies had created a fragrant bower of white and gold. Of the four ushers, two were household faces – a home affairs correspondent and one of Monty's newsreader colleagues – one was a teenage nephew of the groom, and the fourth was Jasper, (with Etonian rising). He handed us our engraved orders of service and slotted us into a pew near the front, with my parents.

'Can I help you do that?' asked Amos.

'I think this is one I have to do on my own, mate.'

'Come on,' said my mother, 'you can help me blow up my cushion.'

I couldn't resist whispering to Jasper, 'The last time we were all at a wedding together was ours – do you remember that?'

'Do I ever. You made me wear breeches.'

'Sorry.'

'It's okay, I forgive you – I had an absolute blast. And I know I was a little sod.'

Verity, praying, blushed on hearing this. She was looking exceptionally pretty in her green Oxfam dress and coral beads. She had tied a long scarf round her head, with the ends hanging over her shoulder. The effect was rather Russian and romantic. I caught Glyn looking at her with an expression of gentle pride.

Becca and Ros were accompanying the bridesmaids, David the bride. In the pew immediately in front were Anthea, and Brian with his son Brett. Someone – his father perhaps – had made him wear a navy double-breasted blazer, and light blue trousers like a golfer's. I could only hope that this was such accepted wedding gear for the young in Canada that Brett wasn't embarrassed by it. But the back of his neck, beneath fiercely short hair, was rather red.

Glyn was leaning across Verity and Amos, listening to my mother. He straightened up and whispered in my ear, 'Best man's a Harley Street gyni, according to Diana – do you think there's any significance in that?'

'Hardly. I don't think kids feature anywhere in Steph's plans.'

'Who said anything about plans?' said Glyn. This made me want to laugh. I concentrated madly on the order of service, like pressing your lip to stop a sneeze. It was the usual non-churchgoers stuff – 'O perfect love', 'God be in my head' and – bizarrely – 'Abide with me'. Perhaps Monty was a football fan.

I looked across at him. He looked elegant and rather pale, next to his best man, who was sitting with his arms folded and his crossed legs sticking out into the aisle. The gyni was heavily built and jowly, with curly grey hair and the complexion of a bon viveur. I was sure he had a fleet of feisty ex-wives, and that he'd get roaring drunk at the reception. He reminded me strongly of Patrick.

Becca arrived, accompanied by a wave of 'Eclat' and a collective intake of breath. 'Budge up.'

'All well?' I asked. 'How's Sinead?'

'Loving it. You'll see in a minute.'

'Are they on their own out there?'

'Mum, please. Ros is with them. And the bloody vicar.'

Verity dipped her head to speak to her sister. 'Becca—'

'What?'

'You look incredible.'

Becca glanced down at herself. 'What, this old thing?' But I could tell she was pleased. She did look incredible. Her simple, brief black suit fitted like a skin. Perilously high black ankle-strap sandals that were no more than a six-inch stiletto, a leather sole and two wisps of strap, enhanced her long, tanned legs and displayed perfect red-painted toenails. The suit had short sleeves, but in a theatrical touch she wore little black silk gloves with a frill at the wrist. Her hair was up, and instead of a hat she wore a flirty black silk nonsense – I think my mother would have called it a 'shush' – which perched on her brazen topknot like an exotic butterfly.

Caro came fussing up the aisle, pretty and wispy in pink and grey. 'Is she here?' asked my mother. Caro shook her head and mouthed, 'On her way.' She looked across at Monty, who raised a hand in salute. He didn't look well.

'He's not good enough for her,' whispered Glyn. 'What do you reckon?'

'Ssh . . .'

'Now where's he going?'

Monty had murmured something to the gyni, and was now walking discreetly, head bent, down the side aisle. The merest rustle of muted, sympathetic laughter carried round the pews.

'It's funny, but he doesn't look like a curry-and-lager man to me,' said Glyn. 'Maybe the best man led him astray.'

Amos asked, penetratingly: 'When's it going to start?'

'Very soon,' said Becca.

'Is that who's going to marry Steph?'

'Yes.'

'Where's he gone?'

'I don't know – sit still! He'll be back in a minute.'

Monty was not back in a minute. He never came back.

He walked out of the church only five minutes before his bride was due to arrive, collected the honeymoon tickets (as we later learned) from his hotel, and went to the aptly named Thai island of Phuket, whence he was never seen again.

It was all in the papers and – it had to be said – Steph never put a foot wrong. Nothing became her like being left at the church door. In interviews she came across as wry, cool, philosophical and curiously sexy. Seeing that pictures of her were going to be taken, she had the good sense to throw her bouquet high in the air and look up at it, so if there were any tears they weren't visible. For a few days she became a kind of female ikon, the embodiment of the strong woman taken in by a weak man, and well shot of him. She seemed not pathetic, but sensible and dignified, maintaining her integrity in the face of what the tabloids called 'Every Woman's Nightmare'. She never said she hadn't loved Monty, she never said a word against him – except that if that was what he was going to do, it was better that he should do it now rather than later. When asked about the dress she said it was far too good to waste, and she would be dyeing it black and wearing it to all the Christmas parties . . . What a woman! What style, what class! Not a dry eye in the house.

Probably only I, in the whole world, could detect the small exhalation of relief in her voice, and the tiny glimmer of gratitude in her eye.

The worst time was the waiting, not knowing. A full half-hour went by before any serious collective doubts arose. Even when the gyni got up out of his seat and strode down the aisle for a recce, he was wearing a smile, and we all chuckled discreetly in acknowledgement of the fact that he was doing his job. A couple of minutes later Caro followed. The organist got a bit desperate and began to play 'Love Changes Everything', which seemed a rather unwise choice, and Becca and Glyn got the giggles. My parents began to feel stiff and stood up in the side aisle, my father perched on the corner of a pew-back as though it were a shooting stick. Amos and Verity began to play 'Stone, Scissors, Paper' and everyone began to talk, the noise level swelling gently but inexorably, like a school assembly when the head's been called away. Brian and Brett turned sideways and craned their necks. Emma actually got up and went into the transept where she stared quite shamelessly over our heads at the south door while talking on her mobile phone.

Anthea leaned over the back of the pew in front. 'What the blue blazes can be going on? Surely she can't be getting an attack of the vapours – a woman her age?'

'Laura said she was like a cat on hot bricks before lunch, didn't you?' remarked Glyn.

'No I didn't. I expect something's happened to the car.'

'I'm going to find out,' announced Becca, rising from her seat and stalking down the aisle. Amos clambered over the rest of us and pelted after her.

Another ten minutes inched by. Glyn said, 'It makes me wish I'd brought my personal stereo. I've got a pile of demos I could be listening to.'

'Here comes your daughter back,' said Anthea.

Even if Becca had been intending to be discreet, which from the expression on her face and the swing of her shoulders seemed unlikely, we were never to know because Amos beat her to it, screeching to a halt and announcing *fortissimo*, 'He's done a runner! Uncle David said the little sod's done a runner!'

Susan, when I told her, was ecstatic.

'No! How sensational! All my life I've dreamed about being present when something like that happened, but I never have! I want to know everything – *everything*!'

I did my best. It needed no embellishment. And because my deepest instinct told me that the events of that afternoon constituted a cock-up rather than a human tragedy, I didn't feel bad about playing up the laughs.

I explained how Caro had swooned, and disappeared between the pews . . . how Glyn and Brian had carried her out of the church in a bizarre echo of the night Glyn and I first met . . . how Emma had made half a dozen phone calls in ten minutes . . . how Verity had knelt down and prayed . . . how Brett had suddenly perked up and passed round a tube of extra strong mints. I described how Anthea whispered 'Bastard!' and then used her best pony-club voice to tell everyone there'd been a change of plan . . . how my mother was heard to murmur thank

God she hadn't fallen for a more expensive hat, and my father looked at his watch and said what was the score now – home in time for tea? How I didn't want to seem too curious, but eventually went outside and found Caro recuperating against a flying buttress, Steph drinking from David's hip-flask and telling the weeping Ros to cut it out or else, Nadine doing cartwheels, Becca directing the salivating news photographers to take pictures of Sinead for Liam with her instamatic, Brian and David conferring in a sensible, manly way and Glyn, tie loosened, hearing the confession of the gyni.

'I saw the piece in the papers,' gasped Susan. 'What a rat! What an absolute shit! He'll never cast news in this town again.'

'No,' I agreed, 'I shouldn't think he will.'

'And your cousin – she sounds like Joan of Arc or something!'

'I wouldn't say that. But she did handle it awfully well.'

'Brilliant . . .' breathed Susan reverently. 'Any woman who can turn a situation like that into a photo opportunity gets my unbounded admiration.' She took a gulp of whatever it was she was drinking. 'And your daughter – that was your daughter, with the legs – she ought to be starring in a skinflick with Brad Pitt, I had no idea she was so stunning!'

'Thank you,' I said modestly. It was clear that whatever Monty's shortcomings, my family's brief connection with him had propelled me into the full glare of Susan's approbation.

'Would she like a job?' asked Susan. 'I'm not kidding – she can be on my team any time she likes.'

'She's got a shocking temper,' I said.

'So have I.'

In all the excitement there was something I'd forgotten to mention to Susan, but I put that right now.

'One other thing,' I said.

'Tell me – I insist!'

So I told her how, just as David was explaining to everyone that they could come back to Ponderosa anyway because it was okay with him if it was okay with Steph, a yellow vintage Rolls had drawn up at the lychgate, quite upstaging the burgundy Mercedes in which the putative bride had arrived.

'Uh-oh,' said Glyn. 'A log-jam of brides.'

But it was more surprising than that. The driver was a long-haired man in a denim shirt – Mad Max. The passenger door opened and out got Josh. He was wearing his usual black jeans and T-shirt, and wicked small round sunglasses with blue lenses.

'Relax everyone, I'm here,' he announced to a largely uninterested audience as Mad Max pulled regally away. It was pretty obvious to me that our son had been on the dope, all the way down. 'We got the job done so I thought hey, why not? Mum, Dad – aren't you going to welcome the prodigal?'

There was something quintessentially English about the way we all carried on regardless. The party back at the Ponderosa was even wilder and more riotous than it would have been had the wedding ceremony been performed. Everyone let rip, and a good proportion were as drunk as skunks. The caterers and the Tuney Loons carried out their appointed tasks with unshaken professionalism. I think everyone was conscious of participating in events on the strength of which they'd be dining out for months or even years. Steph was whirled from partner to partner all night. Brian succumbed early, leaving Ros to soak up the attentions of the gyni who (unsurprisingly) turned out to be celebrating his decree nisi. David worked the room expansively, telling those who admired his calm that he expected Anthea's bloody horseflesh to pay for all this. Becca broke a score of hearts by dancing almost exclusively with her children and taking Brett under her wing for a night he would never forget. The spaced-out but still articulate Josh sat on a table and generously allowed a succession of gorgeous older women to believe that they had the gift when it came to wayward youths. Emma, hat on but shoes off, was all over Glyn like a cheap suit, and periodically asking, 'May I fuck your husband?'

'You're trusting,' said Ros through a mouthful of Coronation Chicken.

'Not really – it's the drink talking.'

'In vino veritas,' remarked Ros sagely, as if she'd just made it up.

At one point, while the gyni attempted to teach everyone

Texan line dancing (he had attended a symposium in Fort Worth in July), Anthea took a group of us over to the stables to admire Morgan Misty III.

'You should see the original to appreciate your painting,' she said.

Verity, Jasper, Amos, Sinead, the parents and I followed her. As we left the unwedding party behind, and the Loons retro-rock gave way to the soft clop and blowing of the horses in the darkened yard, the glowing marquee with its shadowy dancers looked even more like something from another planet.

Several long, inquisitive heads appeared over doors, but it was Misty's we could see most clearly, pale and ghostly with shining dark eyes, at the end of the row. The children began to exclaim and run but Anthea caught Amos's shoulder and put her finger to her lips.

'Quietly. Slow down. It's after lights-out.'

We reached Misty's stall and Verity picked Sinead up to stroke his nose. He whuffled and stretched long lips, nosing around the folds of her dress for a possible treat. Anthea produced a packet of Polo mints from her jacket pocket and distributed them between Sinead and Amos to give to the horse, showing them how to offer them on the palm of the hand.

Jasper said, 'Can I bring him out for a moment?'

Anthea began to shake her head forbiddingly, but then said, 'Just this once.'

Jasper, in his smart striped trousers and braces, but without his tailcoat, went into the stall, put a headcollar on Misty and led him out into the centre of the yard. The sound of the horse's hooves rang out purposefully on the concrete and his ears were pricked so stiffly with excitement that the tips almost met above his head. He was huge – bulky as well as tall – and Jasper looked very slight beside him, but I'd forgotten that of course Jasper had been raised with horses. He leaned confidently into Misty's neck and soothed with his hand the massive nodding head. It was peaceful and pleasing to stand there full of wonder and respect in the dusky stable-yard My father linked his hands beneath his tailcoat and glanced briefly at the horse before gazing at my mother. My mother looked down at her great-grandchildren, enjoying their unspoiled fascination.

'Want a ride, Ver?' asked Jasper.

Anthea sucked her teeth. 'Don't be daft, Jass, this isn't a village fête and he's not some bombproof old hack.'

Verity shook her head. 'I couldn't anyway. I wouldn't know how.'

'I'm only talking to the end and back – go on, Ma.'

'I don't want to,' said Verity. 'Really.'

'I want to,' said Amos predictably. My father, with a considerable expense of effort, picked him up.

'You want to do everything, that's your trouble. Just like your great-gran.' He let Amos go again with a grunt. 'Is he a bit of a handful, then?'

Anthea shook her head. 'No, he's the willingest beast I've had in years. Oh, go on then, to the trough and back.'

It was funny how easily she capitulated and how Verity, given permission, stood on the mounting block and slid on to the horse's back in an easy but careful way that showed she had already imagined it, and had been dying to all along. It was as if we all wanted to see her up there, with her hands clinging on to the coarse white mane, and her legs hanging loose on his great smooth barrel, and the skirt of her green dress spread over his rump like that of a girl in a fairytale.

Jasper led Misty away from us to the trough at the end of the yard. The horse's tail and the girl's hair were two silvery waterfalls in the dark. Even the other horses were quiet and beyond the gentle clop of hooves we could make out a distant, sentimental tune, like the music of the spheres.

They reached the far end as Glyn appeared in the archway.

'Jasper gave Verity a ride,' I said.

'Against my better judgement,' added Anthea.

'No, don't say that . . .' He walked quietly up to the horse and stroked its nose. His caressing hand and his dark head against Misty's moon-coloured neck caused me a sharp pang of longing so bittersweet and intense that I had to look away.

'Magic,' he said softly. 'Magic.'

Only once before had I known the true meaning of the word heartache. That was when we had lost Isobel, and it had been the agony of emptiness and loss, pain feeding on pain until the heart was like a husk, so brittle it threatened to disintegrate altogether. This time was different.

We spent the night at the Ponderosa, but there were so many people staying that we shared a bedroom with Verity and Josh, and the dormitory conditions precluded intimacy, physical or emotional. The next day, when we'd found the story in all the relevant papers, and made the appropriate noises to the stoically overhung Steph, we drove back with Becca and the kids, all three peevish with tiredness. Verity was getting a lift with Jasper, and they'd promised to rouse Josh and bring him back with them – he had college next day.

Glyn asked Becca if she wanted to come back with us to Alderswick Avenue. I hoped she'd refuse, but was still surprised when she did.

'No thanks – I've got stuff to do.'

'It's Sunday, Bex.'

'No thanks.' She closed the car door firmly. The children ran off and she made Amos come back and carry his Wallace and Gromit bag. He did so, gamely dragging it up the path. Looking back as we pulled away, I could see her rummaging irritably for her front-door key while the two of them waited. Sinead peeped round her mother to wave.

'I hope they'll be all right,' I said.

'Of course they will. Why shouldn't they be?'

'She's on edge.'

'She's got a touch of brewer's flu, like the rest of us.'

I felt my eyes fill with more than mere hangover tears. Suddenly I was in trouble, but Glyn handed me his hankie.

When we got home Glyn made coffee and I took mine upstairs and ran a bath. The relief of standing naked and alone in the steam behind a locked door was intense. I took a long, bleak look at myself in the mirror and let the rest of the tears leak out.

Lying in the hot water, with Chopin on the radio, I thought of a game Susan and I sometimes played. We called it 'When I grow up'. We took it in turns to list those things we'd one day do which would mark our final coming of age. They were mostly trivial, like being in control of your hairdresser . . . understanding how the car worked . . . filing your bank statements . . . booking your holiday in January . . . refusing to tip if the service was poor . . . learning to do the crawl . . . and ballroom dancing . . . checking supermarket receipts . . . knowing your NHS number . . . Now, I thought, I was about to add another.

I put on jeans and a sweatshirt and went downstairs. I was almost lightheaded with tiredness, but the jeans revealed that I had lost more weight and this trivial filip to my vanity inched my spirits up. The office door was open and Glyn was standing leaning on his desk, looking through yesterday's mail. He handed me a letter, addressed to both of us, postmarked London.

It was an invitation from Bunny: *Come to my housewarming! High jinx and low company! All the old songs guaranteed!* The RSVP address was in Pimlico, and she'd scrawled a few words underneath it for my benefit: *Don't mock – I'm going to make it fashionable again. B.x.* I smiled as I went into the kitchen and tuned back into Classic FM. I poured myself another coffee from the jug and put the mug in the microwave for a few seconds. The bleeps of the timer coincided with the phone ringing.

Glyn picked it up. I carried my coffee into the sitting-room and sat on the sofa. Sunshine poured in. The tears had drained away now, and tiredness made me calm. The lilting phrases of Chopin rose and fell conversationally in the kitchen. In a moment Glyn would come and sit in here with me, and it would be the first moment of the rest of our lives. Susan was right. Fine resolutions began with small steps.

I heard him put the phone down, and turned as he appeared in the doorway.

'That was Bex – I'm going to go over there.'

'What?'

He came and stood looking down at me, already holding the car-keys. 'Okay? I shan't be long.'

'What's the matter?'

'Mini won't start. It's probably only plugs, but the neighbours aren't there and she's stuck—'

'Can't she wait?'

'Probably, but she's all ready to take the kids swimming, and it won't take a moment.'

'I've heard that before.' I was beginning to sound querulous. 'The others will be back soon.'

He sat down next to me. 'I'm sorry . . . we don't get a lot of peace, do we? But then we never asked for it.'

'She said she had things to do – why does she suddenly need to go to the pool?'

He shrugged. 'Search me. Does it matter? Maybe this is what she had in mind.'

'And when Becca wants something, of course, we all have to jump,' I said waspishly, but Glyn only laughed.

'She wasn't being like that. She said she wouldn't have rung if the kids hadn't been all wound up to go—'

'Very touching.'

He stood up. 'I'm off.'

'Glyn!'

'What?'

I tried to recapture my mood of a few minutes earlier. 'Don't go. Please.'

'What is this, Laura-lou, the Ides of March?'

'No, but we get so little time alone together—'

'That's families.'

'They're grown-up!'

He leaned over me. 'They must like us. And anyway Amos and Sinead aren't grown-up and they want to go swimming. I've said I'll go, now, I'm not going to let them down.'

'What about me?' It was almost a wail.

'I'll see you when I get back.'

Something, as they say, snapped. I stood up and yelled, 'Don't bet on it!'

He turned in the doorway. 'What?'

'Just say no to Becca!'

'I've already said yes.'

Perhaps, even at that stage, if I'd been able to keep it simple, to tell him I loved him, to say that my need was greater than Becca's, it could have ended there. The trouble was I wanted him to know without being told. Looking back, I believe he did understand, but this was grown-up time and the responsibility was mine. We confronted each other across the room.

'You know your trouble?' I said coldly. 'You're for peace at any price.'

'What?' He looked suddenly pale. 'I don't understand – I don't know what you're accusing me of.'

'I'm sick to death of you emerging from every situation smelling of roses because you choose to take the soft option.'

'Laura – don't talk to me like that!' It wasn't a reprimand, but a savage plea, full of anguished resentment. It was like being on some ghastly white-knuckle ride. I was out of control and unable to stop.

'When have you ever been firm, taken a strong line, protected us?'

There was one of those shrill, terrible silences in which my words, a shameful echo of Susan's, reverberated in the air between us. A mockingly beautiful piano sonata rose and fell in the background. It was awful.

'Us?' he said. 'What was I supposed to be protecting you all from?'

'Ourselves!' I turned away because I couldn't bear to look at the pain I'd inflicted for another second.

I believe Glyn said something else, quietly, but I wasn't interested in hearing it. I went, before I could do any more damage. I brushed past him, picked up my keys from the hall and left him standing amidst the wreckage of our grown-up, peaceful Sunday afternoon.

In my own defence I should say that I went first to Susan's. Something told me that she would set me straight – that she would tell me what I needed to hear without fear or favour. Because in the last analysis we each of us wanted the other to win through – to do the right thing. *Schadenfreude* wouldn't come into it when the chips were down. Susan wanted to look across the great divide and see my flag flying bravely in the sunlight. I wanted her to tell me what to do with all the astringency at her command.

But she wasn't there. It was as though she had slammed the door in my face just as I had slammed it in Glyn's. I returned to the Morris and sat there, realizing through a mist of self-pity that I took Susan for granted.

If she had been there I wouldn't have gone near Patrick. If Bunny, or Lucilla, or Mijou – or even, God help me, Annette – had lived anywhere within striking distance, believe me, I would have sought them out instead. It even crossed my mind to hack out to Mutchfield and beat on the door of Gracewell to speak to poor Simon, but there were still sufficient shreds of pride left to prevent me. Instead I drove to Calcutta Road.

Guilt turns the most reasonable person – which even in my calmer moments I didn't consider myself to be – into a raving egomaniac incapable of believing that the world revolves around anything but her own discomfort. I'd left my key to Patrick's at home in my handbag. When no one answered the door here either, I leaned on the bell like an Italian cabbie on his horn, as if the shrill, futile sound might eventually reach him, wherever he was.

Josie came out of the basement and halfway up the area steps.

'He's out.'

'So I gather.'

'Sorree,' she said, with an apologetic grimace. That one word told me how desperate, and how desperately pathetic, I must seem. 'He's been gone since before lunch so I daresay he'll be back soon,' she added. 'Would you like a cup of tea?'

'No. Thank you.'

'Okay.' She went down a couple of steps and then peered up at me again. 'Are you all right?'

'Yes thanks.'

'I'm sure he'll be back soon . . .' she reiterated vaguely, embarrassed, no doubt, by the whole encounter.

As I sat at the wheel, trying to compose myself sufficiently to turn the key in the ignition, I saw Patrick in the rear-view mirror. He was strolling along the pavement with his leisurely, slightly duck-footed gait, two fat books under one arm and a supermarket carrier dangling from the other hand. I transferred my gaze from him to my own reflection, and it was not comforting – I looked exhausted, puffy, red-eyed, and every last unforgiving second of my age. There was no hiding place.

I was in the act of starting the engine when he knocked on the window. He put the carrier bag on the ground and made winding-down motions. I did so and he peered in at me.

'What are you doing here?'

'Passing by.' You could say anything to Patrick and he accepted it – he didn't care enough not to.

'Want to come in?' I shook my head. He was as he'd been when I first met him, in Sunday mode, unshaven and probably unwashed. His breath smelled of beer and fags. There was something written in biro on the back of his left hand. The fingers of his right tapped out a tattoo on the roof of the car.

'During the week?' he asked. 'Wednesday?'

'All right.'

He terminated the tattoo with a brisk tap. 'See you then.'

When I got home the others were back, as I'd predicted. Josh was hogging the phone, but looked up long enough to say, 'There's a message on the answerphone for you. And Dad left this.' He handed me a yellow stick-it.

I read it quickly, and went into the office to play the message. It was from Susan.

'This may not make the papers,' she announced, her voice bubbling over with relish, 'but it's definitely news. Give me a ring for the trailer and I promise to present the main feature over lunch . . .'

I called her on the fax phone. She picked it up after three rings and said, immediately, without asking who it was, 'Sorry to disturb the serenity of a family Sunday, but I simply had to tell you, I met this man!'

After five minutes during which she scarcely drew breath, I replaced the receiver with her shriek of triumph ringing in my ears.

I re-read Glyn's note: *Laura – I've gone over to sort out Becca's car. If no joy I'll take them to the pool. Be back soon. Glyn.*

I wasn't sure if the last sentence was a promise or a request.

The car didn't respond to treatment, and Glyn did, of course, take them swimming. When he got back we didn't exactly behave as if nothing had happened, but we let the matter rest, like an unopened parcel left in the corner of the room. I remember I fell asleep quickly, but slept badly, with one confused dream following on another. The next morning, with Josh's return to college for the autumn term and Glyn's early departure for two days of meetings in Newcastle, there was no opportunity to talk.

I'd had one chance, and blown it. My second would come on Wednesday. After lunch.

I pity the poor souls (whoever they were – I can't remember) who came to me for advice that morning. It was a chronic case of 'Physician, heal thyself'. I went through the motions, but my mind was elsewhere and my heart wasn't in it. And I was poor company for Susan at the Tiffin House, though that scarcely mattered because she was on such a roll herself. My farewell to Patrick more than made up for everything else. Copybook stuff, and all his own fault – if he'd washed a bit more often I'd never have been able to read Susan's phone number on the back of his hand . . . The only thing I lacked was a brass band playing as I marched down the road to the car.

I threw his corkscrew and bottle-opener into a skip on the way home.

What I hoped to find at Alderswick Avenue was a house busy with independent, uncaring life. I was like a child who leaves a warm bed for the thrilling, cold terror of a nocturnal exploration and tries, on her return, to slip into the exact same cosy space she left behind, to make believe the night-fright never happened. Glyn would be back from Newcastle – I wanted to catch his eye across our crowded life, to let him know that I was back where I belonged . . .

But it wasn't to be. There was no comforting biological sludge to burrow back into. No family, no grandchildren. No Glyn. The house was empty.

Its emptiness was a slap in the face, the silence intense and unforgiving. Life had gone on without me. There was no note, and the answering-machine was not on. Everywhere was untidy.

In the kitchen there were unwashed plates and glasses on the
table and the draining-board, and the garden door stood wide
open. In the sitting-room some books of Josh's – *Adam Bede*, *A
Companion to the Metaphysicals*, *To the Lighthouse* – lay sprawled on
the floor, with a lined notepad and a chewed biro. The CD player
was on, though the disc – Human Condition – had finished. There
was a footprint on the notepad.

I went upstairs and changed. The repetitive mewing of a Suzuki
violin class filtered through from next door. Starkle, starkle, little
twink. From our window I could see next-door's garden, an
immaculate micro-landscape of curving lawns and paths, with
islands of patio and border, and a cupola still, in mid-September,
frothing with old-fashioned roses. It had been a good year for
the roses.

I went back downstairs to begin on the kitchen. On the way I
glanced into Verity's room. Something was different – the room
was so tidy and so sparse that small changes were instantly
noticeable. I stepped in and looked around and almost at once
I could see the ghost of a mark on the wall over the bed where
the picture of Our Lady had been removed. The wooden crucifix
that usually stood on the bedside table was gone, too.

Stupidly, I thought for a moment of burglars. But that was
plainly ridiculous. Neither the picture nor the crucifix had any
intrinsic value, and how many petty criminals had turned to
Jesus? Besides which all the eminently pinchable – and saleable
– technology was still in place, in spite of the wide-open back
door and windows. I decided she must have taken the things to
the shelter.

Downstairs I went into the garden for a moment. It had
its usual well-used and not quite kept-up-to-scratch air. But
summer was nearly over and what wasn't done now would
wait till the spring. I pulled off a few deadheads, and in
doing so noticed that 'Isobel', perhaps encouraged by next
door's superabundance, had a few unprecedented late buds,
just starting to open. That reminded me that I still hadn't
taken a picture to put in the frame Susan had given me.
The conditions hadn't been right, but now they were, and I
would do it. In the kitchen I did not, as I normally would
have done, turn on the radio. I felt an almost susperstitious

unwillingness to break the silence. I seemed to be waiting for something.

About half an hour later – it was seven minutes to seven – the phone rang.

It was Glyn, speaking on the mobile.

'Laura, I'm so glad you're back.' His voice was easy and light.

'Where are you?' I asked.

'I'm at Parkfield,' he replied. It was the larger of the two local hospitals. 'We all are. Don't worry.'

Futile advice. All I could say was, 'Oh God . . .'

'No, I mean it. Sinead's had an accident. She's going to be all right. I didn't leave a message or a note because I didn't want to drive you crazy before I had something concrete to tell you . . . Laura-lou?'

I had flopped down on the chair. My face felt cold, my hands were clammy. 'What happened?'

'She baled out of the car without looking, on the road side, and another car hit her. It wasn't the driver's fault – not anybody's fault – but she was bowled along a bit. She's pretty battered, but it could have been a hell of a lot worse.'

'Battered?' My voice was sharp with fear. 'But I mean – how bad is she?'

'She bounced along on the bonnet for about fifty yards before she hit the ground. Actually that probably saved her. She's got a couple of something they call depressed fractures of the skull, and some fairly horrific cuts and bruises, but they've put her through the scanner and she will be perfectly okay in time.'

I didn't know, nor dared to ask, what I should make of that 'in time'. Terrifying visions of wheelchairs, clinics and repeated surgery filled my mind. Sinead was so small . . .

'There's no brain damage,' said Glyn. 'She will be okay. She's not in intensive care, even.'

'I'm coming now,' I said.

'Are you okay to drive? Do you want me to come and pick you up?'

'I'm okay.'

'It's C2, the main children's ward on the ground floor. Take care then. Laura . . .'

'Yes?'

'Be warned, she does look pretty grim – but she will be all right.'

That was the third time he'd said that. Was he protesting too much, repeating it for his own benefit as much as mine?

When I put the phone down my panic translated into a peculiar form of manic energy, like that which accompanies the onset of labour. I finished the washing-up, locked the garden door, closed the windows, tidied the sitting-room and turned on the answering-machine. It only took about ten minutes, but all the same I may have been prevaricating a little – I both did and did not want to be at the hospital. I was afraid of what I'd see there, and of other people's reactions. Did Liam, for instance, know what had happened? My parents? The thought of Becca's reaction terrified me. Had the accident, by any stretch of imagination, been her fault? And what if they were wrong about Sinead?

The drive across town through the gently gathering evening to Parkfield was nightmarish. Every light was red, every driver a learner, every pedestrian a halfwit. I'd never been so conscious of the ordinary, quotidian weave of other people's lives: people walking home, sitting in cars, catching the supermarket, buying papers, eating, drinking, jogging, cycling . . . all enviably carefree, it seemed to me. I tried to tell myself that it probably wasn't so – that there must be divorces, illnesses, beatings, accidents, geriatric parents and handicapped spouses – but as usual, thinking about other people's distress did nothing to alleviate my own. In my mind's eye I ran the imagined sequence of events over and over again like an action replay. I saw Becca in the front seat, checking her face in the mirror before finally turning off the ignition and with it the radio. Sinead seeing someone the other side – one of Karen's lot perhaps, or the children from next door. The wide-eyed smile, the wave, the push on the door (which didn't have childlocks), and her swift, happy leap into the path of the oncoming car . . . Why hadn't she had her seatbelt on? But why worry about that now? I needed to blame someone, because I hadn't been there. I'd been with Patrick, so it couldn't have been my fault – could it? I felt as if the whole thing was retribution, visited on the most innocent, for my wrongdoing. If I had been at home the whole complex chemistry of the afternoon would have been different, and this might not have happened.

I left the car parked illegally just outside the main hospital entrance. The woman on reception directed me to C2 – through the area known bizarrely as the Central Plaza, past the lifts, and turn right through swing-doors. As I approached the doors Glyn and Josh came the other way. Inconsequentially, I noticed for the first time that Josh was now taller than his father. Glyn took my hand and kissed my cheek. His skin felt cool, I remembered his voice on the phone. There was a kind of lightness and sureness about him which was in stark contrast to the fiercely scowling Josh.

'Did you manage to park all right?'

'Not really. Does it matter?'

'No point in making difficulties for ourselves. Got the keys?' I handed them over, and Glyn passed them to Josh. 'Find a space for Mum's car, can you?'

'Thanks, love.' I caught Josh's arm. 'Are you okay?'

'Sure.' He didn't catch my eye but he made a small awkward movement which resulted in his hand touching mine, and I let him go.

'Did you see Roberto with Amos?' asked Glyn, holding the swing-door. 'They went to get something to eat.'

'No. Roberto's here?'

'He just showed up – Becca got Nathan to call the theatre and run him up here.'

'What about his show?'

'It'll go on. It's good that he's here, for Amos.'

'Yes.'

We walked up the ward. On either side were a small kitchen, some lavatories, a sluice, a laundry room and some bathrooms. There was also a visitors' lounge with chairs upholstered in the obligatory ginger and khaki tweed, a sign thanking patrons for not smoking, and a television talking to itself. Further along, the ward opened out and there were two nurses behind a desk in an area off which four bays opened. A woman in jeans, a parent, obviously, walked past us carrying some magazines and a bottle of lemonade in a carrier bag. She and Glyn greeted each other.

He spoke to one of the nurses. 'Heather, this is my wife.'

'Hallo,' said Heather. 'If you're going to Sinead I'll come with you, it's vital functions every twenty minutes at the moment.

Bad as air travel,' she added gaily over her shoulder, 'she won't get a moment's peace!'

Glyn laughed briefly, and didn't catch my eye.

Sinead was currently the only patient in a four-bedded room. There were other people there – I dimly registered Becca, at the head of the bed, and Verity perched on the very edge of a chair. Someone kissed my cheek as Heather went briskly about her business, and Glyn gripped my elbow and said, 'It's not as bad as it looks.'

Just as well, for our grand-daughter looked as though she had no right to be alive. If I hadn't known this was Sinead I wouldn't have recognized her. Where she wasn't black and purple she was red. Her face and head were distorted, as though they were made of plasticine and had been pushed by some gigantic thumb. Her eye-sockets were so swollen that only the thin, blood-encrusted line of her lids marked the position of her eyes, and where one was finely slitted, like a sleeping cat's, the sliver of eyeball showed a horrific, unnatural scarlet. Her nut-brown hair was greasy and dark, and some of it had been cut away above her left ear. There was blood bubbling stickily, with her shallow breathing, at the edges of her nostrils and the corners of her mouth. Bloody saliva and mucus had left pink stains on the pillow and the sheet, and her hands, lying on the checked bedspread, were rimmed with blood. A frame held the bedclothes away from her legs. She was on a drip. It was hard to believe that Sinead was not damaged beyond repair.

Glyn put his arm round my waist. 'Say hallo, she can hear you.'

I couldn't find my voice. Heather, taking Sinead's pulse, said, 'She's a lot prettier now than she was a couple of hours ago, isn't that right, Mr Lewis?' Glyn made some vague noise of assent. 'And she'll be a lot prettier this time tomorrow by the time we've finished with her.'

Becca said. 'Granny's here, Sinead.' She looked up at me commandingly. 'Mum?'

I leaned forward. I'd never felt less adequate to a task in my life. 'Hallo, darling.' I cleared my throat. 'Poor you, you are in a mess. But you're going to be fine.'

The liquid red eye opened a fraction more and the swollen

lips moved. 'She's all there,' said Heather. 'Stand by for fireworks while I take her temperature.'

I wouldn't have called them fireworks exactly, but Sinead wasn't happy. Her head twitched from side to side and she made little whimpering, gargling sounds in her throat. Becca held her hand and tried to soothe her without success. I found it very hard to watch. As I averted my eyes I saw that the missing picture of Our Lady stood propped against the water carafe on the bedside locker. Verity was holding the wooden crucifix in her clasped hands. I caught her eye and she gave me a tense smile, jerking the crucifix in a miniature version of what footballers do with the FA Cup.

By the time Heather took the thermometer out, Sinead was crying – a faint, lost mewing that seemed to come from miles away.

'Good girl,' said Heather. She looked brightly at the rest of us. 'That's a very good sign. All the normal reactions.'

I said, 'Her head looks out of shape . . .'

'So would yours if you had two depressed fractures,' replied Heather. 'But a child's skull is amazingly resilient. It'll pop back into shape like a plastic bottle. By the end of the week you won't know the difference.'

Sinead began to retch. Heather picked up a stainless-steel bowl from the floor and handed it to Becca. 'There you go, Mum. All yours.' She flashed me a collusive she'll-manage sort of look, and rustled away.

I half-expected Becca to hand the bowl to me, or Verity, or at the very least to flinch, but she took it, and lifted her daughter's head as she spewed up a terrifying quantity of dark liquid spattered with tadpoles of congealed blood. I watched with appalled respect. When Sinead had finished, Verity said, 'I'll get rid of that for you.'

'Thanks.'

Verity took the bowl, which Becca had covered with a hospital hand-towel, and disappeared with it. I sank down on the chair she'd vacated and watched as Becca dabbed the worst of the mess off Sinead's chin and neck. Our daughter's blonde hair was scraped back into an elastic band, and the only traces of make-up were shadows of smudged mascara which accentuated her hollow eyes. Her pale face looked older, and wiser – this was a stern, womanly Becca, in control and getting on with it. She did not look as if she'd been crying, and her hands were steady.

Glyn asked, 'Can I get anyone anything – tea or coffee?'

'I could murder a Coke,' said Becca, going to rinse out the facecloth in the basin.

'Tea,' I said. 'Two sugars.'

'Coming right up.'

As he was about to go Becca added, 'I don't want Amos to be too late, he's got school tomorrow. If you see them, can you ask Roberto to bring him along here?'

When Glyn had gone I sat quietly for a moment while Becca soothed Sinead back into the relative calm of her semi-conscious trance.

'Have you told Liam?' I asked.

'Of course, first of all.'

I felt myself gently reproved. 'Is he here?'

'Jasper's gone to pick him up from the workshop.'

Another couple of minutes went by. Gradually, now that the initial shock had worn off, I was aware of the rest of the ward – the brisk comings and goings of the nurses in the central area, the slightly less purposeful movements of worried parents in unfamiliar surroundings, voices in one of the other wards, a toddler crying, the distant chat of the TV. Life went on. I felt a little more able to function.

'Becca, it must have been the most terrible shock – seeing what happened.'

She leaned her elbows on the edge of the bed, staring levelly across at me. 'I tell you, Mum . . . I never want to go through that again as long as I live. I thought she was dead. There was blood coming out of her mouth, and her eyes were open.'

I didn't want to dwell on this image – I had to ask about practical things, the order of events.

'Dad said it wasn't the driver's fault.'

'No,' said Becca baldly. 'It was my fault. I told her to put her belt on instead of doing it myself. I hadn't even started the engine.'

Relief overcame shock with dizzying speed. 'But you would have put it on . . .'

'Yes. Eventually. But I shan't leave it to chance again. She and

Amos were horsing around, not very seriously, and she jumped out of the car to annoy him.'

'Is Amos all right?'

'He was very shocked and weepy to begin with. But Roberto's been a star.'

'And the driver?'

'I felt sorry for her. It must have been ghastly, and there was no one to hold her hand. I got Dad to give her a ring and put her mind at rest.' She stroked Sinead's sticky hair and shot me a sidelong look that contained a glint of the old, bellicose Becca. 'You should have seen the car.'

Verity brought the clean bowl back, and went to look out for Jasper and Liam.

Glyn returned with the drinks, closely followed by Roberto and Amos. Amos went and clambered on Becca's knee, and Roberto took my hands and kissed me on both cheeks.

As Becca began giving Roberto a stream of instructions about the house, the key, and getting Amos to school the next day, Glyn went and sat down on the empty bed next to Sinead's. He looked absolutely bushed, his face dragged down with tiredness. I remembered he'd driven down from Newcastle this afternoon and must only just have got back when this happened.

'I expect this is against the rules,' he said. 'But if I don't sit down I'll need hospital attention anyway.'

Becca hugged and kissed Amos. 'Say goodnight to Sinead.'

'She can't hear me.'

'How do you know?'

'Night, Sinead.' He didn't look at his sister.

'What's the plan?' I asked. 'Can we help?'

'We're going home, aren't we?' said Roberto, answering me but addressing Amos. He had scribbled a list on a page from Becca's diary, and consulted it. 'We're going to pack a bag for Sinead, and get you ready for school.'

'Will you be all right, Roberto?' I asked. 'Are you sure you wouldn't like Amos to come to us?'

'He'll be fine with his daddy,' said Roberto, making the point with an unexpected elegance which robbed it of any potential sting. 'I've got two days off – I owe it to my understudy.'

Becca got up. 'It's a kind offer, Mum, but Amos is better

in his own bed. Perhaps you guys could collect him from
school tomorrow?' she added, handing us a kindly sop to our
grandparental pride. 'I'll come and see you off.'

We said goodbye to them and watched as Amos ran off down
the ward towards the distant swing-doors, in front of his parents.
Roberto put his arm round Becca and she dipped her head on to
his shoulder for a moment.

'How will they get back?' I asked. My mind seemed to be
fighting shy of the important stuff and latching hysterically on
to the inessentials.

'In a taxi,' said Glyn.

'That'll cost.'

'I offered to pay, but Roberto and Bex had enough between
them. They want to be independent.'

'She's doing terribly well.'

'She is.'

We sipped our tea from polystyrene beakers. Heather looked
in. 'Everyone all right?' We nodded dimly. She came to the
bedside and looked down at Sinead. 'Don't get too comfy, young
lady, vital functions again soon.'

The phone rang out in the reception area and she glanced over
her shoulder. 'No one there, excuse me.'

She was back in a minute. 'It's for you, Mrs Lewis – it's your
father.'

'Give them my love,' said Glyn.

My father's voice had a mellow, yielding quality – not
over-emotional, but pliant in preparation for possible shock.
I remembered it from once before.

'Laura . . . how are things?'

'Rather dismaying,' I admitted, 'but under control.'

'And the little 'un?'

'Unrecognizable, but not in any danger, apparently.'

'We spoke to Glyn earlier, and he indicated as much. Now tell
me – is there anything, anything at all, we can do? Your mother
and I may be antediluvian but we're completely at your disposal.
Diana's waving in agreement.'

I could picture her doing so. 'Not at the moment, thanks, Dad.
Everything's under control. Becca's being a tower of strength.'

'It doesn't surprise me,' said my father. 'Hang on, your

mother's trying to say something – what? – oh yes, we'd like to come and see the patient. What's the score on visiting?'

'I believe it's more or less any time between two and five,' I said, 'but it's a bit soon at the moment – she looks and feels pretty terrible—'

'We can take it, you know.'

'Yes, I do know, but it would be pointless, she'll hardly know you're here. We'll give you a ring tomorrow with a progress report and work out a time. You can spend the night with us.'

'All right. Your mother's planning some sort of extravagant surprise in the post, anyway.'

'She'll like that.'

'Goodbye, Laura-lou. Chin up. Our very best love to one and all and especially Isobel.'

As I replaced the phone I saw Becca and Liam coming down the corridor.

Verity and Jasper must have stayed discreetly in the cafeteria. Liam looked absolutely white against his black donkey jacket. The skull-like haircut had grown out a bit, but the resulting spikes, combined with his hollow eyes and spectral pallor, looked like his nerve ends sticking out. I said hallo, and he glared at me briefly to establish the source of the sound, before marching past without reply.

Glyn came out of Sinead's room. 'Hallo, mate, she'll be pleased you're here.' He turned to me. 'Shall we find something to eat?'

We found Jasper and Verity, who had been joined by Josh, at a round table in the Plaza. It was bustling here even at eight-thirty, and the gift shop and general store were still open.

'How was Liam on the way over?' I asked.

Jasper looked rueful. 'I wouldn't have wanted to run out of petrol. Poor chap – nothing I could say was going to make him feel any better. I gave up, and put my foot down.'

'Don't worry,' said Glyn, 'he's always a bit like that. I think it's good for him to have something to be highly strung about.'

'I liked him a lot. A very genuine sort of bloke.'

'He is.'

I turned to Josh. 'Thanks for dealing with the car, love.'

'Least I could do.' He was gruff, holding it together by the skin of his teeth.

'You ought to get home.'

'How is she?'

'The same – but that nice nurse says everything's as it should be.'

'I wouldn't know how nice she is – she seems a bit rough to me.'

His eyes were red. I clutched his bony wrist under the table. 'She's confident – she knows what she's doing. Sinead's in very good hands.'

'Right.'

Verity said, 'What do you think we can do now, to be useful? I don't like to keep asking Becca.'

'I'm sure there isn't anything,' I said. 'You've both been marvellous.'

'We'll look in on Roberto, perhaps – what do you think?'

'Good idea.'

She turned to her brother. 'Fancy a lift, Josh?'

He glanced at us. 'Do you need me?'

Glyn said, 'You'd be surprised how much. But we won't be too long ourselves, all right? See you back at the ranch.'

We stayed in the Plaza another twenty minutes or so, and then walked back to the ward. A composed Liam was sitting where Becca had been, holding Sinead's hand, and Becca was rinsing out the steel bowl in the sink. She gave us a grim smile as we came in.

'The nurse has been doing her stuff again – I have a feeling Sinead's going to chuck up every time.'

Glyn went over to Liam and leaned on the next-door locker, talking to him quietly. Josh stood on the other side of the bed, scowling down at his niece. Becca yawned mightily, scrubbing at her face with her hands, emerging with a grin. 'You don't all have to hang about, you know.'

'We'll go if there's nothing else we can do,' said Verity. 'We thought we might call in on Roberto and Amos to say goodnight.'

'Brilliant, thanks. I told them to ring here just before Amos goes to bed, so if they haven't already done it, will you remind them?'

'We will,' confirmed Jasper, leaning across the steel bowl to kiss Becca's cheek. 'You're staying here?'

'We both are. Normally they only allow one per patient, but as there's no one else in here at the moment I asked if Liam could stay too.'

'Beating the system as usual, Bex,' said Glyn fondly.

'That's me.'

Liam got up and came over. Quite unexpectedly he put an arm round Jasper and hugged him, administering a few quick slaps on the back as he did so. 'Thanks for all you did, mate. I appreciate it. I was in no state to drive.'

'My pleasure.' Jasper returned one of the back-slaps, rather gingerly but with a good grace.

'Now you run along,' said Becca, taking her sister by the arm and steering her gently towards the door. 'Give a big kiss from me to the lads back home, and then go and tear up the town or something.'

'I'm not sure—' began Verity.

'I said or something. Goodnight.' She ushered Josh out. 'Bye, big boy – thanks for everything.'

Glyn accompanied them to the door of the ward. I went to Sinead's bedside and gazed down at her, then at Liam, still ashen-faced, in his chair the other side. Searching for some comfortable words, I found myself saying what everyone else had said to me: 'It's not as bad as it looks.'

'I know that. My sister was knocked off her bike when she was ten. She looked like Boris Karloff for weeks.' His lips twitched. 'Doesn't make it any easier, though.'

'I'm glad you can stay here.'

'I'd have sat in the car park all night anyway.'

I believed him.

A few minutes later Glyn got back with a carrier bag which he handed to Becca. Inside were two rounds of sandwiches, two cans of Coke, a toothbrush, a magazine for young women of independent mind, and a giant T-shirt covered in hearts.

'Thanks, Dad.'

He shrugged. 'Only a few unconsidered trifles – it occurred

to me you hadn't got anything here, and they were closing.'

'I'll get organized tomorrow.'

We said our farewells and promised to be in touch next day. In
the reception area Heather was handing over to the night nurse,
who looked about thirteen.

'This is Sue,' she said. 'She doesn't stand for any nonsense.'
We were now used to her little ways, and smiled, but I was glad
Josh had gone.

In the corridor between the ward and the Plaza we encoun-
ered Griggs coming the other way, carrying an armful of flowers
and a silver helium balloon with 'Get Happy' written on it. Two
student nurses walking past must have recognized him, for there
was a certain amount of ill-concealed gasping and giggling. It was
hard to see what all the excitement was about – he was such a
regular bloke. On the other hand – I glanced at Glyn – there was
nothing wrong in that.

They hailed each other like a couple of long-lost buddies, two
of a kind.

'Where's Bex?' asked Griggs. I didn't know whether he'd
picked up the appellation from Glyn, or if it was simply
coincidence. I recalled how quickly my father's 'Laura-lou'
had been appropriated by Glyn. The air seemed full of signs
and portents.

Glyn was giving him directions. My heart gave a sudden
anxious swoop at the thought of Griggs, trailing clouds of
Britpop glory and bearing gifts, coming face to face with the
stressed and penniless Liam.

Maybe he caught my look – or maybe he was simply a
nice man. 'Is Sinead's dad with them?' he asked. We nodded
anxiously. 'I thought he might be. I'll sneak in and leave these
at the desk.'

'Have you just come from London?' I asked.

'Glasgow.' He saw my expression. 'It's cool, Becca's Mum –
I didn't have to, did I? How's the princess?' We told him, and
he listened with severe, unblinking concentration. I had the
impression he'd remember every detail.

'Wicked shame, isn't it?' There was something comforting in
the unflappable, formulaic quality of his comment. We agreed

that it was, but that the worst was over, no matter how long the future haul.

'Cheerio, then.' He shook Glyn's hand, then mine, and we watched him as he went on his way, the balloon bobbing above his head.

'Good of him,' I said.

'Very.'

'It's a hell of a long way to come, and then not even to see Becca.'

Glyn took my hand and laced his fingers through mine. 'He can afford it, you know.' We hadn't held hands like that in – oh – ages. 'There'll be a record company driver sitting out there waiting for him.'

'All the same.'

'Yes,' said Glyn. 'He's okay, our Griggs.'

We got back at ten. Glyn arrived a couple of minutes before me because we'd had to drive home in two separate cars, but he waited outside, so we walked in together. I was glad I'd tidied the house, even if it had been a sort of madness at the time. It felt calm and welcoming – not, as I so often thought, like a collection of transit camps, but a place where life, rich and endlessly surprising, went on.

Verity was on the stairs to meet us in her bombproof nightie.

'Hallo, how is she?'

'Hanging in there,' said Glyn, 'no cause for alarm.'

Verity came down and put her arms round my neck. 'What an awful, awful, day!'

'Over now, though,' I said.

She nodded against my shoulder. When she straightened up she was in command again. 'Josh has crashed out – he left something for you on the table.'

We said goodnight to her and then went into the kitchen and poured ourselves a scotch each from the slightly dusty bottle reserved for crises and my father. I noticed our tickets for Spain, pinned to the noticeboard.

The something Josh had left for us was his holiday dissertation, contentiously entitled 'Who Wrote Hamlet?' Mr Collins had given him a starred A, with the comment: *I'm sticking my neck out for you, Josh. Your work is highly intelligent and fresh. But if you can't be good, be careful.* Underneath this Josh had scribbled in pencil, for our benefit: *He's got to be joking. Hope all's well at the hospital. Love, Josh.*

We sat facing each other across the table, my hand in Glyn's, resting on the essay. I could feel a warm current flowing through us, creating a circuit.

'I tell you what,' he said. 'When she's older we'll have to tell Sinead.'

'About what?' I asked.

'About the night she had her accident. And how she was the heroine of the hour.'

'Yes.'

'And how amazing everyone was – the whole family.'

'They were, weren't they . . .'

'So much so that her wizened old grandparents realized they must have done something right.'

I knew now that I was going to cry – but it was a release, a letting-go, like sex. It felt wonderful. Glyn made no comment on my tears.

'Yes.'

'And they realized what a great team they were.'

He took my other hand in his. My husband looked every one of his fifty-one years, but in his eyes was that unquenchable spark of boyish optimism which had helped to keep the good ship Lewis afloat for over a quarter of a century.

'You gave me everything I have,' he said. 'Do you know that? All this heaven and hell. I'd be nothing without you.'

'Oh,' I said, sniffing, 'you don't need me . . .'

'That's right, I don't. Any more than you need me. But I want to be here with you. There's nowhere I'd rather be. Got that?'

He leaned forward to kiss me and I smelt his warm whisky-breath on my face.

'I do love you,' I said.

'I know that.'

'Glyn, there's something—'

'I know that too.' He kissed me again, no more than an affirmative touch of the lips. 'But it can wait.'

'All right.'

'Let's go up.'

We stood and he put his arms round me. I relaxed – it felt like the first time I'd done so in months – and felt a dart of desire pierce my dog-tiredness.

His hands moved up and down my back, remembering and reminding. I kissed his face. Just before my mouth found his, he said, 'Welcome back.'

We turned the kitchen light off. And there, outside in the soft, untidy darkness, we saw the pale, calm glow of three white roses, blooming in the moonlight.

20 ∫

'It all goes to show – bring us another glass each, please – you never can tell. I've told you before, Mrs Lewis, my preference has always been for a bit of flash. You can't beat a sharp suit, crisp white cuffs, shiny shoes, a tiepin if possible . . . Remember little Jimmy Mullaney? I know I was wasting my time there, but I did so love his style, he was a pleasure to do business with. I've never quite got over him . . . hey-ho . . . And now along comes this semi-housetrained goon with a sex-drive like a Sherman tank. He is without doubt the challenge I've been waiting for. He ain't seen nothing yet! And the timing is so perfect – you've kept us amused all summer long with your antics with Mr Wrong, and now you're doing exactly what I would have advised and returning renewed and refreshed to your husband. Quite right. That's what wives should do. For a moment you had me worried, did you realize? I had the distinct impression that you might be going off the rails never to return – but no! I've always been a good judge of character and my instincts about you were exactly right. You've done me proud. And I love the way your family all rallied to the flag on that fateful evening – they obviously do you credit in spite of having the morals of polecats (I don't know where they get it from). Do you remember what I said about angels? There you are then. The white rose blooms again, and you're going to take that lovely picture of everyone with "Isobel" in the foreground – well, next spring'll do when Sinead's her beautiful unblemished self. And perhaps you'd be good enough to let me have a copy of the picture, since it features my godchild – I don't mind having to put up with everyone else as well, I've forgiven them all now.

I think I may even have forgiven Glyn for letting everyone do exactly as they like – at least he's *consistently* negligent, I rather like that in a man. I think my new bloke may be consistently negligent. But I'll take him in hand, never fear. I adore him, isn't that ridiculous? My heart beats, my erectile tissues stand to attention, I feel sixteen again. And I'm absolutely beastly to him, of course. I have the idea he's always had things too easy, he has a low threshold of boredom. All men are like small boys, but he's more retarded than most . . . It is I, Susan, who will put a stop to all that malarkey. He's going to have to wait for his fun! Ha . . . ! It's going to be better than the telly, Mrs Lewis. All summer I've listened to you, and now all winter you'll be able to relax and listen to me . . . Incidentally, did I tell you that Simon's having lunch with Brunnhilde on a regular basis? I've completely forgiven her – a nice squeezable menopausal confidante may be exactly what he needs at the moment, and who am I to deny him a bit of comfort, especially when I'm too busy myself? Oh. Do you mind us hanging on a bit longer? Yes, and what I was going to say about angels *was* – I bet you thought Henry was your angel, didn't you? Because it was Henry all along, wasn't it, don't deny it. See how clever I am? I always have your interests at heart, I take our friendship *extremely* seriously. But I am totally, totally discreet. I just had a feeling that you and Henry might be able to make sweet music together and I was right – if you could see your face! Now, that's enough about my present, let's talk about me! Because I'm your angel, Laura! I am!'